# AN EAGLE IN
# A HEN-HOUSE

## SELECTED POLITICAL SPEECHES AND WRITINGS
### OF
### R. B. CUNNINGHAME GRAHAM

Compiled and edited by Lachlan Munro

First edition Ayton Publishing Ltd 2017.

Ayton Publishing,
Hillhead of Ardmiddle,
Turriff,
Aberdeenshire AB53 8AL

www.aytonpublishing.co.uk

© Lachlan Munro, 2017

ISBN 978-1-910601-43-3

# Acknowledgements

Thank you to Dr. Catriona MacDonald, and Dr. Duncan Ross for putting me on the trail of Cunninghame Graham, and without whom this book would not have been written, and to Professors Gerard Carruthers, Laurence Davies, and Cedric Watts, for their help and encouragement. Also, to other mentors and inspirers: Dr. Kathryn Castle, Dr. Kelvin Knight, Dr. Niall MacKenzie, and Virginia Wills, and to my wife Lesley for her support and forbearance.

*"Contempsisti barbarorum gladios; non pertimesces meos."* [1]

---

[1] "You have despised the swords of the barbarians; you won't be terrified by mine." Cicero's 'Second Philippic,' adapted by the humourist and caricaturist Max Beerbohm, in a letter to Cunninghame Graham, dated the 9th of February 1899.

# CONTENTS

In Christmas Week - *The Saturday Review* (2 February 1907).
Set Free - *The Saturday Review* (7 January 1911).

☐☐☐☐☐☐

## THE LABOUR ACTIVIST
A Labour Programme - Introduction to Pamphlet (November 1888).
Speech at Rally in Hyde Park (14 November 1888).
Speech at The Oddfellows Hall, Edinburgh (11 June 1889).
Speech at The Temperance Hall, Shettleston (31 October 1889).
The People's M.P. - *The People's Press* (26 April 1890).
An Idealist – *The Saturday Review* (25 August 1906).
Speech at The St Andrew's Halls, Glasgow, (2 November 1906).
Mr. Graham's Disappointments - Speech in Manchester (6 December 1908).
Patriotism – Letter, *The Saturday Review* (29 January 1910).

☐☐☐☐☐☐

## SOCIAL FREEDOMS and WOMEN'S RIGHTS
Parnell: An Open Letter - *The Labour Elector* (25 January 1890).
Vox Clamantis - *The Saturday Review* (4 March 1905).
Women's Suffrage - Speech at St Andrew's Halls, Glasgow (4 October 1907).
The Real Equality of the Sexes - *The New Age* (July 1908).
The Enemy – *Justice: The Organ of Social Democracy* (13 May, 1913).

☐☐☐☐☐☐

## IRELAND
Home Rule – *The People's Press* (20 December 1890).
An Tighearna: A Memory of Parnell - *Dana* (Dublin) (November 1904).

## BRITISH IMPERIALISM
The Imperial Kailyard: Being a Bitter Satire on English Colonialism (1896).
Fraudesia Magna I - *The Saturday Review* (21 March 1896).
Fraudesia Magna II - *The Saturday Review* (4 April 1896).
Bloody Niggers - *The Social Democrat* (April 1897).
Expansion of Empire - *The Sunday Chronicle* (13 June 1897).
Nationalities and Subject Races Conference – Speech at Caxton Hall, Westminster, (30 June 1910).
Bovril - *Justice: The Organ of Social Democracy* (22 July 1911).

## POSTSCRIPT

There are few men nowadays so well known as Mr R. B. Cunninghame Graham.
*The Sunday Post* (13th of November, 1927).

# EDITORS' PREFACE

William Strang – 'Don Roberto' as Don Quixote (1902).

R. B. Cunninghame Graham was [. . .] a plethora of paradoxes. A romantic and a cynic; an idealist and a sceptic; a Don Quixote and a Hamlet; a nationalist and an internationalist; a socialist and a conservative; a revolutionary and a gradualist; a nobleman and a cowboy; a South American cattle-rancher and horse-trader who was also 'the uncrowned King of Scotland'; a dandy and a convict; a Justice of the Peace who headed a riot; an anti-racist and an anti-Semite; an atheist and a defender of Jesuits.
He opposed the Great War but then worked for the War Office;
he opposed cruelty to animals but selected horses to suffer and die in battlefields;
he was a Scottish landowning aristocrat who advocated the nationalisation of the land;
an anarchist who was proud of his descent from King Robert II;
a Marxist (according to Engels), yet he hoped to see Lenin hanged.
He was a striving radical who declared the futility of such striving:
"It results in nothing at the end," he said.

Professor Cedric Watts, ASLS Conference, Stirling, 4th of July 2015.

The long and glittering life of the protean Robert Bontine Cunninghame Graham (1852-1936), adventurer, campaigner, satirist and wit, spanned nearly nine decades, through the height, and slow decline of Empire, to the Age of the Dictators. Graham's childhood encompassed the Crimean War, the Indian Mutiny, Civil War in America, and, very significantly for British political life, a major extension of the adult male suffrage in 1867 and 1885. His last years embraced the agonies of the First World War, the Jazz Age, the economic boom-and-bust of the 1920s and 30s, and, again of political significance, the granting in two stages, in 1918 and 1928, of the vote to all women. Graham lived through a century of unprecedented technological development, and

8

accelerated modernization, accompanied by enormous social upheaval, but a career in Victorian politics, for a man who freely admitted that he 'was no real politician,'[2] seemed highly unlikely.

His young manhood had been spent careening through the endless seas of grass in South America and Texas, but after an apparently ill-advised marriage, and his inheritance of the Gartmore Estate in 1883 (and with it, enormous debts), in 1885, the new laird was recruited as a Liberal MP for an industrial constituency, and up to the turn of the new century, as a brilliant orator and fearless social critic, he became totally immersed in Parliamentary politics, social issues, and political journalism. Although Graham's years in Parliament were relatively few, he was an active player in politics until the end of his days, being a key figure in the foundation of both the Labour and the Scottish National parties.

On the surface, at least, British society during Graham's time in the House of Commons appeared very different from what we recognise today. Any issue of *Punch* from the late 1880s reveals, behind its advertisements for Bovril and liver pills, Parliamentary portraits and cartoons, forgotten men and forgotten crises, the seeming solidity and complacency of Queen Victoria's world. Bewhiskered gents in top-hats, frock-coats, and stiff collars, proceed their passive, bustled wives; 'orny-'anded working-men, heads bowed, touch their sooty caps, and gaitered parsons vie with cheeky urchins, and sneering 'men of cultchaw.' Politically, Mr. Gladstone (The Grand Old Man) was ubiquitous, Britannia brandishes her trident at the Russian Bear, while Mr. Punch himself casts a knowing and obsequious eye over the unabashed snobbery and racism of that fortress of power and privilege, London, self-appointed Capital of the World. The Scottish writer, George Blake summed it up:

> Britannia ruled the waves, and nobody took much account of rebellious Zulus, Boers, Fuzzy-Wuzzies and such. All the British people had good reason to be content with their international status at least; and such a man as Keir Hardie was obviously mad.[3]

These images, however, concealed a world of huge social inequality, poverty, and exploitation, which was not only filling the sweat-shops and slums, but was destroying communities and culture, ways of life, modes of thought, and types of men, resulting in degradation, alienation, and a loss of individuality. It was a battlefield worthy of this maverick's political sword and pen.

As an accomplished horseman and swordsman, and possessed of a lean muscularity, and the dark-red, pointed beard of an hidalgo, the quarter-Spanish Graham is all too

---

2 'Mr Cunninghame Graham M.P. at Coatbridge,' *The Airdrie Advertiser* (23 November 1889) p.5.
3 George Blake, *Barrie and the Kailyard School* (Arthur Barker Ltd, 1951), p.21.

easily compared to Don Quixote, in the best and the worst senses - noble, gallant, brave, and adventurous, but also a good part mad - a dreamer of impossible dreams, a righter of unrightable wrongs, and (on more than one occasion), a fighter of unbeatable foes. But, Graham was a realist, and knew what life was like on the edge - he had lived rough and ridden hard in South America, Mexico, and Texas, and had seen how the poor and dispossessed had been exploited by greedy landowners, and vicious dictators. He could have done little in the Americas, but on his return to Scotland, this young *escocés errante* found no shortage of injustice, and no shortage of oppressors and their henchmen at whom he could tilt his lance.

His brief career in the House of Commons (which he called 'The National Gasworks') from 1886 until 1892 was thus a traumatic experience, as virtually alone he battled to improve the conditions of working people, and for the right of free speech, against the concerted forces of the British establishment, represented by both main parties, including his own. This led to frustration, anger, and isolation, and on three occasions he was expelled from the Chamber for unparliamentary behaviour. The poet Hugh MacDiarmid likened him to: "a blood-mare among donkeys, or an eagle in a hen-house."[4]

Forced to abandon hope of changing the Liberal Party from within, this iconoclastic aristocrat actively attacked it, and promoted the career of his friend and colleague, Keir Hardie. Together they founded the Scottish Parliamentary Labour Party, and promoted its successor, the Independent Labour Party. However, Graham quickly became disillusioned with the internal dissent, rancour, and pettiness of its new adherents, and he was slowly drawn towards a nascent Scottish nationalism as a more viable means of achieving economic, social, and cultural change.

Graham, as a high-profile personality, became a leading member of the London and Scottish cultural and literary elites, where he counted William Morris, Oscar Wilde,[5] George Bernard Shaw, G. K. Chesterton, Frank Harris, Joseph Conrad,[6] and latterly, Compton MacKenzie and Neil Munro, as personal friends. After leaving Parliament, the skills he had gained from writing for (mostly short-lived) socialist periodicals were harnessed in a new career, as a social commentator, and author of dozens of histories, tales and sketches, collected into over thirty books, which won him great acclaim during his lifetime. However, even some of his innocuous subjects carry a political message.

---

[4] C. M. Grieve, *Contemporary Scottish Studies* (Leonard Parsons, 1926), p.51.
[5] Morris and Wilde, among others, rushed to Bow Street Magistrate's Court to support Graham after 'Bloody Sunday,' and Wilde's wife, Constance, was as supporter throughout the three days of his subsequent trial.
[6] Graham was instrumental in Conrad's literary success, and supported him morally, and it is hinted, financially. Conrad once said of him: 'When I think of Cunninghame Graham, I feel as though I have lived all my life in a dark hole without seeing or knowing anything.'

Here, then, for the first time, readers have the opportunity to view a selection of his political speeches and writings, which let 'Don Roberto' speak for himself in his own voice. It is an extraordinary voice, an heroic voice, a sometimes-shocking voice of coruscating scorn and wit, a revolutionary, angry voice, but above all, it is a modern voice.

In compiling these articles and speeches for publication, I have adopted a policy of retaining Graham's own words, along with his occasional eccentricities of expression and spelling. With the records of his early speeches in newspapers,[7] I have, where I thought it appropriate, included the Press reporting (*in italics*) to set the scene, and the hugger-mugger atmosphere of these often-riotous assemblies.[8] In some cases I have been obliged to transpose his words into the first person, and in one instance, through necessity, assembled them from more than one source.

My hope is that the gentle reader will find Graham's dramatic words to be as surprising in their continuing relevance to our own world, as I have found them to be during my fascinating editorial task, and will enjoy meeting the cast of extraordinary characters, who filled his extraordinary life.

*Lachlan Munro*

---

[7] Local newspapers of the period regularly featured full-length speeches by M.P.s and candidates (including audience reactions), but later, on the national stage, this becomes far less common.

[8] "It is very difficult for a man to sit and hear himself being praised. It is a far easier thing to face a hostile meeting with interruptions, jeers, sneers, and insults – so long as they throw no loose building material about." Cunninghame Graham, *The Scotsman* (3 June, 1929), p.7.

# THE PRENTICE POLITICIAN

Spy Cartoon - *Vanity Fair* - 25 August 1888.

Between the Great Reform Acts of 1832 and 1884, despite the extension of the franchise, political rights had been designed to minimise change. For most of the period, local parties were largely indistinguishable from the personal property of politically-active landed proprietors, who took it for granted that they would play a pre-eminent part in politics, and everyone else did too.

Despite going on to represent an industrial seat, it was from this charmed circle that Graham hailed. Not only did his family have strong links to the Liberal Party, it had a well-known history of radicalism, and his candidacy would have been particularly attractive to the Liberal Party managers (the 'wire-pullers') in industrial constituencies, where any radical appeal to the increasingly disaffected first-time voters, would be more palatable coming from the lips of someone of Graham's pedigree.

In 1885 he was selected as the candidate for Camlachie to the east of Glasgow, but in late July of that year he was invited to address a meeting at Coatbridge in the adjacent constituency of North-West Lanarkshire, another industrial black-spot, with a large Irish immigrant population. He was also aware that many in the audience were Highland crofters who had taken jobs in the south to supplement their meagre incomes from the land.

~

# NORTH-WEST LANARKSHIRE LIBERAL ASSOCIATION
Mr. R. CUNNINGHAME GRAHAM AT COATBRIDGE [9]
*The Airdrie Advertiser*, 15th of August 1885.

*On Tuesday night, Mr. R. Cunninghame Graham of Gartmore, the Liberal candidate for the Camlachie Division of Glasgow, delivered a political address in the Temperance Hall, Coatbridge, under the auspices of the North-West Lanarkshire Liberal Association. Councilor Crawford, Glasgow, vice-president of the association presided. The hall was crowded.* [There then followed a list of attendees and apologies]. *The Secretary (Mr. R. Brown.) read a letter from Colonel Buchanan of Drumpelier who regretted his inability to be present, and said he had no doubt that Mr Graham would receive as patient a hearing and have as satisfactory a meeting as Mr. Parker Smith had last week. (Applause.)*

*The Chairman, in introducing Mr Graham, said it was quite certain they were to have a pretty close contest in North-West Lanark, and although they had not yet decided upon a candidate he hoped they had decided that North-West Lanark should remain a Liberal seat - (Applause.) - and that no division should take place in the ranks of the Liberals. They could not expect to find a man altogether to their pattern, still he hoped they would not endanger the seat to the Liberal cause. When they had agreed upon that they should endeavour to get a representative who would make it his aim to forward Liberal principles, and without a slavish adherence to party would find it to be possible on all important occasions to stick to his guns. (Applause.) Mr Cunninghame Graham, who was cordially received, proceeded with his address. After remarking that he esteemed it a high honour that a 'prentice politician' such as he should be deemed worthy to deliver an address to such an important constituency as that of which Coatbridge formed a part, he went on to deal with some of the chief topics of political interest. His first subject was that of Reform, which must be Progressive Reform:*

### PROGRESSIVE REFORM

I am well aware that the progress of all true reform must be gradual, but I would not have it so gradual as the advance of a crab, nor on the other hand, would I have it to progress by leaps and bounds, to lose itself in the tempestuous torrent of anarchy. I would have its advance as sure and steady as that of time itself. (*Applause.*) The extraordinary difference of class and class, and what so immediately arrests the intention of all foreigners who visit these shores, is, I think, to be attributed to many and various causes, and to none more perhaps than the survival of a mitigated form of the feudal system. This system, to which the French Revolution gave its death-blow in

---

9 "One of the chief and most dismal iron-smelting, engineering, and coal-mining towns in Scotland." Bruce Glasier, *William Morris and the Early Days of the Socialist Movement.* (Longmans, 1921), p.72.

almost every other country of Europe, still flourishes in considerable vigour amongst us. Here, and here almost alone, has the existence of enormous territorial possessions continued, and whilst in other civilised countries we find the land almost exclusively cultivated by the peasants or agricultural labourers themselves, in Great Britain is still to be found a class of feudal magnates who, though they do not still possess the pleasing power of "pit and gallows," as well as other privileges considerably "more honoured in the breach than in the observance," still enjoy privileges such as no class should enjoy to the exclusion of the rest in a civilised country. It is through the survival of these feudal customs that we have seen on every side the extinction of our ancient class of sturdy yeomen, the enclosure of commons, the debarring of the popular rights of way over mountains and waste lands, the devotion of enormous tracts of country to deer forests, and the unrighteous spectacle of much of our Highland population constrained to live on the salvage of the country, and so to speak, situated between the devil and the deep sea. (*Laughter and applause.*)

## LAND LAW REFORM

We must have Land Law Reform. This has always appeared to me that the first reform that should engross reformers' attention is that of our Land Laws, for in regard to this question to me more than any other does the fallacy of the old saying that a man may do what he likes with his own. That fact that no one has the right to do what he likes with his own without consulting the rights and feelings of others. It is the pushing of this assumed right to its logical sequence that has tended more than anything else to the depopulation of our rural districts, and to the crowding together of the inhabitants of our cities.

## FREE TRADE

There are few who will deny that it is the adoption of Free Trade that has raised Great Britain to her present pre-eminence in the commercial world, and I fail to see any reason why the same principle that has proved so eminently successful in commercial matters should not succeed also in matters bucolic. There are few who will deny that it is the adoption of Free Trade in Land.

## FREE TRADE IN LAND

By that I mean I would free land from all the trammels that now beset it - that is to say, I would at once abolish primogeniture, entail, and the power of settlement, and would like to see a cheap and expeditious method of transfer introduced such as is at present in use in our Australian colonies, whereby the arrangements for the transfer of land are as soon concluded as those for the transfer of a bale of cotton.

## LOCAL BOARDS

Nor would I stop there; I would give full power to Municipal Councils to acquire land at a fair valuation in the vicinity of our great cities; and should local boards be established (as I hope they will be) for county government, I would enable them to buy land also in the vicinity of our county towns and larger villages, to let out in small crofts to labourers and those desirous of farming on a small scale. These reforms carried out, I would have great hopes of seeing spring up again amongst us that sturdy class of independent small proprietors, whom I have always looked upon as the bone and sinew of Scotland in time gone by, and who are, at the present time, in France and Germany, and wherever they exist, the strongest force on the side of law and order. (*Applause.*) Again, I would wish to see restored to the Highland population those ancient rights of mountain pasturage that have from time immemorial formed part of the birthright of every Highlander, and the withdrawal of which more than anything else has tended to render miserable and discontented this portion of our fellow-subjects. (*Applause.*)

## IMPOSE A LAND TAX

I would by no means deny that right to the Government to impose a Land Tax if they thought fit, in order to raise the revenue for legitimate objects, being well assured that no Government would ever keep its place in Great Britain for a month that proposed to levy a prohibitive or ruinous tax on any of our national interests. All these reforms, I am well aware, would not content the Communist party, to which I referred before, but it has also appeared to me that these gentlemen have desired the substance to fight the shadow, and that it is not so much love of the poor that inspires them but the hatred of the rich. (*Applause.*)

Being all part and parcel of one kingdom, I can see no reason why English and Scottish men should enjoy privileges that Irishmen do not, nor, on the other hand, do I perceive the reason why Irishmen should have privileges that are denied to the English and Scotch. Therefore, I may begin by stating that I can see no valid reason why Home Rule should be extended to Ireland unless at the same time it is extended to England and Scotland. (*Applause.*) But on the other hand, I do not see why every integral part of the three kingdoms should not enjoy a full and ample measure of local self-government. And I think that if such a measure be carried out, and Ireland divided into three or four self-governing districts, not only would those districts be able to provide for their own wants as to race and creed, but that in the end the invisible bonds, "light as cobwebs but strong as steel," which must for ever bind together two countries geographically situated as Britain and Ireland are, may be strengthened and tightened to the[ir] natural advantage, but with[out] the slightest possible feeling of tension between the two countries. (*Applause.*)

There are, however, many other questions which engross the public attention, and none perhaps more so than the question of the severance of Church and State. Before touching on this extremely ticklish point I wish to say that I have no animosity or personal ill will against the old Kirk of Scotland. The good she has done in the past, the good that she continues to do at present, will, I think, be disputed by nobody. In proposing however, as I would to disestablish the Church, I would by no means have the interests of any living clergyman in the smallest degree interfered with. Whilst heartily advocating disestablishment, I would take care that it was carried out in a wide, generous, and conciliatory manner, and I see no reason to apprehend that that the position of the clergy would be in the least degree inferior either pecuniarily [sic] or socially in the future. (*Applause.*) I cannot believe that even John Knox himself ever contemplated that one division of the Presbyterian religion should hold privileges to which the rest are not admitted, nor do I even think that when we talk as we often do of our forefathers shedding their blood for the old Church of Scotland that they ever did anything of the kind - (*Hear, hear, slight hisses, cries of "Oh." and applause.*) - as it appears to me that what they fought for was the principle of Presbyterianism as

16

opposed to that of Episcopacy - (*Loud applause.*) - and against the imposition of a State Church, the very thing that their descendants would have us keep up. (*Renewed and prolonged applause.*) There is still, however, another aspect of the question, and that is, that the Church is supported from revenues derived from land; and it seems to me that in country districts, although the larger landowners can readily bear the imposition of Church teinds,[10] they often press with undue severity on the smaller heritors, who, we must also take into consideration, if they rate Dissenters, are called upon to support their own church as well. (*Applause.*)

## THE LIQUOR TRAFFIC

I now come to a subject which, in many respects, is the most important before the public's consideration, and that is the one of the control of the liquor traffic.[11] Though I am not a total abstainer myself I so heartily and entirely sympathise with the temperance movement - I so thoroughly admire their spirit of energy, enterprise, and organisation - so firmly do I believe them to be actuated by the purest and most human motives - so much do I think that they have the moral and physical welfare of the nation at heart, that I feel it is the duty of every man who has examined into our vast and terrible social problems, to concur in placing the control of the liquor traffic wholly and unreservedly in the hands of the ratepayers. The evils that drink everywhere causes, its fearful effect on the moral and physical well-being of the whole people, the enormous amount of money that is squandered every year on it; the crime, disease, and misery. Those who have witnessed these are aware what a curse the presence of even one drunkard may prove in a street - the constant annoyance and insult suffered by the wives and daughters of our working classes at the hands of drunkards, will readily understand the reasons that have joined together almost as one man our working classes in the demand that the nation as a whole shall accept the principle of local option.

## FREE EDUCATION

With this question, however, it seems to me is the measure connected that of Free Education, as it is to education that we must look as much as preventative measures

---

10 In Scotland, a tithe derived from farm produce to support the clergy.
11 Drink and drunkenness among the working classes was a major social problem.

for the amelioration of social evils, though in England the recognition by the State of its duty in aiding the spread of national education is only a growth of the last 50 years. In Scotland it is far older. A statute of James IV (the "James of the fiery face" of the Chroniclers[12]) required all freeholders of substance to send their heirs to school, and to keep them there till they had perfect Latin. Again, the first book of Policy, published by the Reformed Church in 1560, appointed a teacher in every parish, and from that time till the present day there have been repeated Acts of Parliament and of Privy Council, dealing with matters of education in Scotland, in which, moreover, in a wide spirit of toleration, no distinction of religious differences was ever made. In spite of all this, however, Scotland is very far from being the country in Europe wherein education is most generally diffused, and though many millions have been spent in the last few years by the Government, the fact still remains that a large percentage of the population is still growing up grossly ignorant. I will not weary you with figures, as it is easy to handle them so as to produce any given result. But surely, with the fact staring us in the face that our present system is quite inadequate to provide education for all, and knowing as we do that the payment of fees in no way covers the expenses incurred by Government - surely with these significant facts before us, no true Liberal - no real well-wisher of his country - would for a moment hesitate to bear his share of the burden.

*Mr. Graham then spoke at considerable length in support of the extension of political rights to women, and said:*

I would exhort you all, till the coming election is over and a Liberal victory is well assured, to sink for the present all petty shades of opinion, and to remember that no section of the party can rightly claim a monopoly of Liberalism, for Liberalism in its widest sense includes all kinds and conditions of progressive thought, from the Whig to the most advanced Radical; and I would call on you to resist the glare and tinsel of a meretricious Imperialism and THE WILES OF AN INVERTEBRATE TORY DEMOCRACY, and to rally round that Homeric statesman,[13] that magician of Mid-Lothian, the quality of whose Liberalism is in no

---

[12] King James II (1430-1460).
[13] A reference to Gladstone.

wise strained, [14] and to whom alone we can look for a wide, catholic, and comprehensive programme, and of whom all Liberal eyes are fixed as on the Pole Star. (*Great applause.*) And, finally, I would call on you one and all to stand fast by the fundamental principles of Liberalism - Toleration, Justice, and Free Trade - those principles that have covered the sea with our navies, that have carried the name of Britain in triumph to the uttermost ends of the civilised and uncivilised worlds, and has enabled our country, like the "Tree Igdrasie," [15] to strike her roots to the foundation of the earth and attain the heavens with her topmost branches, though in the beginning she was but a little island buried in the mist of a northern sea. (*Applause.*)

The influence of the American political economist, philosopher, and journalist, Henry George (1839-1897), who had developed radical theories on land ownership, capital, and trade, runs through Graham's speech.[16] George's book *Progress and Poverty* (1879) sold over 3 million copies, and this, combined with popular speaking tours in Britain and Ireland, is considered by many as the major catalyst for the new breed of British radicals - not the writings of Karl Marx. Philip Snowden recalled: 'Keir Hardie told me that it was *Progress and Poverty* which gave him his first ideas of socialism . . . No book ever written on the social problem made so many converts.'[17] According to Peter Jones, Graham was more strongly influenced by George than any other writer,[18] and certainly, George's belief that progress and poverty marched together is a recurring theme throughout all of Graham's writings. They did however disagree on some fundamental issues, expressed in a very public exchange of letters in *The Star* in late May 1889, in which Graham described himself as: "a follower of Marx."[19]

Graham's speech to the North-West Lanarkshire Liberals bears the hallmarks of a probationary sermon, not the words of a visiting speaker furthering his party's policies (particularly one who despised Gladstone). At the end, the chairman assured the audience that the Association intended to proceed on the matter of selecting a candidate: "with some vigour." A week later, Graham was invited to stand as their candidate, which the Liberals in Camlachie did not oppose.

---

[14] The Merchant of Venice, Act IV, Scene I.
[15] Yggdrasill - a giant mythical tree that connected the nine worlds of Norse cosmology.
[16] It has been claimed that George's proposals were derived from an influential book entitled: *The Theory of Human Progression* (1850) written by an Ayrshire farmer, philosopher, and early Scottish nationalist, Patrick Edward Dove. See: Morrison Davidson, *Concerning Four Precursors of Henry George and the Single Tax* (1902).
[17] Philip Snowden, *An Autobiography* (London, Ivor Nicholson & Watson, 1934), p.49.
[18] Peter d'A Jones, 'Henry George and British Labor Politics' in *The American Journal of Economics and Sociology*, Volume 46, No.2 (April 1987), p.250.
[19] *The Star* (25 May 1889). The Fabian, George Bernard Shaw, also weighed into the argument.

~

From the beginning of his campaign, Graham's natural skills of oratory, and his stream of jokes, drew large crowds, particularly from the classes who were about to cast their vote for the first time. However, his selection was not to everyone's liking among the Liberal party hierarchy. On the 12th of September 1885, Graham was back in Coatbridge, this time at the capacious Theatre Royal, where hundreds of people had to remain outside. The Chairman, Mr. Andrew Stewart (the Managing Director, and part-owner of The Clyde Tube Works, the largest steel tube manufacturers in Britain), welcomed their new candidate. (*Loud Cheers.*) However, in what was a less than enthusiastic endorsement, he regretted having been out of the country for the last six weeks, and not being present when the committee had made its choice of candidate: "Had I been present I might have asked you to delay a little and consider further. But, the selection having been made, I consider it my duty as a Liberal voter to go in with the majority." (*Cheers.*) He then referred to the Conservative opposition in the constituency: "we have a very powerful interest opposed to us [. . .] We are opposed by a family who deserves well of Coatbridge. Perhaps there is no family within Lanarkshire who have done so much for this district as the family to which Mr. Baird[20] belongs have done (*Cheers.*) [. . .] we are indebted to them, and certainly their intelligence and ability have created Coatbridge," but, "Mr. Baird is on the wrong side of politics (*Hear, hear, loud cheers, and slight hissing.*) [. . .] being supported not by the newly enfranchised working people, but by the wealthy proprietors and employers of labour."[21]

Graham proceeded to speak, but may have felt that this introduction was not only guarded, but also rang somewhat hollow, coming from a major industrialist like Andrew Stewart. However, if Stewarts' doubts had been encouraged by Graham's radical views, he would have gained little consolation from what followed. Graham would fight his campaigns on universal suffrage, the payment of M.P.s and election expenses, triennial Parliaments, the abolition of the House of Lords, free secular education with a free daily meal for scholars, a graduated income tax, nationalisation of all land without compensation, Sunday opening of museums, the abolition of mineral royalties, and the disestablishment of the national churches. The North-West Lanarkshire Liberals had chosen their Cavalier in the belief he was a Roundhead, but what they got was a 'Leveller':

---

[20] Graham's Tory opponent was John Baird 'of Knoydart,' (1852–1900), a nephew of ironmaster Alexander Baird of Lochwood, the founder of Coatbridge's industrial wealth. Baird was also an absentee Highland landlord, who had sensationally displayed his feudal instincts in front of The Napier Commission in 1883. Graham and Baird were however on cordial terms, having attended Harrow School together.
[21] According to A. B. Campbell, the Baird dynasty also had a notoriously poor industrial record, *The Lanarkshire Miners: A Social history of Their Trade Unions*, (1979).

# REPRESENTATION of NORTH-WEST LANARKSHIRE
## Mr. CUNNINGHAME GRAHAM AT COATBRIDGE.

*The Airdrie Advertiser*, 19th of September 1885.

### *THE EXTENDED FRANCHISE*

With the coming election looming largely before us, it behoves every one of us as citizens and electors, and as Scotchmen, to ascertain fully in his own mind as to how he is going to exercise the Franchise so recently entrusted to him. I am not one of those who looks with the slightest dread on the accession of voting power, and I hold the stories so freely circulated at the expense of the new electors as but mere old wives' tales not worthy of a sensible man's belief; but to those who look otherwise, and are ever sighing for the good old days of the pocket boroughs and Old Sarum,[22] and deploring the break up of pleasant social relations, as they call them, by the introduction of the popular or democratic element into our Government - to those people, I say, who are always prophesying evil, revolution and other sweetmeats - to these I would point out that, although the same farrago of nonsense was circulated before the Great Reform Bill of 1832, none of the awful catastrophes then so confidently predicted have taken place. (*Cheers.*) This wicked franchise that was to deluge all England with blood, and, involve it in civil war, at the very least, has now been an accomplished fact for fifty years, and at the present moment our national credit and honour stand higher; law and order, life and property are more firmly respected than I believe they ever were before in the history of Great Britain. (*Cheers.*)

### *CONSTITUTIONALISM*

There are those who say our social system is so perfect that any touch would be but to mar, not mend, it; there are those who say that the British Constitution is at the highest state of perfectibility to which a constitution can ever attain, and it is their earnest and only wish to never alter it. If, gentlemen, I knew what the British Constitution was, or if they could explain it to me, perhaps I should be of their opinion, but I have never been able to find out that such a thing as the British Constitution exists or existed. If a constitution is an aggregation of curious,

---

[22] A Wiltshire borough, which, despite being virtually uninhabited, up until 1832, returned a member of Parliament.

cumbrous, and old fashioned laws, certainly we have one. (*Laughter and cheers.*) If on the other hand, perfection is shown in Dukes of Westminster with £1000 a day and in match makers in the East End of London, who after a hard days toil, go to bed hungry – if the agricultural labourers of the Midland Counties of England, divorced from all connection with the soil of his native country, starving on 9s or 10s a week, and herded into one room with his male and female relatives of several generations, is a spectacle for much congratulation, then, certainly we are capable of no improvement. It may be, however, that if an inhabitant of the moon, suddenly landed on our shores, it would seem a subject of some reflection that in Great Britain, the richest country in the world, there are thousands of people who from their pauper birth place to their pauper graves and parish shell coffin, never know what it is to have a full meal. (*Hear, hear, and cheers.*) It might also seem strange to him that in this Christian land, whilst the four corners of the world are ransacked to furnish one repast for the palates of the rich, others are battling with starvation, and that, with shops full of food, granaries full of corn, and markets full of beef within their view. Do not think for a moment that I preach revolution, neither, on the other hand, resignation. Supply and demand, freedom of contract, and all the capitalist watch words, have resulted, according to the people who made them, in the prosperity of the kingdom.

### CAPITAL AND LABOUR

But let us see what that prosperity really means. In my opinion, it means the prosperity of a grasping capitalist class, and the reduction of the great bulk of the population to the position of mere wage slaves (*Cheers.*) Our unexampled generosity, our deification of shoddy [23] has certainly carried the country to a great pitch of commercial pre-eminence, but, whether it has not and is daily rendering the lives of the bulk of the population more unendurable to them, is a moot question. Some will say, is this man going to take up his parable against capital and commerce? My answer is, certainly not. What I should like to see, however, is that capital should be made to disgorge some of the wealth it has wrung out of the labouring classes. (*Cheers.*) Turning to history we see that many things now called radical, socialistic, and

---

[23] Of inferior quality, specifically a cloth made from reconstituted fibres.

of foreign importation, are of sturdy British growth, and in ages gone by had stuck their roots so deeply into the hearts of the people, that only centuries of oppression have been able to uproot them. This is why so many of our modern radical measures have a sort of air of going back to the past, rather than looking forward to the future.

## PAYMENT OF M.P.s

These Radical, indigenous ideas, which are being spoken of with bated breath as Socialistic, were part and parcel of our national existence in these days. For instance, take the question of payment of members of Parliament. We shall find that in the days of Henry III in England 2s [shillings] were paid a day to the burgh member as a salary, and a means of living in London. The knights and county members at the same time received 4s a day for their services. Indeed, so strict were the measures taken, that fines were imposed on those who refused to attend after due election, and from those days down to the so-called glorious revolution of William II, this continued to be the custom. Then, and not till then, was this truly practical custom abolished; and then, and not till then, was the great bulk of the people shut out from a share of representation in the national assembly. (*Cheers.*) At this time, too, under the rule of this glorious foreign king, were the ancient national lands that had survived even the plundering and blundering of the Stuarts, finally alienated, and alienated to whom? To a crowd of needy, greedy, unscrupulous Dutch adventurers. (*Cheers.*) Then, too, it was when the landowners finally succeeded in shifting nearly all the charges for military service from their shoulders to those of the people. In fact, we may say that at this glorious epoch was the most serious blow struck against British freedom. It was then that all Britain for the first time became the absolute prey of the landowners and capitalists, and the sweet boon of a National Debt conferred upon a grateful people. (*Laughter and cheers.*) I appeal to all the new electors, and ask them whether they think they will ever be fairly represented in Westminster till the old British custom of payment of members of Parliament – (*Cries of: "No, no."*) – for their services, and the new one of paying all election expenses out of the rates are established. (*Hear, hear, and cheers.*) This no doubt is flat blasphemy to a certain section – (*A voice, "Never mind."*) – but what is more certain than that a good day's work deserves a good day's wages – (*Cheers, and a voice, "We cannot pay all the members."*) - and

23

that all the arguments so freely used against this popular and democratic measure, such as, we should become deluged with professional politicians, and that the dignity of the House of Commons (does it stand very high now?) would be lost. But on fair examination will these arguments hold water; and they be not mere "celestial music," or in the words of the immortal author of Don Quixote, "Nothing but cakes and paired bread." Is it not pretty clear that it is not entirely love of country that now inspires most of our members of Parliament, and that if they are not exactly paid over much for their services, do they not socially or otherwise sometimes continue to indemnify themselves for the expenses incurred at elections? (*Hear, hear.*) Besides, even if it is on one side a saving to the country at large not to pay its representatives, does the presence of a large number of capitalists whose lives have been spent in the acquisition of wealth, whose ideas, if ever they had any, have now become completely crystallised; or, on the other hand, troops of young men who only enter Parliament on account of the social status it may confer on them, and who are always indisposed about Ascot week, or conveniently paired off for the 12th of August,[24] and whose names at divisions are usually conspicuous by their absence - (*Laughter.*) - tend much to the situation, or throw much light on the discussion of the great social problems that at present beset us. (*Loud cheers.*)

## HOUSE OF LORDS

To an advocate of abolition of primogeniture in succession, it must be pretty clear than an hereditary legislation is an anomaly. (*Cheers.*) Do we confide our teeth to an hereditary dentist's care? Why therefore, our laws to an hereditary legislator, merely because he has taken the trouble to be born, and is the presumed son of his father? (*Laughter and cheers.*) There are two sides from which reform of the House of Lords might come, the inside and the outside. (*Laughter.*) Should we leave the reform to the inside, or to the Lords themselves, they will reform themselves as effectually as Satan would reprove sin. (*Laughter and cheers.*) There is, therefore, the other side, viz., the outside, still left, and that evidently is the side from which to look for reform. (*Cheers.*) Whilst I would no more abolish titles than I would seek to destroy Glasgow Cathedral, as they are relics of

---

[24] 'The Glorious Twelfth,' the start if the grouse-shooting season.

a fast-departing picturesque age, still I would have no new ones created except for life, for what should it profit a man if he lose the whole world[25] and be made Baron Tooting, or some other like epithet of opprobrium - (*Laughter and cheers.*) - but from these titles all legislative powers should be taken away and an elected upper chamber, such as in France or America be instituted." (*Loud cheers.*)

## THE LAND QUESTION

*Mr. Graham then dealt with the nationalisation of land, the restoration of a peasant proprietary, the abolition of primogeniture, settlement and entail, compulsory registration of title, and a cheaper and less cumbersome method of land transfer, holding that power should be given to municipal councils to expropriate urban proprietors at a fair valuation, and to let it out in allotments. He then turned his attention to Ireland:*

## IRELAND

This is a subject so difficult to touch on, and so kittle[26] when touched, that it has always been the one that politicians approach with the greatest reluctance. It is not a subject for much self-congratulation that, since the 12th century, we have vainly endeavoured to rule and pacify a small island such as Ireland, situated within 30 miles of us, and only inhabited, even at present, by 5,500,000 people - that is to say, about the population of London, more or less. In Ireland, as in England and Scotland, one of the first questions to ask has been the land question, but in Ireland it has been intensified by the evil of absenteeism, whereby the greater portion of the revenue of the kingdom has always been spent outside of it; for there, as here, the aggregation of land in a few hands has enabled a small class to exact [word illegible] or competition rents. The history of Ireland has been a history of oppression, misconception, tyranny, and folly, such as the world has hardly ever seen, and such as may well make us blush for the Anglo-Saxon race, and exclaim: 'They manage things far better in France.'[27] It has, I think, been falsely charged on the Irish that they that they are idle and shiftless; but those of us who have seen them in America will at once deny. The great misfortune that has attended our dealings with Ireland has been that all our

---

[25] Mark 8:36
[26] Scots: Ticklish, tricky.
[27] In other words: 'How bad can things be?'

reforms and conciliatory measures have been so long delayed that they appear to have been extorted by force rather than granted willingly, and thus, not unnaturally, all their good effects have been lost. What we have to do at present, having put our hands to the plough not to look back, to endeavour to treat the Irish as we would be treated ourselves - that is to say, as men and as citizens, and not as children (*Cheers and slight hissing.*) The exasperating and puerile vice-regal system should be promptly done away with - (*Hear, hear, and cheers.*) - and full powers granted to the Irish to manage all their internal affairs. (*Cheers.*) It should be the wish of every right-thinking man whilst doing all in his power to maintain the integrity of the empire, at the same time to insist on according to our Irish fellow-subjects their just rights, and the impartial administration of justice without reference to creed, race, or locality. (*Cheers.*) Though long delayed, these measures, once passed, will, I am sure, convince the Irish people that Britons, as Liberals and citizens of the empire, are united in the firm determination to do them justice. (*Cheers.*) To all who regard the question from an unprejudiced standpoint, it must be at once apparent that whilst we owe the Irish many reparations for past wrongs, still separation would be as fatal for them as it would be injurious to us. (*Cries of "No," "Yes," and cheers.*)

### FREE EDUCATION

As you all know that I am a firm advocate of that dangerous and socialistic measure of free education, I will not trouble you with many words about it. But I will warn one and all of you that it is a measure that will involve much self- sacrifice. Do not be deluded for one moment by what some tell you about education being paid for out of the revenues of the churches or any of the like schemes. Education must be paid for by ourselves. We are the State, and it is the State's duty (that is to say our duty) to see that none of its citizens grow up ignorant. It is to education that we must look to refine the people, to shorten the hours of labour, and to join them all in the demand for proper dwelling houses, and, finally, to open their eyes to the fact that co-operation is their stronghold, and it is to that that they must look to free them from the stifling grasp of the capitalists who now enthrall them, and to make them clearly to understand that "the world is weary of work and gold." (*Cheers.*)

It is a curious fact that in Scotland there are no royalties upon minerals, except on gold; but would that there were, and that all coal and iron, and lead belonged to the nation. Unfortunately, we have not been so wise in our generation as the Spanish who, by their ancient "fueros," or national laws, have always considered the minerals in Spain as part of Spain herself, as in fact they are, for is not every shipload of metal sent out of a country an integral part of that country, that can never be regained? (*Cheers.*) Gentlemen, whilst the Dukes of Hamilton are making a monstrous income out of the mines of Lanarkshire, to be spent, God knows how, there are "thirty thousand under ground," toiling in the bowels of the earth for a bare subsistence. (*Hear, hear, and cheers.*) That we can abolish royalties on mines straight off is hardly to be hoped, but that mineral rents should be subjected to increased taxation is a proposition that few will be disposed to delay. (*Cheers.*)

## FOREIGN AFFAIRS

When I have advocated non-intervention in foreign affairs, it has not been in a spirit of indifference or neglect of our vast colonial interests. Every true Briton looks with pride and admiration on our empire, on which, like that of Charles the Fifth, the sun never sets. I do not believe that there lives a man so dead to self-respect and love of country, who would refuse to shed his blood or spend his last shilling for the maintenance of it. (*Cheers.*) What I have deprecated is engaging in useless wars merely to push class or political interests. Should, however, war be necessary (which God forbid that it ever should) to maintain our commerce or uphold our empire, or in the interests of the great mass of the people, it should find a firm advocate in me. (*Cheers.*) Our soldiers and sailors are as much part and parcel of the national life as any other class of the community - round our sailors in particular have the national traditions ever been grouped. Whilst we may place absolute confidence in our army and navy to uphold our national honour abroad, in my opinion it is to the great volunteer movement that we should look for our defence, and to the development of which we should give our utmost care. (*Cheers.*) There should, I think, be little danger from the foreigner whilst we maintain unrivalled supremacy on the sea, and whilst at home we have an unpaid but disciplined army of citizen soldiers, each one animated with the sincere wish to do his duty, and encouraged by the thought that he is fighting for all that is dearest to man, and that Great Britain, extending her influence over the whole known world, has been the envy, the admiration, and the despair of other nations, whilst abroad her commerce and kinship binds her indissolubly to her colonies; at home she is secure from all foreign dangers by the arms of her stalwart sons, and by her natural position "sae fast in the sea.[28] (*Loud and prolonged cheering.*)

~

Graham's chances of success looked encouraging, but ironically, immediately before the election, Charles Stewart Parnell, leader of the Irish Parliamentary Party, issued an order to his newly enfranchised Irish voters in Britain that, in seats where a Conservative was opposed by a Liberal or a radical, they were to cast their votes in favour of the Conservative Party, since they now offered the best hope of progress towards Irish Home Rule. This was a blow that would prove fatal to Graham's chances, as the Irish vote swung solidly behind his opponent. Gladstone scraped back into power, with the support of the Irish MPs, on the basis that he would introduce an Irish Home Rule Bill, but this was defeated, and he resigned. A second election was called for 9th of July 1886, and Graham was again selected as the Liberal candidate for North-West Lanarkshire.

## ELECTION ADDRESS AT COATBRIDGE
*The Coatbridge Express*, 30th of June 1886.

*One of the largest and most enthusiastic meetings which ever crowded the Temperance Hall, Coatbridge, was held there on Monday night, [28th June] the occasion being addressed by Mr. R. B. Cunninghame Graham of Gartmore, the Ministerial [Gladstonian] candidate for the representation of North-West Lanarkshire. The hall was closely packed, and hundreds who were anxious to gain admission were either turned away to the Unionist meeting in the theatre, or lingered at the windows and doors of the Temperance Hall to catch portions of the speeches given therein [. . .] Councilor Reid, who was called to the chair, briefly introduced the candidate to the meeting. Mr. R. B. Cunninghame Graham, who was received with great cheers, said:*

There is only one question before the electors, and it, like Aaron's rod has swallowed up all others. (*Cheers.*) Within the last few months, events have succeeded each other with startling rapidity. Even as a sermon which was short was not counted less acceptable, so I hope will my speech if it were brief. Once again the Liberal party is appealing to this country under the leadership of its same old chief [Gladstone] -

---

[28] Possibly a misquotation from Gawin Douglas's Scottish vernacular translation of *The Aeneid* (1513).

(*Cheers.*) - and I am proud to be again selected to be the Liberal candidate of North-West Lanarkshire. (*Cheers.*) I am also proud that by your assistance I am able once more to fight the battle of freedom, of temperance, and of toleration. (*Cheers.*) I have pleasure in holding up the Democratic flag against privilege and monopoly, and I stand here on behalf of Liberalism, of Home Rule, and of Mr. Gladstone. (*Cheers.*) The question is whether we would restore to Ireland, by acknowledging frankly and honestly, and like men, that we have been wrong - whether we would restore to Ireland that Parliament, which she has formerly enjoyed, the withdrawal of which formed so black and so base a page in our national history, and, indeed, it was the withdrawal of that Parliament which has been the cause of anarchy, agrarian outrage and disturbance - a state of matters which has now existed for the last eight years - or whether we would, on the other hand, pursue the old, old policy of Lord Salisbury - (*Groans.*) - which was twenty years resolute government, prohibition of public meetings, censorship of the press, searching for arms, and a thousand and one fictitious annoyances which were incidental to governing Ireland according to English ideas. (*Cheers*) Had these annoyances been imposed upon Scotland, they would have resulted in civil war - aye, and would have deluged the country in blood from John o' Groats to the Solway. (*Cheers.*) What did Spenser, the poet, in Queen Elizabeth's time say? "Laws shall be fashioned unto the manners and requirements of the people for whom they are meant, otherwise, instead of good, they may work ill, and pervert justice to extreme injustice." (*Cheers.*) This from the first was what had been done with Ireland. English laws, excellently adapted no doubt for England, had been forced upon them, but they were found not to be suitable. It must be remembered that long ago Ireland was in the same position as the Highlands of Scotland. There was no such thing as absolute property in land - the chieftain and his clansmen had equal rights, the land belonging solely to the tribe. (*Cheers.*) And thus they found, owing to this patriarchal system, a freer, a nobler, and a more manly style of manners and customs prevailed in Ireland than there did among the Normans in England. Would that the relationship between chieftain and clansman existed still - would that the landlords of Ireland had not forgotten that the soil of their country ought to be cultivated for the production of food and not exclusively for the production of rent. (*Cheers.*) We cannot call back yesterday. There are no birds in last year's nests - (*Cheers.*) - and what remains

29

for the Liberals to do, having seen the manifest failure and breakdown of the old system, was not to waste time in vain regrets, but to address ourselves as men to changing this state of affairs which has existed for so long. (*Cheers.*) Perhaps some of you might ask - What has this to do with Mr. Gladstone and Home Rule? My answer to the Tory is nothing - (*Laughter.*) - but to the Liberal a great deal. (*Cheers.*) No doubt the Tories will say, as I have heard two of them say, while travelling in a train - "Look here, old fella', it's no good of talking about the Irish, they are an inferior race" - (*Laughter.*) - and the other Tory replied - "Yes old chappie, by Jove they are, and it's all on account of their d——d religion." (*Great laughter.*) Well, there is no good in reasoning with such people - (*Cheers.*) – but if argument is required they would need to say with Shakespeare "There is no conclusive argument for your dull ass but a stout stick."[29] (*Laughter and cheers.*) To a Liberal – and I hope you are all Liberals – (*Cheers.*) – the historical aspect of every question is always useful, because it enables a man to comprehend more completely the feelings and prejudices inherent in a race of people and it enables him to take a clearer and more comprehensive view of the present existing circumstances. There is one issue now before the electorate of this country, and that is – "Gladstone or Salisbury." (*Cheers.*) In other words – "Tory or Liberal." (*Renewed cheers.*) None others are – (*Cheers.*) - because all the various schemes you have heard debated of late are but schemes of private individuals. (*Hear, hear.*) I maintain most emphatically there are only two schemes - namely, those of rival Ministers, "Salisbury and Gladstone" - "Home Rule or coercion." (*Cheers.*) Of course we know there are people in the world who like to see justice done - especially to themselves - (*Laughter.*) - but they are not particularly anxious to see justice done to others. (*Hear, hear.*) All those folks adopt the same platform as a certain young lord did - a man over three score and ten years - a man who from his youth upward has sympathised with the oppressed, whether at home or abroad - a man who is renowned throughout the world for his sympathy with law and order. (*Cheers.*) Did any sane man, looking at the question quietly and dispassionately, see danger in this Home Rule Bill. (*Cries of "No."*) As to the Land Purchase Bill, I refuse to discuss it in its present shape. *(Hear, hear.)* For the present, we might assume that it is dead, but I will be no party to paying the Irish landlords at the

---

[29] A misquotation from Hamlet: Act V, Scene II.

risk and responsibility of the British ratepayer. (*Hear, hear.*) I esteem such a bill as but a sop to the landlords. (*Hear, hear.*) A soap bubble blown up in the air for fools to chase. (*Laughter.*) It has been said that the Nationalist party would not stop there. Mr. Parnell in the House of Commons has accepted the bill on behalf of his party, and are the critics to call Mr. Parnell a liar? I am not disposed to contend for one moment that the possession of absolute power is an unmixed blessing for any man; but I have yet to learn that Mr. Parnell would have absolute power. He would have no power in Ireland other than a moral one. (*Cheers.*) That Mr. Parnell will be the first Prime Minister in Ireland is excessively likely, but like other Prime Ministers he would have to face an opposition; and the mere fact of governing and being responsible for law and order has a very sobering effect. Mr. Parnell will have to face a disorganised and disunited people; he will have a large national debt to meet, and a small revenue to meet it with. More than all of that, if he wishes to separate, he would have to face loyal Ulster - (*Laughter.*) - Major Saunderson - (*Hooting.*) - and Johnson of Ballykilbeg; and besides all of these, he would have to face 30,000 British troops and the strongest fleet that ever rode the sea. (*Cheers.*)

I will now turn to the Birmingham school, and the followers of that political chameleon – Mr. Joseph Chamberlain. (*Laughter and hisses*) The objections of this party are chiefly two. The first I do not consider valid as it is the absurd and degraded 'No Popery' cry; and the second, which is a little more valid, is that if a Parliament was established in Dublin, one of its first Acts will be to impose protective duties upon Irish industries. This was carefully provided for in Mr. Gladstone's scheme; but I do not believe for one moment that a cool-headed statesman like Mr. Parnell would seek to place his country is such a disadvantageous position. But should he do so it would not affect this country, else the whole theory of Free Trade would fall to the ground. Besides, the lesson the Irish would receive from the prompt stagnation from their home manufacturers would soon cure them of their trouble. (*Cheers.*) The keynote of Mr. Gladstone's Irish policy is to be found in trust in the people, and dare to do the right. (*Cheers.*) The bill might be dead, but the principle survives - (*Hear, hear.*) – because of the heroism of one man who has determined to do battle for the liberties of a nation even though he is on the threshold of the grave. (*Cheers.*) If he should fail, and failure is possible, the seed sown will germinate, and produce fruit after many days. Come what may, no one can deprive Mr. Gladstone of the glory of being the first to see clearly in this momentous question. Like Moses, he might see the Promised Land and never enter it. He might fail, but the glory of his failure will remain till the end of time. Who can withhold their sympathy and their admiration, their respect for the heroic old man standing, like Saul, head and shoulders above his countrymen, calm, serene, and alone, gazing over the troubled seas of contemporary politics into the quiet waters of the future in much the same spirit as we might imagine the old Spanish navigator gazed for the first time over the Pacific from the tall peak of Darien.[30] (*Great cheering.*)

This time, the Irish vote swung solidly behind him, and he was elected with a majority of 334. *The Glasgow Herald* expressed both "surprise and disappointment."[31]

~

Graham seems to have been in no great rush to attend Parliament, which reassembled on the 6th of August, and there is no record of him taking the Oath, but, perhaps following the precedent set by Charles Bradlaugh M.P., he may have 'affirmed.'[32] Nor are there any newspaper reports of him being in attendance at the many meetings in Lanarkshire throughout August and September in support of the miners, against the reduction in their wages by 6d a day, due to a slump in the demand for coal; meetings at which a former miner, turned journalist, Keir Hardie, was becoming prominent.

On the 2nd of October *The Airdrie Advertiser* reported:
> We understand that owing to the serious illness of Mrs. Graham, her husband, the member for North West Lanarkshire was unable to be in his place in the House of Commons during the last part of the last session, although we believe he paired in favour of Mr. Parnell's Bill.[33]

Although concern was widely expressed for his wife Gabriele's health, it was a poor start to his parliamentary career, and undermined his supporters' confidence in him.

When Parliament reassembled in 1887, Graham did not join his fellow Liberals, but sat on the cross benches, between the Crofters' Party and the Irish MPs. 'The Address in

---

[30] John Keats, 'On First Looking Into Chapman's Homer.' (1816).

[31] 'General Election Results and Comment,' *The Glasgow Herald* (10 July 1886), p.4.

[32] Charles Bradlaugh (1833-1891), an atheist and republican, and founder of the National Secular Society in 1866. He had been imprisoned in Westminster Clock Tower, and fined for refusing to take the Oath, but was eventually allowed to 'affirm' in 1886. The law was changed in 1888 allowing future affirmations. His funeral was attended by 3,000 mourners, including Mohandas Gandhi.

[33] Presumably, 'The Tenant's Relief (Ireland) Bill.'

Answer to Her Majesty the Queen's Most Gracious Speech,' a debate which dealt with Ireland, British Foreign Policy, and Expenditure, was the ideal opportunity for him "to lose his political virginity," and he rose on the 4th night, on the 1st of February 1887, to make his Maiden Speech, a speech that would his establish his reputation as an orator of wit, originality, and mockery, and it reflected the major themes which had, and would continue to occupy his energies - the plight of the poor, oppression in Ireland, and British imperialism:

## MAJESTY'S MOST GRACIOUS SPEECH. ADJOURNED DEBATE. [34]
[FOURTH NIGHT], 1st of February 1887.
MR. CUNNINGHAME GRAHAM (Lanark, N.W.)

A debate on the Queen's Speech forms the best occasion for a new Member to lose his political virginity (*Laughter.*), and, therefore, I cast himself at once on the forbearance and the generosity of the House.

On glancing over the Queen's Speech, I am struck with the evident desire which prevailed in it to do nothing at all. There was a similarity in its paragraphs to the laissez-faire school of political economy. Not one word was said in the Speech about lightening the taxation under which Her Majesty's lieges at present suffered; not one word to make that taxation more bearable; not one word to bridge over the awful chasm existing between the poor and the rich; not one word of kindly sympathy for the sufferers from the present commercial and agricultural depression (*Hear, hear!*) - nothing but platitudes, nothing but views of society through a little bit of pink glass. To read Her Majesty's Speech, one would think that at this present moment this happy country was passing through one of the most pronounced periods of commercial activity and prosperity it has ever known. One would think that wheat was selling at 50s. a-quarter, and that the price of bread had not gone up. One would think that poverty, drunkenness, prostitution, and wretchedness were in a fair way to be utterly extirpated; and one would think further that Great Britain had made the first important step towards that millennium when the Irish landlord would cease from troubling, and when the landlords and tenants would lie down in amity, and finally be at rest. (*Laughter.*)

Of course, it is matter for congratulation that this country was not suddenly called

---

[34] Transposed into the first person from Hansard and *The Airdrie Advertiser*, (5 February 1887).

upon to enter upon a Quixotic crusade to place Prince Alexander of Battenberg[35] upon the Throne of Bulgaria.

We are thankful for small mercies, and I supposed we must be content. If this unlucky nation had to forego the pleasure of paying for the vagaries of Prince Alexander, it had still a pretty large group of needy Royalties who were placed on the Civil List of this country. (*Laughter and Radical cheers.*)

It is not to be expected that Her Majesty's Government would vouchsafe to the House any idea of when the British troops might be withdrawn from Egypt. That is expecting far too much. But, surely, it would be wise to let the House know when it was intended to withdraw those troops from their inactivity in that pestilential region, and from playing the ungrateful role of oppressors of an already down-trodden nationality. (*Radical cheers.*) But no. The bondholders must have their pound of flesh. We must also protect the so-called high road to India by the Suez Canal, in order that the very last straw might be laid on the unfortunate fellaheen,[36] and that British money and British treasure might be poured out like water. I had forgotten the "cent per cent." (*A Laugh.*) I had forgotten by whose advice we were in Egypt - that it was by the advice of that illustrious statesman and economist who has raised the art of carpet-bagging from its primitive rudeness into a political science, (*Laughter.*) and who so well illustrated the Scriptural injunction, "When they persecute you in one city, flee to another."[37] (*Great Laughter.*)

With reference to our latest filibustering exploit in Burmah, it was a matter of great congratulation - it was something on which a Christian might truly plume himself, to hear that Her Majesty's Government were in process of rapidly suppressing brigandage, which had grown up in the country, and in putting down bands of marauders. "Marauders," like "mobled Queen,"[38] was "good," very good, when applied to poor, unfortunate, misguided people, who, in their pig-headed way, were endeavouring to defend their own country. Does the House recognise how a band of marauders was put down? I do; I have seen it done often. Surely, it can be no great matter of self-

---

[35] A nephew to Tsar Alexander II of Russia, and uncle to Earl Mountbatten of Burma. He was elected Prince of Bulgaria in 1879, but forced to abdicate in 1886. His wish to marry Queen Victoria's daughter, Princess Viktoria of Prussia, was the source of political intrigue, and potential Royal scandal.
[36] Arabic: An agricultural labourer.
[37] Matthew 10:23
[38] Hamlet: Act II, Scene II. 'O, who had seen the mobled [swaddled] queen.'

congratulation for Britons with arms of precision to shoot down naked savages. It can be no feather in a soldier's cap to suppress these unfortunate wretches with all the resources of civilisation at his command. When the telegrams came from Burmah we slapped our hands on our chests, quite regardless of damage to our shirts, (*Applause.*) and talked of British gallantry; and so we laughed like parrots at a bagpiper, when we looked at the sketches in the illustrated papers depicting Natives running away from our troops. A native wounded to death, I take it, and tormented by mosquitoes in the jungle, felt his misery as acutely as the best be-broadclothed gentleman among us, even though he should happen to be a chairman of a School Board; but what is all that to the Government? The Government, like an American hog, must root or die.

The question is, how did this Government come in? That is the humour of it. They came in by the help of the pseudo-Liberals – the crutch-and-toothpick Gentlemen (*Laughter*) – through the assistance of that feeble Union ladder which, having been used and abused, was now about to be cast aside and been kicked into the dunghill. I was delighted to see how the noble Lord (Lord Randolph Churchill)[39] last night treated his Unionist allies – to observe that, having betrayed their master, like Judas Iscariot, there was but one resource left for them, and that was to go out and hang themselves (*Great Laughter.*) – and to see how these superior persons fell out and bespattered one another, and I thought to myself, "How these mugwumps [40] love one another." This Government reminds me of Pope's flies in amber:- "Things in themselves though neither rich nor rare, One wonders how the devil they got there."[41]

The noble Lord [Churchill], with that retiring modesty which was his great characteristic, left the government to seek obscurity or popularity as the case may be. His alleged pretext was economy. Well, it was easy to wish for economy, but to follow it was quite a different affair. What was the use of his preaching economy in the face of an ever-increasing army? (*Radical cheers.*) The army was the first branch of expenditure where economy might be practiced. What should a small democratic State like this want with an army? Its only use could be to wring another million or two out of stout patient ass, the British Public. (*Great Laughter.*)

---

[39] Father of future Prime Minister, Winston Spencer Churchill.
[40] People who stand aloof from sordid party politics.
[41] Alexander Pope: An Epistle to Arbuthnot (1734).

I do not wish to be understood to say a word against the navy, or any money that ought to be spent upon it. (*Cheers.*) I do not impugn the skill of our military officers, or the gallantry, prudence, and daring of our brave troops, but they should not be allowed to exercise their gallantry, bravery, and daring at the public expense. (*Laughter.*) I deprecate still more the spending of any public money to find places for the younger sons of our plutocrats and autocrats. (*Hear, hear.*) I deprecate spending the money of this country to forward the ambition of soldiers and diplomats who made the name of Britain execrated in the four corners of the globe. (*Irish cheers.*)

Personally, I regret the resignation of the noble Lord the Member for South Paddington. He was a type in times of dull uniformity, and from the depth of his obscurity I admire the noble Lord's parabolic course. (*Laughter.*) The noble Lord's resignation has saddened me as children are saddened when they see a rocket spout up, and were all unaware that it would fall down a stick (*Laughter.*) - as was well said by Ben Jonson - "He was a child that so did thrive in grace and feature, (*Laughter.*) As Heaven and nature seemed to strive which owned the creature."[42] Where is the noble Lord now? Yesterday he was, to-day he was not - gone like the froth on licensed victuallers' beer, or the foam on petroleum champagne, leaving Her Majesty's Government, alone and unaided, to wrestle with the difficulties of the situation, and to give "their careful consideration to all the matters" pertaining to their functions. (*Laughter.*)

With respect to Ireland, I have eminent qualifications for dealing with that subject, for many reasons. First of all, I have never been there (*Laughter.*); secondly, sitting next to Nationalist Members, I have gained, of late, something of National colour; and I had once known an Irish commercial traveller, who imparted to me various facts quite unattainable by the general public. I have also gained much information from the hon. Member for Camborne (Mr. Conybeare), who has recently been staying with the nobility and gentry of that country. From these sources, I have conceived a warm respect and regard for that much-abused and downtrodden class - the Irish landlords, who are held in the deepest affection by their tenants. As to the Glenbeigh evictions,[43] the landlords have been held up to most unjust obloquy, as they have ever been most

---

[42] Ben Jonson: An Epitaph on S. P. (1616).
[43] After rent increases of 50%, seventy families on the County Kerry estate of Rowland Winn (later, Lord Headley), who could not pay, were ruthlessly evicted in January 1887, and their houses leveled or burned. This situation had already been brought before the House of Commons on 28 January 1887.

kind to their tenants, whom, in fact, they have kept in cotton wool. It is the pride and the privilege of the Irish landlord to look after the interests, creature as well as spiritual, of his tenants; and, such is the relation of class to class that, so far from turning them out on a bleak, cold winter's night, the landlord has provided his dependents with a fire to warm their hands; only, through a pardonable inadvertence, it was their houses that had furnished the blaze.

The Government has lighted a light that will serve to light the Liberals on their path. The homes destroyed in Glenbeigh were, no doubt, as dear to the poor peasant (*Irish cheers.*) in his lonely village on the stony mountain side in the far west, as is the shoddy mansion in South Kensington to the capitalist, as is Haddon Hall to its owner, or as is Buckingham Palace to the absentee owner of that dreadful building. (*Cheers and great laughter.*) Who can say that the affairs of this handful of obscure tenants in a wind-swept and rain-bedewed, stony corner of Ireland, might not prove to have given the first blow to that society in which one man worked and another enjoyed the fruit - that society in which capital and luxury makes a Heaven for 30,000, and a Hell for 30,000,000 - that society whose crowning achievement is this dreary waste of mud and stucco - with its misery, its want and destitution, its degradation, its prostitution, and its glaring social inequalities - the society which we call London - that society which, by a refinement of irony, has placed the mainspring of human action, almost the power of life and death, and the absolute power to pay labour and to reward honour, behind the grey tweed veil which enshrouded the greasy pocket-book of the capitalist. (*Laughter.*)

~

## REACTIONS TO CUNNINGHAME GRAHAM'S MAIDEN SPEECH

The audacity and eloquence of this speech stunned the House of Commons, and brought a stream of praise from the political diarists:

THE PALL MALL GAZETTE, 9th of February 1887, by 'Looker-on':
The House welcomed the advent of a wit last night. The rising of Mr. Cunninghame Graham, about half-past nine o'clock, was the signal for a mild sensation, the hon. Member being distinguished by a remarkable, not to say eccentric, personality. The chatter and personal criticism soon ceased. He had scarcely spoken a dozen sentences when he had secured the ear of the House, and almost every other sentence

thereafter was punctuated by bursts of general laughter, and occasionally by the sound of party cheers. The speech was not unmarked by irony and sentiment; but it will be remembered by its smartness and wit. The hon. member for Lanarkshire made a most successful maiden speech.

In the same journal, 'Occasional Note':
The really important thing in last night's debate was the discovery of a new Liberal wit, in the person of Mr. Graham, no slight acquisition in these endless nights of dreary talk *de omnibus rebus est quibusdam aliis* [44] just as the night before was remarkable for the discovery of a really clever Tory in the person of Mr. Curzon.[45] Readers of our "Mems about Members" will have been prepared for both apparitions. Our only fear is our "selections" may be spoiled by their immediate successes. No man can be witty if he speaks too often. Even Mr. Labouchere is sometimes flat, and Sir Wilfred Lawson is often watery - unto tears rather than unto laughter. Let Mr. Graham be warned, and not make him too cheap - nor his wit (to use his own expression) "like the froth of the licensed victualler's beer, or the foam on petroleum, champagne.

VANITY FAIR by 'Sir Rougham Rasper, Bart., M.P.', 5th of February 1887.
Advent of a new man. Name: Cunninghame Graham. Description: Scotch Home Rule Visionary. Outward aspect: Something between Grosvenor Gallery aesthete and waiter in Swiss café. Person of "cultchaw," evidently, from tips of taper fingers to loftiest curl of billowy hair, and with sad soulful voice to match. Drawls out some deuced smart things. Effect of speech heightened by air of chastened melancholy. House kept in continuous uproar for more than half-an-hour. Fogeys and fossils eye him askance, and whisper that he ought to be "put down;" but lovers of originality, in all quarters, hail him with satisfaction.' [He added that he would try: 'To make a point of being present whenever Graham obliges.']

A rare dissenting voice was the Conservative *St James's Gazette*:
ST JAMES'S GAZETTE, 3rd of February 1887.
Mr. R. B. Cunninghame Graham, the member for North-West Lanarkshire, sacrificed what he was pleased to call his "political virginity" to the desire to get laughed at in the House of Commons. Some of Mr. Graham's jokes succeeded in evoking laughter, although the more elaborate of them seem to have fallen flat. He called the Liberal Unionists "crutch and toothpick gentlemen," compared Mr. Randolph Churchill to the "froth on licensed victuallers' beer or the foam on petroleum champagne," and imparted the necessary flavour of profanity into his

---

[44] Latin: Concerning all things and certain other matters.
[45] George Curzon (1859-1925). Later, Lord Curzon of Kedleston, Viceroy of India (1899-1905), and Foreign Secretary (1919-1924).

performance by making irrelevant Scripture quotations in the middle of the funniest passages. In respect of taste and ability, as well as in its usefulness as a contribution to the transaction of public business, his speech was exactly on a level with a political song at a music hall; and a music hall is about the only place, outside the House of Commons, where such a performance would be likely to receive a patient hearing.

The toleration which the House of Commons extends to mere buffoonery is difficult to explain. Gratitude is sometimes expressed to these gentlemen for "enlivening the proceedings." Some people may possibly be enlivened by listening to Mr. Graham or Mr. Conybeare; but wit and eloquence must indeed be at a low ebb if this sort of thing is needed to keep our legislators awake. There are no doubt, dull speakers and even depressing speakers to be found in the House. But uniform dullness would be better than dullness relieved by such humour as Mr. Graham's. Mr. Graham and his rivals, however, aim at something more than the applause of their audience and the advertisement of their names. Their third-rate witticisms are intended to be read and repeated by their constituents. Mr. Graham hopes, no doubt, that his tawdry phrases will pass from lip to lip in Lanarkshire, and that his constituents will feel an honest glow of pride in the possession of a member who can keep his brother legislators laughing for half an hour at a time. A quiet man who attends to business, and never speaks until he has something to say, is not the most popular kind of member with a very large class of voters. A man whose name appears prominently in the papers is the ideal member of this class; and they do not greatly care by what quality he obtains this prominence. If he cannot obtain it by eloquence or ability, let him do so by buffoonery. It is for the working classes all over the country to show that those who believe them to prefer a clown to a man of business are mistaken. They owe it to themselves to put a bridle on the Parliamentary buffoon.

~

Graham's impact on the House can be witnessed from an article written the following year, signed: 'Young Parliamentary Hand' which appeared in the hugely successful 'United Ireland,' the imprisonment of whose Editor, William O'Brien, would be the pretext for a momentous demonstration in Trafalgar Square, which became known as 'Bloody Sunday':

PORTRAITS IN THE HOUSE by Young Parliamentary Hand.[46]

From the beginning Cunninghame Graham was regarded as one of the most remarkable men in the new Parliament. His appearance alone singled him out from the ordinary run and ruck of new members who huddled (timidly) together in the lobbies

---

46 *United Ireland*, (3 March 1888), p.6.

of Westminster. They stared in amazement at the stranger who always seemed to be in a hurry. Had Cunninghame Graham only carried himself a little less erectly, if his closely-knit frame had been a little less sinewy, and his movements less limber, he might very well have passed muster as the representative of a certain school of art. But anyone who carried investigation beyond the cursory glance soon noticed muscularity in the body which never came from wielding a paint-brush, a tan upon the firm flesh which never was due to the cool light and shade of stuccoed studios. In fact, the critical observer noted something about Cunninghame Graham that was of a soldierly smack, but not quite soldierly either. That the man was a mighty rider was obvious to the experienced eye in a little, but his movements were not that of a cavalryman: they were freer, less stiff, simpler.

London, more eager than Athens of old for something new, was pleased, at the time, to take a great deal of interest in that curious production of American frontier life, the Cow-boy. Buffalo Bill and his merry men were the heroes of the hour, and in certain circles, while the craze lasted, little was talked or thought but the Cow-boy. The Cow-boy fever ran its course and died away as all such frenzies do in a great capital where people hunger and thirst after any new excitement.

If Cunninghame Graham had been content to call himself 'Mexican Jack' and to sport a sombrero, he would have obtained what the French call a *succès fou*,[47] but he was a man with a mission, and languid London does not love men with missions. He was a Radical in the true sense of the term - a Radical with that touch of Quixotism without which few reforms would ever come to anything. He saw that there was work to be done, and he set himself to do it with the same fiery energy and indomitable determination which he had shown during his former travels in wild lands. He entered Parliament not to play the part of the silent member, but to plead vehemently for all the causes dearest to his heart.

It is needless to say that he made himself at once amazingly unpopular with all the 'classes,' with advocates of things as they are, and that if there was one individual whom the average Tory hated almost a much as any Irish member, it was the impetuous, red-haired Cunninghame Graham.

The Tory press wholeheartedly agreed:

> He is above all things a "misanthropic professional philanthropist," whose love for his fellow man in the abstract is compatible with a limitless capacity for making himself objectionable to individuals in the concrete [. . .] He is unquestionably the most unpopular man in the House of Commons.[48]

---

[47] French: An extraordinary success.
[48] *The Observer* (20 June 1889), p.4.

~

In a unique, candid speech to young Liberals in 1889, Graham spoke about his original motivation (or lack of it) to become a Member of Parliament, and his instant disillusionment. If we accept a measure of light-hearted hyperbole in front of this youthful audience, his simplified explanation as to how and why he became radicalised, has a ring of authenticity.

## Mr. CUNNINGHAME GRAHAM M.P., AT COATBRIDGE.

*The Coatbridge Express*, 8th of June, 1889.[49]

*On Thursday night Mr Graham appeared in the Temperance Hall under the auspices of the Coatbridge Junior Liberal Association of which he is honorary President . . . Mr GRAHAM was right heartily received. The hon. Gentleman, it was evident, had a severe cold, and on rising said that in consequence he was afraid it would be impossible for him to speak at any great length:*

You might wonder why I had ever asked the suffrage of this constituency. Well, when I first came before you, two men more profoundly ignorant of every political question than Mr. Baird and myself you could not possibly have found. (*Laughter.*) Mr. Baird's ignorance was only equal to my own. I had the most profound contempt for politicians, and you might wonder why I wished to join them. I found himself at home at Gartmore actually unemployed, and had the wish, not unnatural in a man of my age, to put Member of Parliament to my name, and get out of the duties as easily as possible. (*Laughter.*) On entering the House the attitude of parties did not in the smallest degree induce me to change my position, and for the first three weeks I took the smallest possible interest in business, for I saw that none of the political parties was in earnest, and intended to fill no pledges they had given to the electors at the election times. This might have gone on with me, but one hot night in July I happened to walk down to Trafalgar Square,[50] and it struck me that on each side they had the carriages with the rich ladies, the great hotels, the business men, carriages and traffic generally, and in the middle in the square three or four hundred people for whom the civilisation of Great Britain had found no place, and who were as surely outcasts as if they had been left on a

---

[49] Transcribed into the first person.
[50] The summer of 1887 was unusually hot, and Britain was in deep recession. Hundreds of unemployed people were camped in Trafalgar Square, where the fountains offered some relief from the heat, and it became a focus for civil unrest. Fear of a socialist revolution led to the outlawing of public meetings in the Square which precipitated the 'Bloody Sunday' riot.

desert island, and I thought, perhaps I was wrong, that this strife of political parties had never done, and never would do, anything for these men, and no matter who sat on the Treasury bench, no matter whether Queen Victoria or Mr. Bradlaugh filled the British throne - (*Laughter.*) – no matter whether parliamentary men were paid or not, no matter whether Parliament was shorter or longer, that all this political strife did not enter into the inner life of those men and women at all. I went back to the House of Commons, where they were discussing some question of foreign policy and party finance and the whole thing seemed to me a sham, and existed for no definite purpose at all; but it seemed that this question of the unemployed of our great cities was the one our statesmen should face. (*Applause.*) It immediately struck me that the most tangible commonsense reform that could be applied was one that would induce the capitalist to employ more labour, and absorb the unemployed into the ranks of the employed. I did not think for a moment that any reform they could introduce would make good working men out of all the present generation. Owing to the wretched homes and ceaseless employment of many, it was almost impossible; but I noticed amongst those in the Square a large number of young men and women, and it seemed a dreadful thought that such should be passing from youth to middle age, and from that to old age, uselessly to themselves and the State, and, having turned over the various past reforms proposed, I did not see any that were satisfactory to meet their case. It seemed to me that this question of the general reduction of the hours of labour would, and I felt that to accomplish it some one would have to go to the men themselves and endeavor to band them together. The true slave is the man who has got to work all his time for some one else, and are there not many who have to do that? The readiest weapon to attack slavery of that nature was this general reduction of the hours of labour. There were some capitalists who had already perceived the benefits to be derived from this movement, but in the opposition to it there was practically no difference between the two parties.

# THE RADICAL MP & POLITICAL JOURNALIST

"Thinking of the 'Orny 'Anded One."
*Punch* (28 July 1888)

Soon after his apparent epiphany, Graham marked himself out as being at the extreme end of the broad church of Liberalism. Although strongly democratic, radical, and anti-imperialist, his utterances before and immediately after entering Parliament were ill-defined, but, after meeting William Morris,[51] on the 7th of February 1887,[52] he found, for the moment, at least some political focus. On the 3rd of April, in Glasgow, Graham became the first sitting MP to chair a 'socialist' meeting,[53] and Morris was the main speaker. However, Morris noted in his diary:

> Cunninghame Graham M.P. took the chair for me, which was thought bold on a Sunday and a Socialist meeting; he declared himself to be not a socialist *because* he

---

[51] William Morris (1834-1896). English textile designer, author, and socialist. A central figure in the Arts & Crafts movement.

[52] Morris wrote in his Diary: 'I ought to have noted that on the day that Parliament met, a young and new M.P., Cunninghame Graham by name, called on me by appointment to pump me on the subject of Socialism. A brisk sort of young man; the other day he makes his maiden speech and produced quite an impression by its brilliancy & socialistic hints.'

[53] Also considered remarkable for being held on a Sunday, in a sabbatarian country. It was not particularly bold; Sunday Society lectures were very popular in parts of Scotland.

agreed with the Owenite doctrine of man being made by circumstances; which seemed strange, & I rather took him up on that point.[54]

Undoubtedly, William Morris was a major influence on the development of Graham's ideas, however, neither Morris nor Graham were political dogmatists *per se*. Engels described Morris as: 'a settled sentimental socialist,'[55] and James Redmond insists: 'that Morris's socialism had a compassionate rather than ideological basis in no way mitigated the seriousness, even violence of his conviction,[56] a description, and qualification, that could equally be applied to Graham. Morris had freely admitted that he had been ignorant of economics and 'suffered agonies of confusion of the brain' trying to understand Marx's economic theories.[57] Another description of Morris, this time by H. M. Hyndman,[58] might also be pertinent: 'What was inartistic and untrue jarred upon him so acutely that he was driven to try and put it right all at once.'[59] Both men's moral principles were formed in response to their physical and spiritual environments, and their political convictions from their reaction to the social conditions they encountered, and each had adopted the ideas and language of socialism to suit their fundamentally compassionate and moral impulses. This is where Morris's influence was most significant, not in economic or even social theories, but, for two men from privileged backgrounds, and imbued with aesthetic temperaments and instincts, in providing Graham with an intellectual and philosophical foundation (and perhaps, justification from an older and already famous figure) which could support his radicalism. More tangibly, however, may have been Morris's influence on Graham's future literary output, which, although quite distinctive from Morris's, until the end of his life, resounded with echoes of Morris's (and his own) disdain for civilisation, and progress.

On occasions Graham would describe himself as a socialist,[60] but Hugh MacDiarmid wrote that Graham's socialism was not based on an adequate theory of social causation.[61] At his trial after Bloody Sunday, Graham's co-defendant John Burns had said of him: "He is a social reformer. I am a Socialist."[62] Graham's artist friend Will

---

[54] William Morris's Socialist Diary, 27 April 1887.
[55] Friedrich Engels, Paul and Laura Lafargue: *Correspondence Vol.II*, ed. Émile Bottogelli (Lawrence & Wishart, 1959), p.370.
[56] James Redmond, *Introduction* to Morris's *The News from Nowhere* (Routledge & Kegan Paul, 1977), p.xi.
[57] Morris, *How I Became a Socialist*, p.10. Also Bruce Glasier, *William Morris and the Early Socialist Movement* (1921), p.32.
[58] Henry Mayers Hyndman (1842 -1921) An English writer and Marxist politician. Hyndman was the controversial and domineering founder of the Social Democratic Federation, of which Morris was an active member until his resignation in December 1884 to form The Socialist League. In his influential book, *Origins of the Labour Party 1880-1900*. (Oxford University, 1965), p.24, Henry Pelling, describes Hyndman and Henry Champion as 'Tory Socialists.'
[59] H. M. Hyndman, Introduction to William Morris's *How I Became A Socialist* (1896), p.6.
[60] *The Scotsman* (23 September, 1899), p.12
[61] Hugh MacDiarmid, *Cunninghame Graham: A Centenary Study* (The Caledonian Press, 1952), p.9.
[62] Burns, who had defended himself, added from the dock: "I do not wish to seek shelter behind a man of his social position."

Rothenstein wrote that '[Joseph] Conrad knew that Cunninghame Graham was more cynic than idealist and was by nature an aristocrat, whose socialism was *a symbol* of his contempt for a feeble aristocracy and a blatant plutocracy.'[63] Malcolm Muggeridge wrote of Graham that: 'Few men would have found a classless, Socialist society as unpleasant as he.'[64] It was a fierce sense of injustice, for which socialism, as a general idea, seemed to provide potential solutions, that inspired him, but he was all too aware that these beliefs were at odds his own circumstances, which left him vulnerable to accusations of hypocrisy. *The Scotsman* was only too ready to bring this to public attention:

> He is the hero of the hour. His suspension from the House of Commons and his broken head in Trafalgar Square have won him the boundless admiration of all who regard the law as their enemy, and existing institutions as so many Jerichos to be overthrown by shouting and blowing of trumpets. Whether Mr Graham believes that rent is robbery and profit plunder is uncertain. He has not yet given a practical proof of his faith in the Socialist gospel. He has made great efforts to gain credence as an apostle of some of its doctrines; but he lacks one thing yet in order to compel the faith of the sceptical. If he is a sincere enthusiast, and not a mere windbag, he ought to give the only testimony that is worth anything as proof of sincerity. He should part his property among the poor. What is the use of posing as a leader among those who preach that rent is robbery, while he goes on drawing his rents? [65]

At a public meeting in Glasgow in June 1892, during Graham's campaign to win Camlachie as a 'Labour' candidate, an elector asked: 'Seeing Mr Graham had stated that he was in favour of land nationalisation without compensation, would he show a good example and throw up his own land?' Graham replied that he would not, he was in favour of land nationalisation – not charity, but justice – "*If he threw up his land he would be shutting his mouth.*"[66] Therein lies the extraordinary double paradox in which Graham found himself; in an era of deference to power and money, particularly 'old' money, it had been his aristocratic, 'landed' pedigree that had undoubtedly propelled him into a position of power where he could condemn the very system that had put him there, but knowing full well that without his privileged position, he would have been ignored as a crank.

Increasingly, however, the plight of the unemployed, and the pay and conditions of workers, particularly the miners, fired his thoughts and campaigns, and later, his pen. Also, the inability of ordinary people to make their voices heard, which he saw as crucial if the cause of the working classes was to be advanced. It was also a more

63 William Rothenstein, *Men and Memories 1900-1922* (London: Faber & Faber, 1932), p.165. Editor's italics.
64 Malcolm Muggeridge, *Time And Tide* (28 March 1936), p.440.
65 *The Scotsman* (6 December 1887), p.4. *The Glasgow Evening News* (25 June 1892), p.5.
66 *The Glasgow Evening News* (25 June 1892), p5

substantial stick with which to beat the British establishment, than the constant but nebulous condition of the poor.

Before he had the chance to speak in the House on behalf of the miners of his constituency, he had asked the Under Secretary of State on the 3rd of May 1887 if the police had special instructions to break up Socialist meetings, or if they acted on their own authority.[67] His first real opportunity, however, for an intervention was on the 12th of May, in support of a Bill presented by James Stuart, the Scottish-born MP for Shoreditch, which contended that the police had been unduly interfering with open-air Socialist meetings in London, and that this had been ordered from very high up.

## HANSARD: PUBLIC MEETINGS (Metropolis) SOCIALIST MEETINGS ON OPEN SPACES, 12th of May 1887.

MR. CUNNINGHAME GRAHAM (Lanark N.W.)

Mr. Speaker, I claim the indulgence of this House for a few moments to say a few words on this question, which I consider a most important one, and I do so all the more readily as I am not in the habit of trespassing often, or at great length, upon the patience and time of this House. I can quite imagine hon. Gentlemen opposite will say, what is the good of making a row about a lot of poor devils of Socialists? I do not think that anything very serious has been charged against these Socialists, though your Socialist is a fearful wild fowl. It is not long ago that the hon. Gentleman the junior Member for Northampton (Mr. Bradlaugh) was looked upon as Lucifer or Beelzebub, and hon. Gentlemen opposite said they could never sit with him in this House. Now they manage to take their dinners with him, and digest them very well; and I dare say the day is not far distant when we shall see the hon. Gentleman the junior Member for Northampton occupying a place above the Gangway, and not below it. I believe that those Socialists have been dispersed in their meetings simply and solely because they are poor, because their doctrines are not popular, and because no one cares to stand up and incur the odium of speaking for them. England is a free country thanks to Heaven! It is a free country for a man to starve in, that is a boon you can never take away from him, but it appears in the future it is not going to be a free country to hold public meetings in.

---

[67] Hansard: Questions - Law And Police Socialist Meetings, Instructions to Police (3 May 1887).

What with the closure in the House of Commons, coercion in Ireland, and the suppression of meetings in London, we are getting to an almost Russian pitch of freedom. And, Sir, should we succeed in arriving at the priceless boon of that freedom, we cannot wonder if the people at last shake themselves clear of their apathy, and take the matter a little into their own hands; I think it is not unlikely that, while we are talking here, the people will make a determined effort to assert their undoubted rights. I do not suggest that the people of England are ripe for revolution yet; they will be soon enough, especially in face of the Bills which are now presented to this House; but I do say that I can see no just motive whatever, that because a man's doctrine, or political faith, differs in some measure from that held by the rest of the community, free speech, which has always been considered the birthright of an Englishman, should be denied to him. Neither do I say that the police have acted on their own motion in this matter; we know perfectly well who stands behind them; we know that by the way in which questions have been dealt with, by the paltry, shuffling manner in which they have been put off and I am not here to say one word against the police of London; I consider them to be one of the finest bodies of men in the Kingdom; I am here to compassionate with them in having to do such dirty work as to break up meetings, and to behave in a manner which cannot but be repugnant to their feelings.

Now, I think every hon. Member of this House knows Buffalo Bill Colonel Cody[68] and I would suggest, very respectfully, to this House that a select deputation of the Unionist Party should wait upon Colonel Cody to ask him for the loan of a few thoroughbred Unionist Indians to coerce the people of London. As this House, after all, represents but a small portion of the community, and as nothing is gained nowadays without agitation, I hope the public will not let this matter rest, but will agitate and bring it before the attention of this House, so that we shall be obliged to concede freedom of speech and the right of meeting to every class of the community

---

[68] 'Buffalo Bill's Wild West' had officially opened in London three days earlier, causing a sensation in the capital. Graham had first met William 'Buffalo Bill' Cody when fording the Pecos River at Horsehead Crossing, Texas, in 1880, when he was ranching cattle in San Antonio, prior to being burnt out by Mescalero Apaches. In her biography, *The People's Laird* (2005), Anne Taylor writes of this speech: "This last suggestion seemed to have no other purpose than to remind the House that here was a man who had ridden with Buffalo Bill Cody, herded cattle on the Texas ranges, and was acquainted with real, not stage, Indians. Thus it would incur the charge of playing to the gallery - 'making a figure' was how *The Airdrie Advertiser* more politely put it - seems not to have occurred to Robert who had not yet grasped the effect his colourful personality and forceful language had upon his audiences." Graham entertained Cody in The Glasgow Art Club, during his show's second visit to Glasgow between the 1st and 6th of August, 1904.

~

The opportunity to fulfill his commitment to the miners did not arrive until the 15<sup>th</sup> of August during the marathon Coal Mines, Regulation Bill, which contained over fifty clauses, dealing with general working conditions, including the inspection of mines, but it was a Bill introduced by the Liberals who were now in opposition, supported by Irish M.P.s. Graham was active throughout the long hours of the debates, speaking nineteen times in support of proposals, and put forward clauses such as the care of working horses, the dangers caused by the use of unskilled labour, the detention of workers underground after the finish of their shift, secondary ventilation to the mines, the banning of workers purchasing sub-standard lamps, and the setting up of an accident and insurance fund. He also put forward a clause to refer disputes to stipendiary magistrates, and, that miners' homes should not be tied to their employment:

## AMENDMENT TO COAL MINES REGULATION BILL
HOUSE OF COMMONS: 3<sup>rd</sup> of September 1887.

In Scotland, no workman shall be employed below ground in any mine to which this Act applies (except in cases of emergency) for a longer period than eight consecutive hours, and for more than eight hours in any twenty-four hours, when the mine is worked on the single shift system. The period of such employment shall be deemed to begin at the time of leaving the surface, and to end at the time of returning to the surface.

I know this clause will meet with considerable opposition; but it is a singular fact that all the Members for Lanarkshire, irrespective of Party, are agreed upon the question. The clause is framed to avoid opposition as far as possible. It is framed to apply only to Scotland, where there are 65,000 miners, men who dig the coal we talk about here, united as one man in their demand for the clause. I do not claim for one moment to represent the miners of Scotland more than any of the other Members for Scotland who have miners in their constituencies, except on this one clause; and on that I am their spokesman. I know that not a single voice will be raised from the miners in Scotland to controvert or traverse one single proposal that I should lay before the House. It is said that I am asking for a new thing. One would think I wished to subvert the Constitution by taking out the Mace from the Table and pawning it, or something of that sort. It is said that Parliament has never interfered with adult labour, and that this was a question which should be left to individual exertion, and that the miners in Scotland are strong enough to agitate for themselves and to get what they want carried into law. Whether or not the miners in England are strong enough to agitate for themselves and get their wishes carried out, the miners in Scotland were not able to do so. In proof of that I allude to the strike now going on amongst the Broxburn shale miners. These men had lowered the hours of labour by organisation. What has happened? They are now on strike, simply and solely because their employers have been able to break up their organisation, and will not open the mines, unless the miners consented to work 9 hours from bank to bank. More than that, 800 of them are this very day being evicted from their homes. And in what condition? Anyone who knows the miners of Scotland will know the miserable condition those men are in, and little by little they had disposed of their wretched goods and chattels. I appeal to anyone who has seen the eviction of a miner's family, whether a wretched rickety table, a dirty chair, and a few pots and pans do not constitute their whole household goods? In the face of a scene like that, they are to have political economy supply and demand and the mumbo-jumbo of books thrust down their throats. We sit here prating and prating, and 65,000 men who have come to us in their simple faith are to go away empty-handed. We have been challenged to produce a single instance where a properly accredited body of working men have passed a resolution in favour of the Eight Hours Movement. [69]

The Trades Unions Congress at Nottingham in 1883 unanimously passed a resolution to that effect, and the Trades Council of Glasgow in January of this year unanimously passed a similar resolution. Are those not properly accredited bodies of workmen, whose opinions go for something on this subject? But I suppose it will be said that trades unions, as a whole, have not spoken out, and given us their opinion. Far be it for me to attack trades unions; but I wish to supplement trades unionism. Where trades unionism is too weak to protect the working classes, I wish Parliament to step in and give them that protection by giving them an eight hours' day. It has been said that we would be opening the gate to other questions of a vastly wider scope by accepting

---

[69] Graham campaigned continually for the eight hour working day as the first step in a programme of much wider social reform: 'accepting it as the battle ground on which the first real skirmish of Capital and Labour (in our time) will be fought.' *The Labour Elector* (8 February 1890), p.93.

this Amendment. If we did so, I for one would be glad, because I wish to see this principle applied to every trade in the country. But before sitting down I would like to say this. If we pass this eight hours' clause, and I have great hopes we will do so, it will not interfere one jot, tittle, or iota with any other district where the men had already obtained by their own exertions what I now seek for these miners in Scotland. The clause only fixes a maximum. It does not force the men to work up to that maximum, but, of course, it says that beyond eight hours they should not work in the mine. It is a question of great importance to the future welfare of the miners in Scotland, and if Hon. Members opposite, who, I am willing to believe, are anxious to do what they can for the miners, cannot vote for it, I entreat you not to vote against it, but to walk out, and not defeat those who really knew what they were talking about.

On this question I am a practical man, and those who disagree with me are the academicians. The question is none of my raising. For my sins and yours, I have been speaking lately in every mining district in Scotland, at some 63 or 64 meetings, and at every one of them a resolution was unanimously carried in favour of eight hours a-day. The miners of Scotland are looking to this House to help them in this matter, and I hope every Member will bring a fair and unbiased judgment to bear upon the question.[70]

Graham concluded with these words:

I can tell (the Home Secretary) the miners look forward to the time when the Government will take over the mines and machinery and work them for the benefit of the people and not for the selfish ends of a few capitalists.

His Amendment was doomed from the outset, but the final flourish put the last nail in its coffin, and it was greeted with jeers and laughter by many in his own party, but Taylor writes: 'in all probability [this] was the first time nationalisation of the coal mining industry was taken seriously by anyone in the House of Commons.'[71]

---

[70] Hansard: Coal Mines, &c. Regulation Bill. (3 September 1887).
[71] Anne Taylor, *The People's Laird: A Life of Robert Bontine Cunninghame Graham* (The Tobias Press, 2005), p.159.

~

# EXPULSION FROM THE HOUSE OF COMMONS
12th of September 1887.

Graham's frenetic interruptions and incendiary language had already been adversely reported in a London daily newspaper on the 17th of August, under the title 'Mr. Graham's Eccentricities,' where he was described as bobbing up and down in the chamber to catch the Speaker's eye and intervene in the proceedings, and pacing around the lobbies: "at a pace seldom seen in Parliamentary circles." The Chairman of Committees eventually asked him to sit down, accusing him of having no idea of correct procedure, and after this rebuke: "the MP for North-West Lanarkshire vanished like a bubble that is blown away." Graham had already been criticised for his 'Buffalo Bill-like performances [. . .] gestures, postures, and unrefined Yankeeisms,' in a letter to *The Coatbridge Express*,[72] but the London article was reprinted in *The Airdrie Advertiser*, and undoubtedly damaged his reputation in the constituency. However, at this time Graham had also been desperately campaigning inside and outside Parliament to save the life of a young Polish Jew named Israel Lipski, who was about to hang for the brutal murder of a woman on dubious evidence.

Greater disappointment and anger were to follow, however, when the amended Bill came back from the Lords on the 12th of September, minus several of the clauses that Graham had campaigned for. The Secretary of State was in the process of accepting the Lords' amendments when Graham interrupted:

"Does the hon. Gentleman really intend to tell the House that after all the work and all the debates here our decisions are to be reversed by a small number of noble "minors" in "another place?"[73]

Despite objections from other MPs, the Secretary of State continued to accept the Lords' amendments and whittle away all the efforts that members of the Commons had debated. Again Graham interrupted:

"I really wish to know what this house intends to do for the safety on miners. We are not going, upon the question of safety hooks, to be put off by a consideration as to the speed of the winding, put off simply on the recommendation, not of a court of practical miners, not of those who represent the working miners, but simply because eight or ten old gentlemen, who know nothing of the subject."

---

[72] Letter to the Editor, *The Coatbridge Express* (3 August 1887), p.3.
[73] The House of Lords.

He was called to order and warned about describing the Lords in that manner, but again Graham intervened:

"I shall certainly not disobey your ruling, Sir; but what I wish to ask the right hon. Gentleman the Home Secretary is whether we are going to do something for the miners, whether as he has been appealed to by the miner's Representatives, he will not fake heart, and venture to move to disagree with those gentlemen to whom we owe so much respect."

The Secretary of State continued to accept the Lords ruling that it was not necessary for to have independent inspectors of mines, when again Graham objected:

"I am sorry to have to inflict any remarks of mine upon the House at 3 o'clock in the morning, but I feel bound to do so because I consider that the wishes of 60,000 miners in Scotland should be studied before the convenience of the Gentlemen sitting here . . . It is all very well for the Home Secretary to seek to stifle our arguments by using the name of the hon. member for Morpeth. Nobody respects him more than I do myself, but he does not speak for Scotland on this matter. I do, and I tell this House plainly, on behalf of the whole mining population of Scotland, that this Amendment will be opposed to the bitter end."

He concluded:

"It does seem a curious thing that an Assembly which is not elected by popular vote should dare to dictate to us, who are elected."

At this, the Speaker, having cautioned him twice, called "Order" and asked Graham to withdraw the words "Dare to dictate." Graham said that it was a matter of conscience and would not apologise. He was then 'named,' and W. H. Smith[74] made the Motion that he "be suspended from the Service of the House," which won by 157 Ayes to 44 Noes. Graham apologised for any perceived discourtesy to the Speaker, but would not retract his words about the House of Lords, and withdrew.

~

Graham's exasperation with the House of Commons in general, and the Liberal Party in particular, grew, and he regarded them as no better than the Tories, stating that he saw no difference between them "except the better cut of the Conservatives' boots," adding: "If a hat were dropped from the House of Commons on the Liberal benches, it would fall on the bald head of a millionaire." While in prison (see "Bloody Sunday" below) he

---

[74] William Henry Smith (1825-1891) was an English bookseller and newsagent of the family firm W H Smith & Son, who expanded the firm by selling books and newspapers at railway stations. Elected a Member of Parliament in 1868, within ten years he had risen to the position of First Lord of the Admiralty. Due to his lack of experience in naval matters, W. S. Gilbert parodied him as 'Sir Joseph Porter K.C.B.' in the comic opera H.M.S. Pinafore (1878). By the mid 1880s, he was twice Secretary of State for War, but by the time of Cunninghame Graham's outburst he was First Lord of the Treasury and Leader of the House of Commons.

wrote an article entitled: 'Has The Liberal Party A Future?' in riposte to an article a month earlier in the same publication by R. B. Haldane.[75] It was tantamount to a suicide note among the Liberal party establishment.

## HAS THE LIBERAL PARTY A FUTURE?
*The Contemporary Review*, February 1888.

No sensible man can be much exercised as to whether the Liberal Party - *qua* party - has a future or not. If the Liberal party is to be the party of humanity - the party that is to redress social inequalities, to make equal laws, to remove the stigma of poverty, to check vice in high places, to allow men to make us rich by their work without our taxing them before they begin, to stand between the employer and the employed, the landlord and the tenant, the poor and the police, why, then may it live a thousand years, and, above all, may the salaries of its officials resist the touchstone of common sense as long as possible! But, an[d][76] it will not do this, why, let it go, in God's name, and relegate itself to the limbo of all worn-out parties! That the old is passing away is, of course, since time was time, a truism; but it is because the Liberal party seems indisposed to admit this, and is seeking to restrain the new ideas in old brain-pans, that the children's teeth are being set on edge with the sour grapes of individualism, while the stomachs cry out for a satisfying meal of Socialism. *Laissez-faire* is a very pretty device in a book, or a study, but a poor thing in practice; *laissez-faire* the Corn Laws and the Factories Acts, *laissez-faire* the Irish and Highland landlords and the chaos of London no-government, and you will in a short time have to face a civil war or a revolution. The Liberals have of late concerned themselves too little with the condition of the people question, have been too apt to pay too much attention to lines of figures without souls, to say to those who say that party is on the increase, "My dear sir, you must be mistaken. Incomes of £2000 a year are far more prevalent (for it would seem to be epidemic) than they were ten years ago. Let us settle the Irish question, and get back, for God's sake, to

---

[75] Richard Burdon Haldane (1856-1928), Scottish lawyer, politician, and philosopher. At this time he was Liberal M.P. for Haddingtonshire (East Lothian), but later, Secretary of State for War, and Lord Chancellor. In a letter to his mother, dated 25 October, 1887, Haldane wrote that Graham's speeches were: 'doing a great deal of mischief all over Scotland.' Haldane of Cloan Papers, NLS, MSS 5940, f.101. Despite this, Haldane had stood bail for Graham following his arrest in Trafalgar Square, and given evidence in Graham's favour at the subsequent trial, which set back his own legal career. In later life he became a Labour supporter.
[76] The article was rushed into print, and shows signs of not having been proof-read.

our proper place in Downing Street, and all will yet be well." But although the one consistent and ardent aspiration of the Liberal politician is to throw the adverse party out of its comfortable armchairs in Downing Street and to rest there himself, still we cannot but feel that that inconsistent and dissentient Liberal party, in spite of the well-meant endeavours of those who form it, and who would still thrust into the mouths of a democracy to whom she has given a shadow of power by enfranchisement, the threadbare maxims of Adam Smith and Ricardo,[77] and who would still like to sit comfortably and hatch political eggs in the good old-fashioned Liberal political way, is at war not only with itself and the Tory, but with vestiges of more advanced political tendency which cling on to the edge of the garment.

The Liberal party, as a party, is severely threatened, and the signal of dissolution, inevitable and complete, will be the death of its leader [Gladstone], who still unites under his banner all shades of Liberal thought, whether tending towards moderation or advancement. But at his death, with no one to combine these heterogeneous elements, with not one man of weight or influence to guide the Liberal party, it is easy to see its ultimate fate. Into the Tory ranks will crowd most of these adverse elements, without order, and tumultuously, to array themselves against the common enemy, which time, education, and the past political events of this year are rapidly forming into an enemy of irresistible strength - the democracy and the wage-earners of Great Britain - and which, regarded as to its ultimate outcome, means civil war - war betwixt the classes and the masses. Events seem to be rapidly tending towards this climax.

I doubt all optimistic views. I believe that never before in England have the relations between the State and the people been so intimate and so strained - I doubt whether the Spirit of Hate and Fear animating the one, and the Spirit of Menace and Discontent the other, have ever encountered each other before with such virulent pressure as at this moment. The people dislike and distrust politicians - Liberal as well as Tory. They have begun to realise what manner of men these are whom they so tamely submit to rule them, and the submission is being lit up by inquiries and ugly questions, which are being asked at this moment in every workmen's club in the land.

This, then, explains the fear - nay, positive hatred - for those theories which are at

---

[77] British political economists.

present being debated by every intelligent workman in the kingdom: Nationalisation of capital, nationalisation of land, and State regulation of wages and hours. No wonder that the Liberal party will *transiger* [78] with any one or anything - with coercion in London, with coercion in Ireland - rather than admit these pestilent and popular doctrines - mark the last adjective, Liberal! - within their political-economical catechism.

That the State is at some peculiar turning-point of its history - that the enfranchisement of the working-man and the power it gives him is being realised by his accommodating M.P.s, Mr. Haldane proves to us. He says that nearly all the Scotch members who represented mining constituencies voted in favour of the eight hours clause, *independently of party* - mark that! - and adds, "Indeed, in some of these constituencies the choice for the member lay between doing so and most seriously endangering his seat." Now, can anyone seriously think that these men voted for this clause *con amore*? [79] No; they knew that if they did not, the miners had the power, the strength, and the organisation to throw them out.

If this is wrong, then the whole system of the franchise is wrong; but if it is right, what is to become of the Liberal party in the future? Will it, as a party, go on from step to step and from trade to trade, as they become organised, voting to retain its power whilst limiting the principle, or will it frankly at once recognise that it only exists for the good of the people, and not for its own benefit?

It is alleged that this new movement amongst the miners of Scotland (which is also spreading all over England) is one of the difficulties with which the Liberal party has to contend. Why should this be so? Long ere this, those of the Liberal party who have any perception must have been prepared for this movement. Did any sensible body of men imagine for an instant that a class of men like the miners, whose conditions of labour are so exceptional, and whose facilities for organisation are so extensive, would be content to sit down quietly with the franchise in their possession, either not using it or merely using it to return A. or B. to power? The miners argued this: We wanted an Eight Hours Bill, we saw at once that only a demonstration of force would constrain any considerable body of men to vote for it. They saw clearly that between Liberal capitalist and Tory aristocrat the miner would be left as before in his darkness every

---

[78] French: Compromise.
[79] Italian: With enthusiasm.

hour of the week in a narrow seam for an indefinite number of hours per day. They knew that the Roman miner, though a slave, was at least well fed and cared for whilst he had strength to work, and they saw that they, in spite of Christianity and Liberalism, were treated as but parts of the machinery of the mine, with this difference, that the machinery had cost money and they had not. What wonder, therefore, that, having appealed from Tory demands to Liberal sympathy, they fell back upon themselves! What else is to be expected from all the rest of the trades in the kingdom?

Recollect that the miners, like the rest of the working classes, are not the least taken in when the Liberals plume themselves on the grant of the franchise. They know that had not the Liberals conceded it, the Tories would have been forced to do so, and they bitterly resent the incompleteness of the gift and the foolish restrictions with which it was hampered.

Ireland in all these questions is the example that the working-classes must keep before their eyes. They have seen Ireland hold the balance betwixt the parties, and they remember that in the ignoble struggle for place and power that took place two years ago, both parties showed they were squeezable, and they were determined themselves in the future to be the squeezers and not the squeezed.

As they themselves labour, whilst politicians only talk, they are not averse to State regulation of the hours of work. As their wages rapidly tend to this devoutly to be desired consummation of the political barometer - namely, the reproduction point – they are not afraid of the State regulating wages. This for two reasons - firstly, that the State would not only fix a minimum, and that minimum would have to be not less than 5s. per day, whereas now the maximum hardly exceeds that; secondly, because they hope that day by day more of their own class will enter Parliament. They look with little dread at the State nationalisation of mineral capital and mineral royalties, because, having no capital themselves, they fail to see why their work should merely go to maintain the life and the faculty of reproduction in themselves, whilst a class of men exactly similar to themselves is enriched by it. Were there any remarkable intellectual superiority of their employers over themselves, then perhaps they would think otherwise; but it is to be wondered at, when the division between them is only of a tailor's making, and they see their employers are as dead to refinement and to acts of humanity as they can be themselves, that they exclaim, "We have been muzzled long enough, chained long enough,

56

worked long enough for them," and that they are now inclined to demand a little of the profits, and a tolerable chance of an old age whose only support shall not consist in the parish shillings?

Can any Liberal - and if he can, I ask what good is he to the people? - defend the system of mineral rents? It may be that there is something to be said for the ownership of the surface of the earth. A landlord can drain, improve, fence; but what can any man do for the minerals? Can he create them? If so, why does he not create them everywhere? Can he increase them? All he can do is to charge rent - that is to say, impose a tax on the others who wish to work them. There is an old saying of the time of Wat Tyler,[80] "I wolde that there were never a priest in Englande." Be that as it may, the miner might well say, "I wolde that there were no owner of land," for it is by the folly of the lawyers, with their "De cœlo usque ad centum,"[81] that this source of national wealth was allowed to be diverted from the society to the individual.

The cup of our iniquity has been filled to running over in the proposition to nationalise the land. What, touch the land! As soon touch the fixed stars, the heavens, the House of Lords, or the rest of the hereditary bodies.

It would be difficult, however, even for a political economist to nationalise the minerals and not the land, for where do the minerals begin and the land end, or the minerals end and the land begin? Again, at what distance below the surface should the rights of the individual end, and the rights of the State begin?

This is not the place for a dissertation on the means whereby the land may be acquired by the State; but to whom does the land belong? To the wealthy and titled proprietor, who buys and sells it as a speculation (and with it the human souls - or have the poor souls? - on it), who may have some moldering old house or some modern stucco abomination in which he receives for three weeks in the year that so-called society which follows, like carrion crows, wherever there is food or drink, and appearance of wealth, the men to slaughter pheasants, and the women to rival their professional sisters in the pursuit of the slaughterers, and both of them to laugh at their host when the last cigar is smoked, the last glass of wine drunk, and they have got away with the smallest possible amount of tipping compatible with the social status of an English lady or gentleman.

---

[80] Leader of 'The Peasant's Revolt' of 1381.
[81] Latin: From the sky to the centre (of the earth).

57

(And there clearly can be no lady or gentleman rich enough to be really self-respecting outside these islands.)

To whom does the land belong? To the owner, who has paid the land and blood money, or to Hodge,[82] born on the soil, who knows no other life, cares for no other land, lives but to enrich with his work and to fertilise with his body in death the acres on which he has passed his life: Hodge, whose aspirations stray no further than the clump of elms out yonder that he sees from his window, who has watched the miracle of Nature being wrought day by day, hour by hour, from his lead-paned window, who on the same spot has watched the change to spring to autumn as solid and as unmoved as a tree, who loves every brown clod in the fields with the love of an animal, greater because inarticulate. The land, *ne déplaise* [83] the Liberal and Conservative parties, would seem to belong as of birthright to Hodge, because it can neither prosper without him, nor he without it - witness his son's case in the cities.

But to return to these self-same pestilent miners - these foolish fellows who care nothing for large families, not Karl Marx, nor Malthus, fellows whose only idea is to get enough to eat. The unlooked-for weapon has been put into their hands; they mean to use it, and in the fight all differences of Orange and Catholic, Liberal and Conservative, will be laid aside.

The miners are not inspired idiots. They thoroughly understand the import of the changes they seek to bring about. They are thoroughly aware that the theories of Karl Marx do not state that population presses on subsistence; but, on the contrary, point to the opposite statement, that there is enough for all were it more equally distributed, and, whilst thoroughly grasping the fact that union is strength, only value their unions as a means of bringing pressure on Parliament, which, to their uneducated minds, seems not a mysterious Mumbo Jumbo of high-toned and well-dressed individuals, but really the assembly of 600 of the public servants sent there to do their bidding, which, if it does not do so, 6000 underground (in Scotland) are determined to know the reason why.

The new democracy seems not to reverence Liberalism as we once knew it, but Gladstone. It is the name, the personality of the man that holds them.

---

[82] The 19th century stereotype of an English agricultural labourer.
[83] French: Displease.

His very shortcomings they condone, but nothing but the deepest scorn is manifest for those timorous, miserable, invertebrate animals who, whilst posing as Liberal leaders, are really Tories at heart; who have seen the poor bludgeoned and outraged in London, the crofters driven to desperation, the Welsh farmers infuriated, and have said not a word; too timorous to risk a newspaper reviling, too utterly empty to be able to face the pin-prick of public opinion, so that an immediate collapse brings about one thing only - at any price and at any cost return to Downing Street, and a fat salary - incompetent leaders, as useful to a democracy as a blind dog to a blind beggar; as utterly illiberal and far less honest than the most antiquated Tory, content, for his sole function, to force down people's throats, as by advertisement those who sell Bazaar tea would condemn us to drink it, their shallow and petty schemes which can result alone in their own personal achievements. No, if the Liberal party has a future, it must get rid of these nobodies, and show that it has no fear of modern thought; it must pledge itself to an Eight Hours Bill, institute a municipality for London, nationalise the land, and commence public works for the unemployed; and then, if it has good luck, it may regain the confidence of the democracy - that is to say, if some other party has not been beforehand in the field.

Graham had openly attacked his own party and presaged the growth of a party of labour, one that he had been actively encouraging to become a force in the House of Commons, although, for the moment he and Hardie still considered this to be best achieved from within the Liberal fold.[84] He certainly had grass-roots support by his appeals to the radical element, and in December 1888, at Cumnock in Ayrshire, led by a torchlight procession and a brass band, the miners presented him with an illuminated address, and in February 1888 ordinary members of the Scottish Liberal Association passed a resolution of support against his imprisonment, *The Scotsman* referring to them as "riff-raff."[85] His position as a Liberal M.P., however, was coming under increasing strain, and in a letter to the Chairman of the North-West Lanarkshire Liberal Association, dated the 14th of March 1890, he formally severed his connection with them, thanking them for their support: "of one whose views were not always in accord with yours and theirs." This split had apparently been coordinated with his Labour colleagues, for, on the same day, Shaw Maxwell M.P. and Keir Hardie, wrote to propose

---

[84] This idea of a party within a party was by no means unique among the Liberals, the most significant precedent being Joseph Chamberlain's National Liberal Federation, formed in 1877.
[85] *The Scotsman* (9 February 1888), p.4.

putting up a 'Labour' candidate in Graham's place at the next General Election.[86] At this stage, Graham apparently had no intention of standing for Labour, as he believed only working-class men should fill that role: "and then I would be content to retire to a quiet country life at Gartmore."[87] He would be obliged to reconsider.

~

Away from local politics, where previously he had found it almost impossible to get into print, with his increasing fame (or rather, notoriety), particularly after 'Bloody Sunday,' and his attack on his own party, he was embraced by the denizens of the London radical demi-monde, rubbing shoulders with Karl Marx's daughter Eleanor, and her partner Edward Aveling,[88] the anarchist, Prince Kropotkin, Henry Hyndman, and activists such as Annie Besant,[89] and the trade-unionist Tom Mann. This was a world in flux, where various brands of socialism vied for prominence, where organisations proliferated then disappeared as quickly, where alliances developed then sundered, among the same small group of mostly middle-class intellectuals, idealists, and faddists. If a week was a long time in politics, then a year was a lifetime in the precarious world of socialist publishing into which he now plunged. But, while the demands of writing for these little-read journals were exhausting, they would prove an ideal training ground for his future literary career.

## THE PEOPLE'S PARLIAMENT
*The People's Press*, 21st of June 1890.

Temperance is a safe subject. It is nice to be temperate, sober, and chaste (vicariously), and this our legislators see. Hence, the rush of men to speak on the subject. Anything is popular in Parliament that tends to improve the masses from above. Anything that tends to make them the social equals of honourable gentlemen, anything that makes them independent of the upper classes is, of course, "Taboo."

You know we sit to legislate for, not to do the will of the electors. On this matter, the Whigs and Tories are agreed. Each of them is certain of one thing (if of nothing else), that he is not a delegate. I should think not, indeed. Why should he? A man who

---

[86] *The Coatbridge Express* (19 March 1890), p.2.
[87] *The Airdrie Advertiser* (23 November 1889), p.5.
[88] In 1898, 'Tussy' Marx committed suicide, apparently because of Aveling's infidelities. It may have been a suicide pact that Aveling, for his part, did not go through with.
[89] Annie Besant, (1847-1933). An English socialist, writer and orator, theosophist, women's rights activist, birth-control pioneer, and supporter of Irish and Indian independence.

has bought an article of any sort does not consider himself in the position of the delegate of the miller. We have all bought our constituencies, paid dear for them, too, in some instances; therefore we are clear we are not delegates.

The electors, too, are equally clear on their part, that they are going to get little or no good out of us. Hence their custom to make us all patrons of cricket and football clubs at a guinea (a guinea is so much nicer on a list than £1) a club.

Hence, too, the inordinate love they develop in us for opening bazaars (£5. 5s a speech) and charitable institutions. All this has the effect of making "safe subjects" popular as themes to speak upon in the People's Parliament.

Naturally a man who has paid a large sum to represent the north-eastern division of East Middlesex, does not want to imperil his capital. He has sunk a certain amount in the purchase of his seat and he wants to get in again. Quite as naturally he has been returned by a combination of middle-class men calling themselves (purely for the sake of euphony) Liberals or Tories. These gentlemen, mostly local tradesmen, lawyers, or employers of labour; or, if it is a country district, Tories, lawyers, and parsons, do not view with much favour a regular downright Eight Hours' Bloke.

The Tories and parsons look on a man who wishes that the State should own the land as they would on the devil. *Retro Satanas*[90] in both cases, then. Speak we, therefore, on the temperance questions, even though we take our "Stone Fence," our "Santa Cruz Sour"[91] or our humbler but perhaps as exhilarating, 'alf-and-'alf.[92] Hence, "Danks" (Waddy, M.P., his real name) rising like Venus from the sea foam, beautiful, despite his sixty years and bottle-nose, in chemists' windows, finds it convenient to spout temperance, finds it wise to place himself on return from circuit, before the public gaze. No compensation, he roars. Oh wily "Danks." He owns no public houses, prattleth sweetly of Liberal parties, pleads at the bar, poses before the House (and Lords), and is a very pleasant, pointless representative. A Wesleyan withal, not a very persecuting type though.

The Tories jeer him. "Danks" (we call him "Danks" behind the scenes), draped in his long black coat as if it were a toga, starts and defies the thunder. He'll speak two

---

[90] Latin: 'Back Satan.' The medieval formula for exorcism. Also a witty prose device for 'don't tempt me.'
[91] Rum-based cocktails.
[92] A quarter gill of whisky, and a half pint of beer 'chaser.'

hours if Tory members jeer. Oh, awful prospect, one hour of "Danks" far better than a thousand; Lockwood[93] drops his sketch half finished, members retreat in awe, and the great temperance speech drips on. Thus and in this way is a question of this sort debatable. Strange how the lawyers distinguish themselves in our national conventions. Tory Ambrose equals Liberal Danks. Fire, fury, sound, and nonsense balance cant, drivel, and hypocrisy. Never did I listen to two such speeches. Taken on the whole, the lawyers make the worst show in the House of Commons. Hardly one of them has any convictions except on briefs. None of them rise above the mere party level. All of them speak on safe subjects.

The curse of law, as Belfort Bax[94] so ably styles it, is well exemplified in Parliament. *Nisi prius*,[95] from Matthews, Russell, and Webster, to Gedge and Waddy.

There is an ancient custom in Boston and New York. On Independence Day, a regiment of men dressed in the custom of the last century, and known as "Putnam's Phalanx," parade the streets. It is comic, but so comic that the judicious weep. To see their bourgeois (reactionaries to a man) strut through the streets, with fife and drum, assuming to be patriots is really fine. To see our "Putnam's Phalanx," our brigade of Devil's Own, swarm like bees (or devils) in the People's Parliament, always makes me wish the galleries as at Madrid held 2,000 people. I wish it, for no ushers can control so many, and the applause bursts out, and censure also when a fool speaks.

Our Parliament is All Fool's Paradise. Those who make safe speeches, the lawyers, guinea pigs, and others, get quiet hearing. Why? Because the place wants a purge. Some say force is no remedy. Was there no use of it in '93.

How long would "Danks" and Ambrose "Putnam's" phalanx and the rest of them have gone out without the pestilent irruption of the *sans culotte* [96] hosts.

Think not, sweet Oxonian juvenal, I wish the mob to try conclusions with the Maxim Gun. I only state a fact, most undeniable; it is this - that People's Parliament is a ship of fools, and in it, when safe questions are debated, speakers rise like trout at

---

[93] Sir Frank Lockwood, lawyer, and Liberal M.P. for York, he was also a talented caricaturist who contributed to *Punch*. In May 1895 he was the lead counsel in the successful prosecution of Graham's friend Oscar Wilde for gross indecency.
[94] Ernest Belfort Bax (1854-1926) English Socialist, barrister, historian, philosopher and journalist. He was editor of *Justice*, the organ of the Social Democratic Federation, to which Graham occasionally contributed.
[95] Latin: 'Unless before.' Usually a legal term.
[96] French: Without breeches - the common people.

flies in a mere. And all the time outside, the Eight-Hour blokes fight on and lack advancement. I too am for temperance, sobriety, and all that (as De Quincey was); still, would that we have a day or two just now and then to edge in somewhat of the people's matters.

I am almost aweary, not of the sun,[97] for I scarce see it once or twice a week, but of the dreary drip, drip, drip of words, the apathy of workmen, and the fair, steady, blowing breeze of popular applause, that swells the sails of our ship of fools, the People's Parliament. Surely it is getting almost time to take to boarding-pikes (by ballot, if you will) and capture it.'

~

His writing for socialist journals reached a peak of one article a week from the beginning of 1889, until the demise of *The People's Press* in February 1891, when the pace slowed considerably. In each, despite his conversational style, the righteous anger never abates, the hatred of injustice runs deep; coruscating sarcasm and jocular disdain tussle with wild analogy to drive home his points. Although presumably aimed at working class readers, he makes no concessions to the uneducated, and a typical piece might run the gamut from South American history to socialist ideology to Gilbert & Sullivan, from Russian peasant traditions to the castrato Farinelli, decorated with his beloved literary allusions, all tumbled together with panache and showmanship.[98] We might be forgiven for suspecting that this 'prentice politician' was engaged in learning a different trade. However, his quick-fire, often slapdash style, was creating problems:

### The "Star" on Cunninghame Graham's "Copy."
*The People's Press*, 3rd of September 1890.

Mr. Cunninghame Graham, says our contemporary the *Star*, has unwittingly gone within an ace of bringing about a strike and causing a revolution in his office. He sent us a letter the other day from Liverpool. That letter was 24 pages long, and was headed "Dancing and Barricades." It has made everyone dance who touched it, and still remains an insurmountable barricade. It cannot be read. Mr. Graham's handwriting is sometimes crotchety, but this specimen of his calligraphy was about as legible as Egyptian hieroglyphics. The letter has been touring about the office for several days - from the editor to the printer, from the printer to the reader, from the reader to the sub-editor,

---

[97] A paraphrase from Macbeth: Act 5, Scene 5.
[98] 'But still I might have finished all those sentences; not broken off to moralise right in the middle of the tale; split less infinitives, and remembered those rules of grammar that I have disregarded, as freely as a democratic leader tramps on the rights of the poor taxables who put him into power.' Cunninghame Graham, *Rodeo* p.xvi.

and back to the printer again in a cycle - a cycle which threatened to end in revolution. Everyone has wrestled with it, but no one has been able to dig a continuous story out of it. The head printer put on his glasses and tore his hair over it, until he now wears an aged look and a wig. And expert comp was called in, but the only evidence he gave was that in Clowes' office [?] the men refused to set Mr. Graham's copy. A strike was ordered at once unless the copy was withdrawn. It was withdrawn and handed to the reader, who found his occupation gone, and gave notice. The sub-editor has had a tussle with it, took it home to sleep over, but has not slept or worked since. The application of a microscope only diminished the legibility, and a magnifying glass only increased our difficulties. The copy remained undecipherable.

(We tearfully sympathise with the men of the *Star*. Two of our own most valued men, after a prolonged struggle with one of Graham's articles, retired to the peaceful seclusion of a padded room at Colney Hatch.[99]- Ed. *People's Press*.)

---

[99] Colney Hatch Lunatic Asylum (later, Friern Hospital) in North London.

☐☐☐☐☐

# BLOODY SUNDAY

Free speech, Home Rule for Ireland, and the introduction of an Eight Hours Bill were the main platforms on which Graham campaigned, but the turning point in his political career was undoubtedly the riot in Trafalgar Square on the 13th of November 1887 (later known as 'Bloody Sunday'), when several marches converged in support of the imprisoned Irish nationalist William O'Brien M.P. In what looks like an impetuous, almost suicidal act, born out of extreme frustration with his experiences in the House of Commons, Graham charged the police cordons and was severely beaten.[100] He, and fellow protestor John Burns, were charged with "Unlawful assembly, assault of the police, along with other 'evil-disposed' persons, thereby endangering public peace," and jailed for six weeks in Pentonville Prison[101] (while Graham still held the office of Justice of the Peace in three counties, and Deputy-Lieutenant of Dunbartonshire). William Morris wrote of the event: 'His conduct will long be remembered, one would hope, by lovers of freedom; but he must expect for some time to come to be a pariah among

---

[100] Sir Edward Reed M.P. wrote the following account in *The Pall Mall Gazette*: 'After Mr. Graham's arrest was complete, one policeman after another, two certainly [. . .] stepped up from behind and struck him in the head [. . .] with a violence and brutality which was shocking to behold. Even after this, and when some five or six other police were dragging him into the Square, another from behind seized him most needlessly by the hair [. . .] and dragged his head back, and in that condition he was forced forward many yards.' It had been a blow to the head, while on military service in Ireland, that had confined Graham's father to an institution, under restraint, until his premature death, and family and friends feared that history might repeat itself.

[101] They were released after four and a half weeks, on the 18th of February, for good behaviour. Graham's prison experiences were recalled in his essay 'Sursum Corda,' published in *The Saturday Review* (19 June, 1897), pp.681-83.

M.P.s. To do him justice he is not likely to care much about that.'[102]

Of all the events in his extraordinary life, it was his actions in Trafalgar Square that created the greatest sensation. A 'London Correspondent' to *The Coatbridge Express* wrote: 'One of the most popular men in London at present is Mr Cunninghame Graham,' [103] and on his release from prison, he was given a hero's reception. However, although he enjoyed adulation amongst the rank and file, many senior members of the Liberal party were not amused:

> Sir, I must express my indignation at the second resolution which was proposed at the conference on Tuesday, viz – "That this Council of the Scottish Liberal Association protests against the imprisonment of Mr. R. B. Cunninghame Graham, M.P., for his attempt to vindicate the right of public meeting in Trafalgar Square, London." The above individual is not a political martyr, he has been imprisoned like any disorderly person, and like many sound Liberals, I regret his locks have not been cut, as it might help to cool his ardour. The recognition of such a person will do a great deal of harm to the Liberal party, and the Council had surely very little to talk about when they had such a miserable second resolution to propose. It would have been quite in order, if the following words had been added: "That the Council also protests against the imprisonment of drunks and disorderlies connected with the Liberal party." I am, &c, A Chairman of a Liberal Association[104]

Two weeks after leaving prison, Graham was back in the House of Commons defending his actions:

**MOTIONS. PUBLIC MEETINGS IN THE METROPOLIS. ADJOURNED DEBATE**, 2nd of March 1888.

I do not claim, like the hon. Member for the Bordealey Division of Birmingham (Mr. Jesse Collings), to know what people think, but I should like, with the leave of the House, to endeavour to justify my conduct and that of the people of London in the events which had occurred during the last four months. I wish to free the people from the aspersions cast upon them of being revolutionary. I look upon those events as being important rather in their social than in their political aspects. You have had some ingenious and eloquent speeches from the lawyers on both sides of the House. The right hon. and learned Gentleman the Member for Bury (Sir Henry James), in a

[102] *The Commonweal*, 26 November 1887, p.377.
[103] *The Coatbridge Express* (7 December 1887) p.1
[104] *The Coatbridge Express* (22 February 1888) p.1

nice piece of special pleading, put the question before you from his point of view; but while he was tearing his passion to tatters,[105] I can not but remember that the right hon. and learned Gentleman has been accustomed to impart passion and pathos into his speeches all the days of his life, according as his brief was marked 50 or 500 guineas. The right hon. and learned Gentleman has challenged any man in the House to be the guarantee for public order and peace, were a meeting held in Trafalgar Square. It was a curious thing that Her Majesty's Government is unable to answer for peace and order; but I relied so much upon the law-abiding qualities of the working population of London that I will endeavour, were I allowed to do so by the Government, to hold a meeting in Trafalgar Square, and, as a private man, if riot or damage ensues, I will pay for it with his person, or in any way the Government might think fit.

I have some little right to be heard on this question. For what I considered my duty I was beaten and assaulted in the sight of London. I was put to great inconvenience and expense, and had to serve a month's imprisonment. (*Laughter, and cries of "We have him to keep the people in order!"*) I can tell right hon. Gentlemen who laughed at the poor that the people of London looked at the question from a vastly different aspect. Was it wonderful that the people of London did not attach the same importance to legal argument that this House was disposed to attach to it? What did the proletariat of London know of the legal aspect of the question? They have seen what they considered, rightly or wrongly, right turned against them. They have seen themselves beaten down on a place where they thought they had the right to assemble for merely expressing that right which their fathers had exercised for 40 years. Would they have been worthy to be called Englishmen had they failed to remonstrate? Was it wonderful that a little bitterness had been imported into their speeches and remonstrances, when they had seen, as I have done, the women and children beaten down by police? In dealing with the conduct of the police, it would ill befit me to make an attack upon them. I do not intend to do so. A policeman is a man to be pitied. Surely a man who lives execrated amongst his fellows is an object to be pitied. I deplore not the conduct of the police, but of those who set them on. I would attack not even the Government, but the social system that has forced the best of our

---

[105] Hamlet, Act 3, Scene 2.

young men into the police and the best of our young women into the streets. In the future Government will have to pay their janissaries better, or else they will not be able to recruit them from the people of England when they came to apprehend the duties that the acceptance of the blood money entailed upon them. There is one point, however, which I consider totally indefensible on the part of the Government, and that was why, during the long, useless guard on the 13th November, the police were kept on the Square without food or refreshment? There was a design in that the design being deliberately to create a feeling of hatred between the police and the people. If that was the design of the Government they have succeeded (*Laughter, and cries of "We are glad of it!"*) and, having sown the wind, it was not his fault if perchance they reap the whirlwind. If the temper of the Government is to laugh at the sufferings of the poor of London, and to suppress all free speech there as they are endeavouring to do in Ireland, I deplore it, and I deplore it as a partisan of law and order, because free speech is the only safety-valve for so large and dense a population as that of London. The inevitable result will be that secret societies will be formed here, as in Russia, and I would be the first to deplore that. Hon. Gentlemen need not flatter themselves that the same spirit of hatred that was growing up betwixt class and class in Russia is not growing up here in England. I appeal to anyone who had followed the social and political movements of the day to say that the proletariat of London was not as well able to judge upon social circumstances as the proletariat of Russia. They are not deceived by phrases. They estimate a cheat upon the Stock Exchange and the Turf with the habitual criminals in our gaols, and they fail to see the difference between the titled whore of Belgravia and the poor prostitute of Regent Street, except as regarded sympathy and censure. And when they see such a bitter spirit of hatred at work, and it was at work, I would put it to you whether it was safe to shut up the only safety-valve that was left to the people that, namely, of expressing their feelings in public meeting? The Government has endeavoured to confuse the issue by representing the working men's clubs as bodies of revolutionaries and organised plunderers. I indignantly deny this, and assert that if they had not been interfered with the meeting would have been as orderly and legal as any meeting that was ever held in the Square. I do not wish to say that the trial and sentence passed upon me was not a perfectly fair and legal one from the Judge's point of view; but it requires more than a finding of a Judge and jury to lay at rest for ever the question of free meeting in the capital of the British Empire. I was been tried on three counts of assault on the police, causing a riot, and illegal assembly; but the good sense and honesty of a British jury acquitted me instantly on the counts of assault and riot; therefore, I fail to see how any fair-minded man could come forward with the stale argument of a riot having been caused either by my action or that of the working men of London.[106]

What sort of riot could it be when 60,000 men were to have assembled, and all the properties which the hon. and learned Attorney General (Sir Richard Webster) could produce in Court were two pokers, a piece of iron in paper, and a piece of wood with nails in it? That was a formidable array of weapons with which to subvert the British Constitution. There was an illegal assembly, however, and that was the assembly of 4,000 police and soldiery in the middle of the Metropolis, for no adequate reason, and in times of high peace. That there was no bloodshed or damage to property was not the result of the Government's action, but of the good conduct, the good temper, and the self-denial of the people under great provocation. But the real question was not touched at my trial, and the Government has not raised it in Mr. Saunders's case, because he presume they thought they had no chance of succeeding. Why has he not been allowed to raise the question in a legal way? I have hitherto had no opportunity of defending myself in this House; but he will now, in the little time left him, endeavour to show that there was no other course open to me than that which I pursued. I totally deny that my meeting had any connection with those that went before. It seems to me that the objection to my meeting arose from the fear of the Government that in London there would be a large vote of sympathy passed with one of the most prominent victims of their Irish administration. I challenge anyone to say what Statute or unwritten law I broke on that occasion. I was found guilty of the obsolete offence of illegal assembly. I admit it was bad taste of the people of London to parade their insolent starvation in the face of the rich and trading portions of the town. They should have starved in their garrets, as have no doubt many Members of Her Majesty's Government and most of the upper classes would have wished them to do.

---

[106] This is disingenuous, for it was not as unplanned as Graham states. Immediately prior to the riot, at a meeting in Broxburn, he said that he planned to "test" the authorities in Trafalgar Square. *The Airdrie Advertiser* (12 November 1887), p.4.

(*Cries of "Order!" and "Divide!"*) I am not in the habit of asking for mercy at the hands of any man; but the masses of the City of London look to the Speaker for justice on this occasion. They look to him to let me, their advocate, lay their case before the House; and I appeal to the Speaker now, and I know I should not appeal in vain. The son of him who gave the people free bread would not deny their Representative free speech, at least in Parliament. It had been charged against me that I had stirred up a lot of ignorant men to dash their heads against a wall. It has been charged against me that I had spoken sedition, and that I was a revolutionary. If to be revolutionary is to wish to ameliorate the condition of the poor of this City, to wish for a more democratic form of government, to wish that Members of Parliament should be paid for their services, to wish to pass Liberal measures of a similar nature, then I am a revolutionary. It has also been urged that I have stirred up men to break the law. That is an absolute and foundation-less calumny. I would not ask for any more indulgence from that House, but would thank you for the courteous way in which you have listened to a man struggling with weakness endeavouring to place before you what he considers a more serious aspect of a Constitutional question; and I would only renew the pledge I have given before in public, but in no spirit of challenge to this House, and no spirit of disrespect to the Speaker, that a time will come, and I say it with confidence, certainly being able to fulfill his pledge, when I will hold a meeting of as many men as Trafalgar Square would contain, and when the Government of the country, no matter whether Whig or Tory so greatly should public opinion have developed by that time, would be but too glad to assist him in keeping law and order on that occasion.

TRIAL SCENES AT THE OLD BAILEY. FROM A CONTEMPORARY SKETCH.

Almost a year after the incident, Graham gave an equally partial account of events in William Morris's publication *The Commonweal*:

## BLOODY SUNDAY

*The Commonweal*, 10<sup>th</sup> of November 1888.

Except the facts known to the public, I fear I can tell little of the occurrences in Trafalgar Square last November. As to the reason why three men were killed, many sent to prison, three hundred or so arrested, and several condemned to penal servitude; the retail trade of the metropolis thrown into disorder, the troops called out; as to why many men and *women* were beaten and brutalised on the public streets, the wherefore that the powers that be chose to expose their capital to the chance of being sacked and burnt by an angry populace - I confess I am still in the dark. The more I think, the more I cannot tell. It may be that Sir Charles Dogberry had heard of, and wished to imitate, the behaviour of the negro pilot who came aboard a ship in the West Indies, and immediately gave the order, "Haul um jib up, Mr. Mate," and then, amid the curses of the crew, instantly remarked, "Haul um jib down, Mr. Mate": giving as his reason that he wished to show his authority.

What I can tell you is merely this, that I was in Birmingham and read in the morning papers that a meeting having for its object to petition the Government for the release of Mr. William O'Brien, M.P., had suddenly been proclaimed without rhyme or reason. At that time I was a newly elected Liberal member. I had heard members of my party, men who at that time I respected and believed to be in earnest talking big at meetings and telling lies about what they intended to do in Ireland that autumn. I had read Mr. Gladstone's speech at Nottingham, in which he had expressly said that coercion would not be confined to Ireland, but would also be applied to England if the people were supine. I had read this, and - fool that I was - I believed it; for at the time I did not know that Liberals, Tories, and Unionists were three bands of thimbleriggers.[107] I did not know that the fooleries of Harcourt and the platitudes of Morley were anything else but the utterances of good dull men, who at least believed in themselves. I was soon to be undeceived.

To return to my meeting. I came up to London, hearing that the meeting was held

---

[107] Fairground tricksters.

under the auspices of the Radical clubs of London in conjunction with the Irish National League. Now, one would have thought that I should have met at every political club in London the local Liberal member encouraging his constituents. One would have though that the boasters and braggers from the country constituencies would have rushed up to town to redeem their vaunts on public platforms. I expected that it would be thought as cruel and tyrannical to break up a meeting, at which thousands of Irishmen were to be present, in London as it would be in Ireland. I thought that freedom of speech and the right of public meeting were facts in themselves, about which politicians were agreed. I did not know the meanness of the whole crew even at that time. I was not aware that freedom of speech and public meeting were nothing to them but stalking-horses to hide themselves behind, and under cover of which to crawl into Downing Street. I soon found however that the Liberal Party was a complete cur, that what they excelled in doing was singing "Gloria Gladstone in excelsis," and talking about what they intended to do in Ireland. You see, the sea divided them from Ireland, and one is always brave when no danger is at hand. However, political capital was to be made out of London, it appeared; therefore Mr. Shaw Leferve thought it better to vapour[108] and obtain a cheap notoriety in Ireland, where he knew he was quite safe, than to help his fellow-townsmen - he is I think a Londoner - in London, where there might have been some incurred.

Finding myself deserted by all my colleagues, with the exception of Mr. Conybeare and Walter McLaren, who would have been at the meeting had they been able, and at that time not knowing many of the Radicals, I turned to the Socialists, some of whom I did know, and hearing their procession was to arrive at St. Martin's Church at a certain time, I determined to join it.

What happened is known to all: how no procession reached the square; how they were all illegally attacked and broken up, some of them several miles from the Square; how in spite of every constitutional right, and without a shadow of a pretext, banners and instruments were destroyed, and not a farthing of compensation ever given, though the loss fell on poor people. It will be remembered too, how the police,

---

[108] Disappear.

acting under the orders of Sir Charles Dogberry,[109] the Christian soldier (sic!), felled men and women, and in some cases little children, to the ground. I wonder if Mr. Henry Matthews, the pious Catholic Home Secretary, approved of this, and how he broached the matter to his priest when he went to confession? It will not be forgotten the sort of bloody assize that followed, and how Judge Edlin[110] wrote himself down ass [sic] by the folly of his sentences. No one will forget the trial and condemnation of George Harrison, and his sentence of five years' penal servitude on the oath of one policeman, eleven independent witnesses being of no avail to save him. Then the pantomimic trial of John Burns and myself, and our condemnation by Mr. Justice Charles Shallow, also on the testimony of professional witnesses, and for an obsolete offence. It is still, I think, fresh in the memory of all, how with the help of all the professional perjurers in London, all the arms collected from the vast crowd amounted to three pokers, one piece of wood, and an oyster knife. How I failed to join the procession, and having met Messrs. Burns and Hyndman by accident, proceeded to the Square; how we were assaulted and knocked about and sent to prison, is a matter of notoriety in London.

I can tell no more of the incidents of the day than any other spectator. I walked across the street with Burns, was joined by no one as far as I remember, and found myself a prisoner in the Square with a broken head. Whilst in there, though, I had ample time to observe a great deal. I watched the crowd and police pretty carefully; I saw repeated charges made at a perfectly unarmed and helpless crowd; I saw policemen not of their own accord, but under the express orders of their superiors, repeatedly strike women and children; I saw them invariably choose those for assault who seemed least able to retaliate. One incident struck me with considerable force and disgust. As I was being led out of the crowd a poor woman asked a police inspector (I think) or a sergeant if he had seen a child she had lost. His answer was to tell her she was a "damned whore," and knock her down. I never till that time completely realised how utterly servile and cowardly an English crowd is. I venture to say that had it occurred in any other country in the world, the man would have been torn to pieces. But no!

---

[109] A character in Shakespeare's 'Much Ado About Nothing.' The constable in charge of Messina's night watch.
[110] Sir Peter Henry Edlin (1818-1903). A severe judge.

73

in England we are so completely accustomed to bow the knee before wealth and riches, to repeat to ourselves we are a free nation, that in the end we have got to believe it, and the grossest acts of injustice may be perpetrated under our very eyes, and we will still slap our manly chests and congratulate ourselves that Britain is the home of Liberty.

Other things I saw that pleased me better than this. I saw that the police were afraid; I saw on more than one occasion that the officials had to strike their free British men to make them obey orders; I saw that the horses were clumsy and badly bitted, and of no use whatever in a stone street; and lastly, I am almost certain I observed several of the police officers to be armed with pistols, which I believe is against the law. I saw much too, to moralise me. The tops of the houses and hotels were crowded with well-dressed women, who clapped their hands and cheered with delight when some miserable and half-starved working man was knocked down and trodden under foot. This I saw as I stood on almost the identical spot where a few weeks ago the Government unveiled the statue of Gordon,[111] not daring to pay honour to one of the greatest latter-day Englishmen because they feared the assembling of a crowd to do him honour, because, I suppose for both political parties the comments on the death of a man sacrificed to their petty party broils would have seemed awkward. As I stood there, I saw the gross, over-fed faces at the club and hotel windows, as I heard the meretricious laughter of the Christian women on the housetops (it is a significant feature of the decadence of England, that not one woman of the upper classes raised her protest by pen or on platform to deprecate the treatment of her unarmed fellow-countrymen; so, all their pity was for the police.) I thought yet, still - I have heard that these poor working men, these Irishmen and Radicals have votes, and perhaps even souls, and it seemed impossible but that some day these poor deceived, beaten, down-trodden slaves would turn upon their oppressors and demand why they had made their England so hideous, why they ate and drank to repletion, and left nothing but work, starvation, kicks, and curses for their Christian brethren? Somewhat in this style I thought; this I saw as I stood wiping the blood out of my eyes in Trafalgar Square. What I did not see was entirely owing to the quietness of the crowd. I did not see

---

[111] General Gordon of Khartoum.

houses burning; I did not see pistols cracking. I did not see this - not because of any precautions the authorities had taken, for they had taken none, but because it was the first time such a scene had been witnessed in London during this generation.

Now, whilst thanking the "Commonweal" for giving me so much space, I can only say that I do not contemplate the renewal of such a scene with much pleasure. "You can beat a cow until she is mad," says the old proverb; and even a Londoner may turn at last. I hope that there may be no occasion for him to turn in my life-time, but I know that if he is not forced to do so, he will have only himself to thank for having avoided it. No party will help him, no one cares for him; rich nobles, City, West End, infidels, Turks, and Jews combine to cheat him, and he stands quiet as a tree, helpless as a sheep, bearing it all and paying for it all. This, then, is all I can tell you of the great riots (sic) in Trafalgar Square, where three men were killed, 300 kicked, wounded, and arrested, and which had no result, so far as I can see, but to make the Liberal Party as odious and despised as the Tory party in the Metropolis. All honour to the Socialists for being the first body of Englishmen in the Metropolis to have determined that the death of three Englishmen, killed by the folly of Sir Charles Dogberry and worthy Mr. Verges, the Home Secretary, shall not go unregarded, and I hope unpunished.

~

The events in Trafalgar Square was a bone that Graham had no intention of burying, and for the rest of the Parliamentary year, he gnawed and gnawed away at it, and at every opportunity, questioned Sir Charles Warren's competence and legality, and proclaimed the rights of Free Speech, in the face of continuing police harassment of Socialist gatherings. (*The Saturday Review*, which was already referring to him as a 'statesman and prose-poet,' reported that the police transferred several hundred men to Trafalgar Square, every time he drew near.[112]) Even with the resignation of Sir Charles on the 9th of November over criticism that he had mishandled the 'Jack the Ripper' case, Graham was not finished with him, or the Home Secretary, and five days later his opportunity came:

---

112 'Relief For the Police,' *The Saturday Review* (12 May 1888), p.558.

## SPEECH CENSURING COMMISSIONER OF POLICE:
HOUSE OF COMMONS, 14th of November, 1888.[113]

I would ask the House to believe that in censuring the conduct of the late Commissioner of Police I am not actuated by any personal spite. I believe that Sir Charles Warren is an honourable and straightforward man, and a man of courage; but at the same time he is the most ill-fitted man, perhaps, in the British Empire to fill such a position. I say this with a free conscience that in this gentleman's dismissal I have had neither heart [?] nor part, and if I were asked suddenly to answer the popular cry of "Who killed Cock Warren?" I should say "Gent-Davis." But I trust that the Government will not send him in *partibus infidelium* [114] and so commit some unfortunate infidels at a distance to a charge of a military officer who has not scrupled to over-ride our constitution, and to treat British citizens half a mile from the House as if they were rebels in some island in the South Sea. The police outrages for which the right hon. Gentleman the Home Secretary took upon himself the responsibility, have borne fruit, and only last night there was a meeting at Clerkenwell Green, and the retiring procession was dispersed with violence by the police for no cause whatever. I must ask the attention of the House for a few minutes whilst I read from the columns of The Daily News. I know The Daily News is not an Anarchist paper, but a hard and fast, buying in the cheapest and selling in the poorest, bourgeois sheet, a very dull paper since it has not been served up with the sauce of Andrew Lang. I was present at a meeting last night with Mr. Morris, the poet, at Clerkenwell Green, which was attended by 15,000 or 16,000 persons, a meeting to protest against any interference with the right of public meeting in Trafalgar Square, to express satisfaction at the dismissal of Sir Charles Warren, and to call for the resignation of the right hon. Gentleman the Home Secretary. The Daily News' account of what transpired is as follows: "Considerable satisfaction was evinced at the retirement of Sir Charles Warren, and the hope was repeatedly expressed that Mr. Matthews would

---

[113] Transcribed into direct speech from the report in Hansard.
[114] Latin: 'In the region of the unbelievers.' Warren held several posts after this, including command of the British garrison at Singapore. Described by General Sir Redvers Buller as "a duffer," he was also in command at the disastrous British engagement with the Boers at Spion Kop in Natal Province, South Africa, in January 1900, during the Second Boer War. The slaughter is memorialised in the word 'Kop,' a colloquial name for a number of steep terraces and stands at English football grounds.

quickly follow his example. A large body of foot and mounted police was stationed in the vicinity, but they did not exercise their authority until the proceedings were far advanced." I finished my speech at 9 o'clock, and spoke subsequently in the House. The events I shall now read occurred about 10 o'clock. "At about half-past ten the speaking at one of the platforms came to an end, and the East Finsbury contingent thereupon re-formed itself into a procession and started from the Green with banners flying, drums beating, and a few lighted torches held aloft. Six mounted and a dozen or so foot police immediately charged the procession, and amid a scene of much animation the torches were extinguished, the drums silenced, and the banners lowered. A large crowd bore round to the right and proceeded up the King's Cross Road, accompanied by a number of police, including three patrols, who made repeated efforts to disperse the gathering. The people, however, held together, and proceeded in a body towards the Pentonville Road. On arriving outside the police station the number of constables was largely recruited, and the Superintendent in charge gave orders to his men to scatter the crowd. Several charges were at once made, a few blows being exchanged, and in a few minutes the road was cleared." I would ask the House whether this does not sound more like a description of what might be expected to take place at Donnybrook Fair,[115] or at a rowdy meeting in Texas, or in the Rio Grande, than in the capital of the civilised world? The right hon. Gentleman the Home Secretary stated that he was responsible for all that the police did. Is he satisfied with having upon his shoulders the responsibility for such doings as these, in which the violence of the Police Force fell upon the poorest classes of Her Majesty's subjects? I would ask the right hon. Gentleman the Home Secretary whether he contemplates with much satisfaction the assurance he gave last night with regard to this responsibility? I would assure the right hon. Gentleman of the circumstance which cannot be within his knowledge. It is this: For the last year I have urged at many meetings, and have pleaded in private with men of the more violent section of advance in this country, on behalf of the right hon. Gentleman, and I do not hesitate to say before God and this House, that I have stood between the right hon. Gentleman the Home Secretary and death many times. But how can I be responsible for men of this kind in the future? Is it not likely

---

[115] An annual fair held on the southern outskirts of Dublin, synonymous with brawling.

77

that if this state of things is allowed to continue, and British citizens are allowed to be beaten down at a public meeting without the reading of the Riot Act, the people will turn in the end, and we shall have some frightful horror such as occurred in Chicago[116] to debate in this House. God grant that this thing may not go any further. The right hon. Gentleman the Home Secretary, who is so ready to assume responsibility for the Acts of Sir Charles Warren, has assumed responsibility for the blood of the two men who were killed through this man's folly last November; but I appeal to the right hon. Gentleman, as the responsible Minister of the Crown to whom the last appeal is to be made, on behalf of the poor, destitute, miserable, starving, down-trodden citizens, for whom the Government of this country exists, and by whom the Government is maintained, to take them under his protection, and to put a stop now and at once, before worse happens, to a state of things which cannot but lead to social turmoil, and to a state of things vastly different from that for which we pray every day in this House, namely, the peace, tranquility, and prosperity of this realm. Is it the object of the present Government to put down the right of public meeting in the open air altogether? The danger of holding meetings out of doors is getting so great that I am beginning to shrink from it. *(Hear, hear!)* What I mean is, that I shall be unable to get speakers. Even Members of Parliament are beginning to shrink from taking part in public meetings out of doors in this land of liberty and free speech. There appears to be a great and growing tendency to interfere with the right of public meeting in the abstract, and the people are not disposed to tamely submit to this. I do not know whether I shall be supported by the Front Opposition Bench on this subject, though I cannot help saying that it might be well if something is said by the Liberal Leaders to show that there is more than a difference of mere name between the two Parties. When I read the story of the Good Samaritan, I often admire most the conduct of the good, honest thief who knocked the wayfarer down, rather than that of the Levite who pretended not to see the wounded man. In discussing this question of the Chief Commissioner, I am not at all sure that the people of London are any more safe under those who knocked them down than under their pretended friends who refused to see

---

[116] 'The Haymarket Affair.' A riot in the aftermath of a bombing at Haymarket Square, Chicago, in May 1887. Four 'conspirators' were subsequently hanged. It is generally considered as the event that began the May Day labour rallies in America.

them when they were on the ground. It is said that political partisans who aspire to office would crawl through a public sewer to obtain it, and I can assure the Liberal Front Bench that before they change places with right hon. Gentlemen sitting opposite to them, if I have any influence, I would be instrumental in emptying such mud on their heads here in London that it might choke some of them, or, at all events, the savour would stick to them during their political lives. It is, I understood, intended to increase the Estimate for police to £20,000. But there is no necessity for this. At present there is a policeman for every 500 of the population, and if that is not sufficient, London must be one of the most revolutionary cities the world ever knew, instead of, as I believe it to be, one of the most quiet and peaceful. With the exception of Ireland, of St. Petersburg, and the Eastern portion of Moscow, there is no city in the world with so large a proportion of police. It is a very great mistake to suppose that by these high-handed measures the police are rallying the small shopkeepers to their sides. On the contrary, so far from this agitation against the militarism of the police being confined to the lowest of the population, it has found an explosive echo in the hearts of the small shopkeepers, who know that the whole of their capital might be destroyed in an hour's riot, and that the causes of such riots would be the unnecessary interference with what the people have been accustomed to consider their constitutional rights. I would warn hon. Members, Conservatives as well as Liberals, of the desirability of considering whether it is not a dangerous thing to push the populace of London as it has been pushed during the last year; and whether it is a good thing to press upon the people of this Metropolis that there is a blood feud between rich and poor."

~

**BLOODY SUNDAY: L' Envoi : TWENTY YEARS ON**
*The New Age*, 19th of November 1908.

When I read again my article of 20 years ago which appeared in the "Commonweal" through the kindness of my great and revered friend William Morris, I confess that, like Warren Hastings,[117] I am surprised at my moderation.

I did not say half enough in condemnation of the brutal conduct of the Tory

---

[117] An English statesman (1732-1818). The first Governor of Bengal.

Government then in power, or of the base treachery and cowardice of the Liberals, who refused all help.

Now as then, I preferred, actually preferred, the thieves amongst whom the wayfaring man fell on his way to Samaria (I think) to the Liberal Pharisees who passed by without helping me.

You can at least fight with a highway robber, and if he beats you it's a fortune of war. Against a cowardly sneak and Pharisee, the state of your stomach deprives one of the power of doing anything but retch.

A Tory Government has been succeeded by a Liberal Government. That is to say, the hogs who were gorging and growling outside the national food troughs twenty years ago have ousted the hogs who had eaten and were lying warming their bellies in the sun. Since that time the British Empire has several times been put up to the ignoble Dutch auction known as a general election, and we, the free and independent citizens have been bought and sold again.

England is a big prize. Let it not be forgotten that though the actual "trading" amongst our politicians is not so large as it is in some other countries over the counter, that the jug and bottle department is always open.

After twenty years' experience, I am more and more convinced that our politicians do not work (sic) for nothing.

What have we gained after twenty years on the path to Liberty? Denshawai[118], Zululand, the Boer War, the suppression of free speech and the liberty of the Press in India are the answers.

We are the same hypocrites. The Tories are just as ready to coerce, the Liberals as cowardly and impotent to defend.

To their credit can be paid the killing at the Featherstone Pit.[119] This makes them equal with their sweet enemies now out of power. Should the necessity arise, the Liberals would be just as active in suppressing free speech in London as the Tories were

---

[118] 'The Denshawai Incident' (13 June 1906). A dispute between British army officers and a local Egyptian population, over the shooting of pigeons. Twenty-six villagers were flogged and given hard labour, and four were hanged, all of which would inflame Egyptian national sentiment.

[119] A parish in the City of Wakefield in West Yorkshire, the site of the 'Featherstone Massacre' of 12th September 1893, where two young men were killed by soldiers. Graham addressed a crowd of mourners from an upturned apple cart following the funerals, and made his 'Revolutions are not made with rosewater' speech. He also commemorated the deaths in his sketch: 'A Yorkshire Tragedy.'

twenty years ago.

Nothing has changed. Only the bottle-holders of to-day would be the butchers of yesterday, and instead of Tory policemen jumping the guts out of a prisoner or knocking down a woman in the streets and calling her a "bloody whore," the ministering angel would be a Liberal.'

~

We can perhaps leave the last word on 'Bloody Sunday' to George Bernard Shaw:

Cunninghame Graham is the hero of his own book; but I have not made him the hero of my play, because so incredible a personage must have destroyed its likelihood - such as it is. There are moments when I do not believe myself in his existence. And yet he must be real; for I have seen him with these eyes; and I am one of the few men living who can decipher the curious alphabet in which he writes his private letters. The man is on public record too. The battle of Trafalgar Square, in which he personally and bodily assailed civilization as represented by concentrated military and constabular forces of the capital of the world, can scarcely be forgotten by the more discreet spectators, of whom I was one. On that occasion, civilization, qualitatively his inferior, was so quantitatively so huge in excess of him that it put him in prison, but had not sense enough to keep him there.[120]

~

Now, after his release from prison, Graham threw himself with messianic zeal into socialist propagandising, first, on platforms the length and breadth of Britain, often addressing ten meetings a week, and he continued to campaign for Keir Hardie as a miner's representative in Parliament, as early as July 1887.[121]

His support for the miners had established him as a champion of the working classes, and *The Manchester Guardian* reported on the 1st of February 1888: "The announcement that the Scotch miners are going to present a handsome testimonial to Mr. Cunninghame Graham, M.P. is not mainly concerned with Trafalgar Square. Mr. Graham is regarded as their thick-and-thin champion in the matter of the Eight Hours Bill."[122]

---

[120] G. B. Shaw, *Notes to Captain Brassbound's Conversion: Sources of the Play.* (August 1900).
[121] *The Coatbridge Express* (9 November 1887), p.1.
[122] *The Manchester Guardian* (1 February 1888), p.5.

# SOCIAL COMMENTATOR

An officer of the NSPCC (founded 1889) with a starved child.

Graham's anger and zeal were fired by the poverty, squalor, and degradation he saw all around him, as he campaigned up and down the country, particularly in Central Scotland. A shocked witness to this was the Londoner John Burns, the man with whom Graham had charged the police lines in Trafalgar Square. In June 1892, during his visit to Glasgow to support Graham's unsuccessful election campaign in Camlachie, Burns and Graham walked the city streets between 11pm on a Saturday night, and 2am on the Sunday morning:

> I have seen every phase of life during the years he had been a public man, but never had I seen such sights – no, not even in the East End of London – as came under my observation We estimated that during the three hours walk about the by-ways and back-ways of Glasgow, we saw some 5,000 [inebriated] persons – men, women, and children. Of this number 400 were blind, speechlessly drunk [. . .] all these unfortunates were scrambling, fighting, cursing, and swearing, and making the place a perfect hell. Another 500 had more drink than was good for them, and I was ashamed to say that of the drunken persons 30 were under the aged of 13. [. . .] Accompanied by a stalwart Highland policeman, we were shown some of the most

vile dens that the mind can conceive. We went into brothels, and in some of these places, which were unfit for human habitation, I saw some sixteen people to a room. Upon seeing such a state of affairs I could not help exclaiming "My God, no wonder these people drink." (A tearful Burns is also reported to have exclaimed: "My God, does Scotland stand where it did?")[123]

The only substantive solution put forward was control of the liquor traffic, and intervention by the churches and charities to try to comfort the poor, as in this lecture by the Medical Officer of Health in Scotland, James B. Russell in 1888:

> I have said the only hope for Glasgow lies in the Church, which alone has the hand endowed with virtue to convey healing to those social sores. [. . .] The constantly increasing proportion of the population of this country which is concentrating round our towns constitutes one of the most anxious features of the times. Be assured if the Church neglects this field, the devil and his ministers will not. Those one and two roomed houses are filled with restless, uncomfortable souls, wakening up to the contrast between their misery and the luxury of their neighbours, and ready to grasp at any theory or project however wild, which promises material relief. Nihilism, Communism, Socialism, Mr. [Henry] George, [Charles] Bradlaugh, *even Cunninghame Graham* - any sort "of Morrison's Pill"[124] will be eagerly swallowed. [125]

~

Concern had been growing over the harsh working conditions amongst the nail and chain-makers of Cradley Heath in 'the Black Country,' in the West Midlands, particularly for female labour. A damning Board of Trade Report was published, prompting Graham to visit Cradley Heath to see for himself:

## A PLEA FOR THE CHAINMAKERS
Pamphlet, December 1888.

The condition of the people at Cradley Heath has been well known for the last fifty years to the public. Disraeli called it Hell-Hole. Royal Commissions not a few have reported on it. Radicals have questioned about it. Philanthropists have sighed and passed on. Clergymen of various denominations have passed lives of modest usefulness endeavouring to divert the minds of the people from the ills they endure

---

[123] Transcribed into the first person from *The Glasgow Evening News*, (13 June, 1892). p.3.
[124] A popular quack medicine compounded from vegetables, invented by the Scot, James Morison (1770-1840).
[125] 'Life in One Room, or Some Serious Thoughts For the Citizens of Glasgow.' Lecture delivered to the Park Parish Literary Institute, Glasgow, 27 of February 1888. Editor's italics.

in this world, to the prospective happiness they may enjoy in the next. But nothing has, so far as I am aware, ever been attempted in a practical way to improve their condition.

Royal Commissions, reports, etc., are excellent things in their way, but there is little use in them if they are not acted upon and merely serve to swell the pile of correspondence in the pigeon-holes of some office in Downing Street. Such is their general fate.

I have never gone to Cradley Heath without coming away in the lowest spirits. The mud is the blackest and most clinging, the roads the slushiest and ruttiest, the look of desolation the most appalling , of any place I have ever seen.

An able pamphlet written some years ago, called "Chains and Slavery," [126] puts forth the condition of the people better than I can. It would require a Zola to write their epic, and a Millet to paint their outward semblance. Still they would fail. An Englishman alone could, I think, render their dumb protest into fitting words, and such an Englishman has not yet been found.

Wages, it is said, have risen all over England. The condition of the wage-earners has bettered ten-fold, say the economists. It may be so, but what, then, must have been the condition of the Cradley Heath chain-makers fifty years ago?

Let me try to place before you Cradley Heath.

A long, straggling, poverty-stricken, red brick, Worcestershire village. Houses all aslant, with the subsidences of the coal workings underneath. Houses! yes, houses, because people live in them. But such dens! Ill-ventilated, squalid, insanitary, crowded; an air of listlessness hanging over everything. Not a pig, not a chicken, not a dog to be seen. A fit place in which to preach thrift, and economy, and abstinence! Oh, yes, especially abstinence - but from what?

Something picturesque withal about these wretched houses, something old-world about the shops where the people slave. Something of pre-machinery days in the deliberate tenacity with which the chains are made. The crowded little workshop, with its four or five "hearths," its bellows, its anvils, its trough of black water, its miserable baby cradled in a starch box. The pile of chains in the corner, the fire of small coals, the

---

[126] A quotation from Robert Burns' 'Scots Wha Hae.'

thin, sweating girl, or boy, or old man (every one seems either very young or very old at Cradley, age seems to follow so hard on youth). The roof without ceiling, the smell of bad drainage, the fumes of reeking human beings pent in a close space - such is a Cradley Heath workshop.

Mud, dirt, desolation, unpaved streets, filthy courts, narrow reeking alleys, thin unkempt women, listless men with open shirts showing hairy chests. Mud, dirt; dirt and more mud - such is Cradley as regards its streets.

Work, work, always; ever increasing; badly paid; from early dawn till after dark; from childhood to old age, and this is the chain they forge. Stunted forms, flattened figures, sallow complexion, twisted legs from working the treadle hammer, are the outward and visible signs of which the chain and nailmakers' dull, dogged, despairing resignation, born of apathy and hunger, is the inward and spiritual grace.

To sum up the position briefly. Failure of civilisation to humanise; failure of commercialism to procure a subsistence; failure of religion to console; failure of Parliament to intervene; failure of individual effort to help; failure of our whole social system.

But the time has come, the electric light of public opinion is turned for the moment upon Hell-Hole. What will it do? Merely flash off again, and leave the darkness more intense? Or will it bring life and health and hope?

I have little doubt there are many philanthropic people ready to help these poor folk if their case were widely known. Truly, they lack advancement, but not charity.

I have always contended that what is wanted at Cradley is the temporary advance of some portion of the wealth that the district has created. It should be remembered that very little small chain is made in any other part of England. It should be remembered that many profits, apart from the legitimate cost of distribution, are made off small chain before it reaches the consumer, and that if those profits remained with the producer no charity would be needed. All parties in the State alike condemn the middleman. Well, an opportunity has presented itself to get rid of him in the district. But not by praying, not by reading reports, or poring over statistics. Action! Action is what is wanted, and prompt action too.

What says Mr. Burnett's report in reference to the various Commissions, Reports, Select Committees, etc.? "The general drift of these reports and of the evidence is to the effect that for at least 150 years the condition of the nailors has been wretched in the extreme, except during brief seasons." Wretched during 150 years; during all the period of England's commercial supremacy; during the rise of the machine industry; whilst the steam engine was supplanting the stage coach; whilst discoveries to lighten labour (sic) were being made - during all this time these men were hammering away making nails, and were wretched, were starving, worse, I say, than savages, for in their distress savages see no wealth about them.

"It may be said," says Burnett, "that excepting the abatement [mark the word abatement, it should have been abolition] of the truck system [127] and the excessive employment of children, all the evils then complained of as existing in the nail and chain trade exist to-day intensified to some extent by increased population and the pressure of outside competition, whether from abroad or increased application of machinery to the work of production." "Evils intensified!" a good reason, I suppose, to do nothing and to prate of not interfering with the course of trade; to twaddle about supply and demand, and so forth. I have no doubt that to some it may seem as foolish to throw doubt on the laws of supply and demand, etc., as on the law of gravitation, but whilst one is an established scientific fact - easily established by throwing a stone into the air - the other law is merely a rhapsody of words, merely a piece of defensive armour invented by fools who, in the main, knew nothing of what they wrote, and seized upon by knaves eager to strengthen themselves in the possession of their ill-gotten gains.

And all this has been known for years. Liberals and Tories alike have known it, and have done nothing. Nothing has been done, or will be done. I fear, while the bulk of both parties are rich men and employers of labour. Anyhow, the present state of this district is a scandal to both parties, a satire on civilisation, and makes one doubt whether Parliament, as we now know it, with its stupid fuss, its stupid men, and its foolish measures, is any advantage to the poor at all.

But there is a greater than Parliament; there is the power that made Parliament and can remake it; the power that pays for the green covered seats, the Speaker's wig, the

---

[127] Whereby employees were paid in tokens or produce from a company store (or 'Tommy Shop'), rather than in money. Despite legislation, the system persisted into the 20th century.

mace and all the other baubles; and if Parliament is deaf, the masters of Parliament - the people of England - will, if they read this dull pamphlet, at least be able to judge of the true state of the case. Perhaps the way to put things best before them is to Mr. Burnett's report:-

Harrison, aged 53, and his daughter Elisa, 28 . . . work in a dark little shop in a most insanitary and filthy court . . . making nails . . . had to work late and early to earn 15s. per week between them, out of which they had to pay 2s. for breese (small coal) . . . family of seven . . . lived mostly on tea, and bread and bacon. On Sundays they might be able to get a morsel of meat, or "beef cheek," to boil and make soup with . . . Eliza enumerates as chief items of expenditure: two lbs. of tea at 6p., 4lbs. of sugar 2d. 1s. 10d for coals, 2s. for house rent, and 1s. 6d. for bacon.

No fear, I should think, of pauperising these people by helping them; little chance of undermining their self-reliance, so dear to Englishmen (rich ones).

Joseph Marson, 83 . . . had been 75 years a nailor . . . nails he had known at 2s a bundle, now only 8d . . . could earn 2s. 6d. a week when he could get nails to make, and got 2s. 6d. a week from the parish.

Five shillings a week is generous pay at 83, after a life of toil. Still, God forbid, we should interfere with the course of trade. The weakest to the wall, my worthies. You see this old man was the victim of an "economic pressure," therefore let us bow down before "economic pressures" when they do not touch ourselves. Let us, if we be Tory Pharisees, talk of the greatness of the empire - it appears that the shop where he worked for 75 years was all the empire citizen Marson knew. If we be Liberal Politicians, let us refuse to interfere with supply and demand. In either case, Joseph Marson will soon be in a pauper's coffin and will have obtained that freehold land measuring 6 feet by 2½ , that is the only one obtainable by most Englishmen.

John Lavender, nailer, 24 . . . and his wife making 3½ inch spike nails . . . by their joint efforts can make 18s. a week, working 15 hours per day . . . Rent and breese would run to about 2s. 9 d. per week. So that a good pair of workers, under specially favourable conditions, could only clear 15s. 3d. between them in a week of from 60 to 70 hours' unremitting toil.

It is good for a man to bear the yoke in his youth (how about women?). Let them work on, good souls; parish coffins await them: skilly[128] (a nourishing diet) awaits them in the workhouse; and, best of all, the praise of all well-meaning thick-headed men who know that labour ennobleth man, but are determined to be as little noble themselves as possible. Again:-

One little shop was in full swing . . . four young women, all clean and newly washed had just resumed nail making after tea. Three of them at nails known as "forties," that is, 40lbs to the 1,000. The nails are 3 inches long, and the price 2s. 1d per bundle of 54lbs. These young women seem very skillful workers, and the rapidity with which they can beat, point, cut off and head the nails, seems like the very culmination of manual dexterity. By working from six in the morning to nine at night, they can each make a bundle in two days, or about 6s. 3d per week. Out of that 5d per week for breese, 2d each for rent of shop, and about 4d. per week for repair of tools. The clear earnings of these young women, skillful, persistent, unwearying workers, their arms thin but hardened by unceasing toil, their chests flat, their faces pallid, and their palms and fingers case-hardened by bellows, hammer, and rod, will run to 5s. 5d. per week when in full work. Their hours of toil are supposed to be limited by Act of Parliament.

These fair young women must be indeed noble, if work can do it.

I will quote one more instance from the report, this time of a chainmaker, a desperate, wicked old rascal as will be seen:-

An old man of 68, named Blunt . . . been a chainmaker 54 years . . . is making bare 3 - 8 chains, for which he can get 3 s. 6d. a cwt., and can make 1½ cwt. a week. In an outburst of passionate revolt against the hardness of his lot, he declares: "I often feel inclined to put myself away."

What a disgusting old man! Does he not know that to repine[129] is unmanly and un-English? Has he not heard the clergyman preaching contentment? Did he never hear the ultimate fate of the suicide? I hate to hear of such cases. Perhaps the unthankful old dog will be getting questions asked in Parliament, and parading his insolent starvation in that august assembly, coming between us and the Irish Question. Why can he not turn his face to the wall, curse God, and die, like many another professing but starving

---

[128] A thin soup.
[129] Express feelings of discontent.

Christian has to do in this famed land?

Passing from Cradley Heath to Cradley proper (says the report) I mount to Anvil Yard, a region of squalor and dirt far surpassing anything I had yet seen. Rents are high here, and range from 3s. to 4s. In one case, a covered drain running past the end of a dwelling-house struck damp through the house from floor to ceiling: open drains everywhere carrying off household refuse, and curious privies, with overflowing ash-pits, loading the atmosphere with the most pungent odours. Here, also, are the domestic workshops, built on to the houses, so that the occupant can step at once from kitchen to anvil.

All this, too, from a Government report, prepared for that smuggest and most Philistine of legislative assemblies - the British House of Commons.

However, I have seen it all - and worse. I have seen three generations of chainmakers, from the old man of 70 to the boy of 13, working in one shop. I have seen the pallid, flat-chested girls, and I have waded through the black clinging mud of Anvil Yard. I have wondered at the patience of these unfortunate people, and I have marveled at the supineness of Parliament, which for the last fifty years has known of their condition, and done nothing.

I challenge contradiction to my statement that the average earnings in the chainmaking trade, after deducting cost of fuel, repair of tools, etc., are: of women 4s. to 5s. 6d., with many as low as 2s. 6d.; of men, many as low as 5s., the average from 10s. to 13s., while the maximum earned by a few of the most skillful at the best quality of work is 17s. to 20s. These sums are earned by an average of twelve to fifteen hours' hard work per day. These, too, are the present figures, which are the highest earned for many years.

It now remains for me to state to what I think their misery is due, and to try to propose a remedy.

Of course, primarily, the fault is in our social system that regards toil as good in itself instead of as a necessary evil, that permits free trade in human flesh, that hugs itself with complacency as it repeats the capitalist dogma that competition is the soul of business. Of course application of machinery has rendered the living of the nailmakers more precarious. But it is not with the chainmakers. Small chains are not made by machinery. If a dog chain made at Cradley Heath for a penny, or at most twopence, is sold in London to the dowager to lead her phlegmatic pug for 1s., surely some one must make a dishonestly large profit out of it. I do not assert that any one person has the "legitimate shent per shent"[130] out of it, but there are a large number of small profits made as it passes through the hands of agents and dealers, most of whom are unnecessary to its distribution. Hence it will be seen that any plan that aims at helping the chainmakers must include also a scheme for eliminating the middlemen. The truck system, too, still flourishes in the district, with the usual consequences. These reasons, the want of union, the rapacity of employers, the introduction of female labour, the scandalous neglect of Parliament to act upon the evidence of the various commissions and reports it has received, are, I think, the chief causes of the misery of the district.

As for these remedies, they are not so easily to be found. Mr. Burnett, in his report, speaks of the desirability of introducing the factory system, and further on, if I understand him rightly, seems to deprecate any legislation.

To introduce the factory system without legislation would do more harm than good. The factory system under some benevolent, go-as-you-please, supply and demand, church and chapel-going capitalist, would indeed be handing over the poor people to be more sweated than ever. I can easily imagine the abolition of the domestic workshop system and the introduction of factories on the free competitive system being used still further to sweat the people, for without doubt there is still marrow in their bones for the clever man of business to extract if he had the chance. The factory system that I look for is one under the direct control of a local authority created by the Government and elected by the chain and nail makers themselves.

I can imagine that the very idea of such a scheme would be as pleasing to the ordinary middle-class Liberal or Tory, as was the mass to the lug of Jennie Geddes.[131] A Government exists, however, I suppose, for some other purpose than to waste the

---

[130] 'Cent per cent,' or 'shent per shent' were commonly used by Graham to indicate his hatred of capitalist profiteering. The latter carries an anti-Semitic inference, although Graham had several close Jewish friends.
[131] A market-trader, who, on Sunday the 23 July 1637, threw her stool at the head of the Dean of Edinburgh in St Giles' Cathedral, in protest over the first public use of 'The Booke of Common Prayer' in Scotland, with the words: "De'il gie you colic, the wame o' ye, fause thief; daur ye say Mass in my lug?" This act is reputed to have sparked the riot that led to 'The Wars of the Three Kingdoms,' which included The English Civil War.

nation's money in armies, in ironclads[132] (to be sold soon as scrap iron), in pensions, and in Jubilees. Surely some portion of the wealth that has been wrung out of this unlucky district might be put at its disposal in the form of a loan. Perhaps, though, their patience has had its usual reward - neglect. If there had been no park-railings to pull down or landlords to boycott, the result might have been different. Why should the Government not create a local authority with power to deal with the difficulty, as suggested by Mr. Mahon?

These men ask no charity, only the right to live by their own work. Land might be acquired, and factories built in which the hours of labour could be limited, and the employment of women and children regulated. By the application of the steam fan, the hard degrading toil of many of the boys and girls could be dispensed with. Agents could be employed to buy the iron, fuel, and other materials for the workers, and the sale and distribution as well as the production of chains managed. In this way the workers would escape the foggers,[133] sweaters, warehousemen, middlemen - and whatever else the parasites be called.

I believe all this could be done, and done easily, too, despite the cries sure to be raised of Socialism and the like. I can imagine, though, the rage of the sweaters and the capitalists when they see a chance of their victims escaping them any other way than by death.

I know the pressure that would be brought to bear upon Parliament by the employers of labour on both sides of the House. I can fancy the cries of "Utopian," of "waste of public money," of "Protection," etc.

Gracefully, too, would come these arguments from the House of Commons that is to advance £5,000,000 to buy out Irish landlords and establish smaller ones; from a House of Commons that is prepared to vote £300,000 for river drainage in Ireland; from a House of Commons that has already voted £1,000 to encourage the Donegal Cottage Industries. No, the fact is, there is no party capital to be made out of the Chainmakers, and therefore neither party of political mountebanks will move in the matter.

There is another plan that might be adopted, though I confess it does not so

---

[132] Steel warships.
[133] Middle-men, gang-masters, suppliers of cheap labour.

much commend itself to me. Co-operative works have already been started in the district on a small scale, but are languishing for lack of capital. The Government might advance a sum, by the way of grant or loan, to aid these societies.

I am not bigotedly attached to either of these schemes and if the Government does not like them, let them or any individual produce a better, and I am sure no one will support it more enthusiastically than myself, if it is really likely to help these people.

Something, however, must be done, and done quickly, to cure this disgrace to England, this scandal to civilisation. Something that may place the chainmaker of Cradley at least on a level with the Hottentot; that may put life and hope into the hearts of the flat-chested, pallid-faced women; that may restore life and animation to the muddy, unpaved, deserted streets of Cradley; that may bring joy to its desolate homes; that may end the misery of this, the most miserable people in all miserable England.

Graham tried to lay these appalling conditions before the House of Commons, but was thwarted, and things came to a head on the 1st of December 1888. *The Scotsman*, under the headline EXTRAORDINARY SCENE, reported on Graham's request in the House to the First Lord of the Treasury W. H. Smith that a day be given to discuss the chainmakers of Cradley Heath. Smith replied that the matter was being given earnest consideration by the Government, but that no time would be allocated. In reply, Graham said:

"That does not answer the question. I simply ask whether the right hon. Gentleman will afford facilities for the discussion of the motion of one of his own supporters. If he does not do so, then I can only characterise his action as a dishonourable trick' (*Cries of "Order"*)

The SPEAKER: The hon. gentleman is behaving in a most unparliamentary manner by using language of that kind. (*Hear, hear and loud cries of "Withdraw"*)

Mr. CUNNINGHAME GRAHAM: I never withdraw.[134] I say what I mean. (*Renewed cries of "Order" and "Name"*)

The SPEAKER: I must ask the hon. Gentleman to withdraw an expression which is not Parliamentary. "Dishonourable trick" is not a Parliamentary expression. (*Cheers*)

Mr. CUNNINGHAME GRAHAM: I wish, as on a former occasion, to acquit myself of any discourtesy to you, sir, but I feel bound to characterise the action of the hon. Gentleman as a "dishonourable trick." (*Loud cries of "Order" and "Withdraw"*)

The SPEAKER: I must ask the hon. gentleman to withdraw that expression.

Mr CUNNINGHAME GRAHAM: I refuse to withdraw. (*Cries of "Name"*)

---

[134] George Bernard Shaw borrowed the expression "I never withdraw" for his play 'Arms And The Man' (1894).

The SPEAKER: Then I must ask the hon. Member to withdraw from this House.

Mr. CUNNINGHAME GRAHAM: Certainly, sir.[135] [Some reports add: "I will go to Cradley Heath."[136]]

~

## THE BLOODY CITY

*The People's Press*, 16th of August 1890.

In view of the great Eight Hours demonstration to be held in Liverpool during the week of the Trades Union Congress, the dockers write to Mr. Hugh, the secretary of their union, for a motto for their new banner. A pious Scotchman, beside his Karl Marx (he) keeps his Bible; if perhaps he respects one, he venerates the other. I shall not attempt to assert the respect and veneration between the two ponderous tomes. However, to his Bible in this instance did Mr. Hugh repair, and after a smart tussle with it, aided by a concordance (Cruden), extracted the following pithy motto, from that amiable, if mixed prophet, the blessed Nahum[137]

"The Bloody City is full of lies and robbery."

It may be - I do not know - I only say it may be - there are other bloody cities besides Liverpool, in which lust, lies, and robbery are rife enough. Is it not a robbery that machinery, which should help a man - nay, which should help the human race - should be applied and used as it is in Liverpool and in London. Your curious inventor ties a towel round his head, sits late into the night, plans me a nice machine. Straight your capitalist, who never found out anything in all his life but ways to live on other people's meat, buys it from him. Then this machine, that should have lightened toil and been a blessing, proves a curse. In Liverpool, for instance, a grain elevator does the work of 50 men with six. What happens? Merely this, 40 and more wretches out of work. Hours remain long, as long as usual, for the six men in work; the other 44 go to find other trades, perhaps to starve, or stretch their damned luxurious Christian limbs in

---

135 Hansard: Nailers and Small Chainmakers: New Rules of Procedure. Standing Order 27 (Disorderly Conduct) Mr. Cunninghame Graham Ordered to Withdraw. 1st of December 1888.
136 The Book of Nahum is the seventh book of the twelve minor prophets of the Hebrew Bible. 'The Bloody City' refers to Nineveh.

137 *The Yorkshire Gazette* (8 December 1888), p.11.

the workhouse. Is not this robbery? Is not this a lie - a lie on civilisation, a lie on our progress? The gain is there, the capitalist saves the wages of the forty-four, and still works long hours with the six.

Now in London at the docks we hear there is a new machine intended to coal a ship, by which two-thirds the wages will be saved. Will any human toil be saved? Not it.

"The Bloody City is full of lies and robbery!"

How shall we check this? How shall we prevent the robbery, how nail the lies upon the counter of men's understanding? In a month the Trades' Union Congress will be held. All the reactionary forces will be there. All the wise, reverent fools will lay their addled heads together to cheat the working classes, to preach to these of moderation, of hell fire, of foreign trade, of mutual respect and interest 'twixt the employer and the sweaty, sweated labourer. I must once again proclaim the truth, the naked, open, unpalatable truth. There is no possible community of interest between the employers and employed. One grinds the workman down, scrimps him of his pay, forces him to toil, day out, day in, for a bare pittance. The other cheats his employer, scamps his work, steals the material when possible, tries by any shift to get his pay, and withhold his work.

"The Bloody City is full of lies and robbery!"

Who's wrong? What's wrong? Is it the employer or employed? Or both? My answer is, the system; the base, vile, commercial system that sees God in gold; that thinks a million or ten million cotton bobbins a year atone for lives spent in toil, in miserable surroundings. It is false. No bobbins, no dung forks, no sardine boxes, no shoddy clothes produced at 9s. 6d. the suit, no boots with paper soles, even though cheap, weigh in the scale against the misery that cries out to us from -

"Every Bloody City that is full of lies and robbery!"

Talking to a doctor the other day, he asked, how do you think I spend my life? I answered him, in purging merchants who have swilled too much turtle soup at civic banquets, in writing prescriptions for my lady's lap-dog, in placing sticking plaster carefully on the rich child's (rich child, all children should and might be rich) finger. He answered me, "Some of these I do no doubt, but keep your caustic wit in reserve for your fellow fools in Parliament. I spend half my time at least (gratuitously) in patching up our failures in hospital. Our failures? Yes, in doctoring the poor. Are not the poor our failures? (He spoke of Glasgow and great cities.) In doctoring these, 75 per cent of whom have had no chance, whose maladies are perpetual want of food, whose chief disease is want of work. Those who, when they can get work, work far too long. These long hours, said he, are the curse of all our poor. Cannot you fellows up in Parliament pass laws to stop this? What do you do?" I answered, "Nothing."

"Our Bloody City (Westminster) is full of lies and robbery!"

We pass our time yawning, drinking tea, talking scandal, discussing Lady Dando's legs, or something of that sort. If we pretend to work, it is all fooling, substituting "if" for "and," moving that such and such an Act come into force in March instead of April. Then at the fag end of the session we have a "rump" of foolish addle-headed men with a determination of polysyllables to the mouth. A set of men than none listen to on any serious subject, but who to gain notoriety must needs come in and waste the nation's time with trumpery tales of local folly, petty accounts, fit to be registered in petty courts; anything in fact to get their names before the public and remind their constituents they are not dead.

This, and a stopped measure or so conceived by Government, completes our session's duty. My doctor (a good fellow, one of the old kind of men, a lectorian, nurtured perhaps on porridge at the Northern University) slaps his hand upon the table, and calls out: "Why, damn you all then, do you never talk of labour? Do you not recognise that you can change all this, can equalise the wealth, can make men's lives more tolerable? "Labour", said I, "Oh, yes, we do sometimes talk of it (it's true we all live off and on it), sometimes in a strike we talk of sending troops to crush the strikers. Sometimes we say that labour should be free, we mean, of course, free to compete for us. Sometimes when a collier kicks his wife to death, or a poor working wench smothers her new-born child, we say the working classes are a dreadful lot. You say we should reduce the power of labour. Reduce the hours of labour? *Pas si bête.* That would be the beginning of the end. Then would Bradlaugh, Morley, and all the Tory crows (backed silently by the rich Liberals) rise and fume, and sweat, and make a dreadful pother, about Stuart Mill, and Malthus, and all the writers of the dismal science, now dead and damned for dullness. "And the workmen everywhere," quoth he, "Would they not rise, and say salvation lay in this reduction of long hours? Would they not stem, strive, and strive and stem, till it were done?" "Perhaps," said I, and so the conversation ended, and we separated, he to his hospital, and patching human failures, I to push the Eight Hours movement, and to strive to take his work away from him (blackleg, you see) by getting shorter hours, and thus decreasing the output of our factories.

Anyhow, in Liverpool we can do work. It is true Burns, Mann, and Tillett, leaders of the new blood, are free, and can do their best against the old moderate go-as-Gladstone-pleases Liberal gang. It would be a scandal, knowing as we do that the men of every other country in the world are marching under the Eight Hours flag, that Britain (and Ireland) should hold back. It would be a shame, knowing that, in this Eight Hours question and by means of it alone, the working classes can be freed from their hard lives, and have the profits they create, participate in the increased leisure that machinery can bring, if we hold back.

This congress can and must be captured. A new secretary is to be elected. Look to it, gas stokers, look to it, dockers of Liverpool and London! Look to all the various trades that during the past eighteen months have organised. Elect a Socialist if possible. If not, elect Charles Fenwick. He is honest; timid a little, perhaps, but still a man. Determined to do right, responsibility that spoils many will ripen him. It will give him freedom from the thraldom of his old-fashioned union in the north, which keeps him back. He would move with the times had he the power; and they, once free from the old world attachments which now bind them and keep them back behind the body of the working classes, would move too. If young men go as delegates, let them heed no talk of want of head. Time gives a head, but cannot put sense into an empty brain-pan, even though the chin is like a furze bush.

Speak out your opinions. Remember you are there not as yourselves, but as the delegate of others, and they trust you. Disregard all remarks about a fall in wages. Did wages fall after the ten hours movement? Besides, who says that wages are to fall? Is it not the same employers, who in the past have themselves done their best to bring them down? Heed not foreign competition. In every other country, the same eight hours movement is afloat, in some perhaps as much or more advanced than here. Think of the days when in your childhood, in the factory or the mine, yourselves waited watching eagerly (to be little slaves) till the wished- for bell would free you from your daily slavery. Resolve, at least, the generation after you shall not be spoiled and sweated as you have been, and remember that there are two ways, and two ways only to achieve this. Either by violent revolution, which is alien to the spirit of tradition of your race, or else by legal action. Individual effort can never do it. Has it done it? How many of you now work short hours? Those of you who do, at what sacrifice have you achieved your shorter hours? Granted that Parliaments are bad, that Whigs and Tories are a heap of cheats, that Radicals for the most part are a set of prating fools. Alter it then; send your own men. Do as the miners of the north have done, who if they are behind in economics, still in politics are first. Capture the Congress; pan an eight hour resolution at it; you can do it. Lay your commands on me, or whom you like, to present it in Parliament, and we can turn the dull place upside down before a year be out. When sitting at Congress, close your eyes and think a bit; think of your native city, I care not which it be or where it is, and ask yourself: Is it not true, as Nahum said of old of his,

"My Bloody city is full of lies and robbery."

~

## THE REPTILE PRESS
*The People's Press*, 14th of February 1891.

Yes, it has come to this, that in the main the mighty lever has become a reptile.

No matter if over tea and toast in Bouverie Street the ancient lady tells her yarns, or if the name be *Standard*, *Times*, or *Star*, the Press is dead against "the infernal poor."

The "infernal poor" - not that if you want a charity subscription the Press is lacking, not it. Not that if "individual effort" is your fate, you will lack support. But let the "infernal poor" only talk of "rights" and then the editorial thunder rumbles and all the hacks of Grub-street amble out - from Andrew Lang[138] to Greenwood[139] – to write them down.

It is, perhaps, a cruel thing to say, but it would seem that the press is nobbled, nobbled by the capitalists, and now, instead of being an instrument of freedom, it has become a reptile of the basest sort.

---

[138] Andrew Lang (1844-1912). Scottish historian, novelist, critic, and folklorist.
[139] James Greenwood (1832-1929). English social explorer and journalist.

What is the real function of the press? To chronicle small beer, to tell us who is dead and damned, or hanged, or married, to print the lists of shares, to let the public know what theatres are open, and when glove fight and the football match comes off, and if her gracious Majesty in the east wind has deigned to walk upon the slopes. In fact to be a pimp of news for the public at a penny.

Render to Caesar what is his'n and to the editor his penny, but give him not your conscience in his keeping.

I do not want to tilt against the Press, only to warn folk against its reptile attitude on Labour questions, and to show the reason for it. The press is owned by and run by the wealthy middle class, the Bourgeois. What wonder, therefore, that its sympathies are with the Bourgeois and against the people? That is but natural. What is strange, therefore, is that working men should be received with a written sentiment that spoken from a platform they would not endure for a moment.

Who is it that writes the article that puts the workmen's case in an odious light before the public?

Who calls out for "law-'n'-order" and more police at the docks?

Who is it in the reports of Parliament, speaks of "stirring speeches" by men the electorate knows are fools and cannot speak a sentence to their own constituents!

Often some trembling miserable man with a wife and children, dependent on him, forced to do anything to give them bread.

Sometimes a Tory working for a Liberal paper; sometimes a Whig in chains to a Tory; sometimes a Socialist cursing them both, yet doomed to write or stare - for this, the reptile Press.

Yet when the workman reads the trash - say an attack on Burns, or Mann, or Hardie - by some unknown scribbler, he begins to doubt and think his trusted friend a rogue

Does any mortal of the working classes really wish to know what Mr. Robinson of the *Daily News*, or the editor of the *Star*, *Times*, or *Standard* thinks on a labour question? If he pauses to reflect, he knows the editor must be against him and his class, and that all his efforts will be directed to keep workmen down and save the Bourgeois from attack.

No matter if for party purposes a paper now and then pretends to take the side of the poor - the "infernal poor" - it is always for a purpose and to make capital for the party it belongs to. How many papers are there which, in their offices, give the work to union printers unless they are obliged? Take the instance of the *Scottish Leader*, a paper never tired of bawling (howling?) about Ireland and the Crofters. Comes a dispute with the Edinburgh Printer's Society, and immediately all union men are packed out of the office and the printing sent to other papers and a manifesto appears about the tyranny of trade unionists!

Yes, trade unionism is a pretty soap bubble to blow before men's eyes to lead them from the track of Socialism, but let it break out in "our office" and that's another pair of boots. "Thou shalt not criticise the Press." "Thou shalt not doubt a statement in the Press."

"Thou shalt bow down and worship and believe implicitly each and every syllable that is printed in the Press" - the Reptile Press!

A lie becomes almost the truth in type. All that is printed is the truth. "Thou shalt reverence all that appertains to the Press, all pressmen, all reporters, editors, comps, newsboys, and printer's devils."

It is advisable to say black's white if you see it in the Press, or it may chance you are a Tory in disguise. Look at the fate of Burns in Scotland. Merely because he dared to venture that every single individual of the Scottish Press was not immaculate, that boycott was put on.

These printer's devils take too much upon themselves.

In the fight that is to come - that is going on - which has forced the Government, so it is said, to search abroad for a Liberal policy - the working class must realise that the Press will be against them always. Whig will smite Tory. Tory gird at Whig. But both will be against the working class.

Let the workmen think, if during any strike they ever read an article in any of the great papers that really gave them satisfaction? If there was not always at the end of it some caution as to methods, some hint of violence - if in fact the reptile did not manifest itself in some part or another of the composition? In any labour fight, let but a working man overstep the law - which, by the way, he did not make - and then the friendliest newspaper, instead of finding excuses for his pardonable ignorance, is full of threats, big words, and talk of police and military.

It is time for the gentry of the Press to know that almost all the laws of England are hated and detested by the working class. Men are not all born blind, O Reptile Press!

They know the laws of England in the main are cruel and unjust, and made of design to keep the "infernal poor" in order - such

as, for instance, the Conspiracy Law, which the "People's Parliament" refused to modify the other day. I can understand, if Burns or Mann or Hardie or any well-tried leader of the people were editor of a paper, that the working classes might be eager to know what their opinion was upon a Labour question.

In France, where articles on politics are signed, the workman knows that the opinions he is reading are those of some trusted or mistrusted person. In the one case, because he knows the record of the man who writes, the writing helps him to make up his mind. Thus it is that in France in spite of unjust law, and all the tyranny of the middle class republic and of Papa Constans,[140] there is in politics a solidarity amongst working men not to be found in England. In France no article in a newspaper can gammon any working man to vote for his employer, no matter what he calls himself, because some series of signed articles by some well-known man, has made, let us say the theory of surplus value, plain to him, and he recognises that the employer lives on the surplus value, and that the workman makes it, and that therefore between the two, there can only be war.

That is not all.

In England here, the Reptile Press, often for a wretched wage, for years and years, sucks at the brain and ideas of some clever man, then quarrels with him and casts him on the world, without a name, position, or a living. In France, where articles are signed, this cannot be.

Rochefort,[141] the man who drove the first nail into the coffin of the infamous Second Empire, was only a struggling pressman at the first. In England, probably he would be struggling still. Take the case of Massingham,[142] ex-editor of the *Star*, a first-rate writer, the man perhaps who made the *Star*. Colman and Stewart and the capitalistic

---

[140] Jean Antoine Ernest Constans (1833-1913). A French statesman.
[141] Victor Henri Rochefort (1831-1913). A radical French journalist: "the prince of press controversy."
[142] Henry William Massingham (1860-1924), an English journalist. He would later become the Editor of *The Daily Chronicle*, but was forced to resign because of his opposition to the Boer War. He again lost the editorship of *The Nation* due to his support of The Labour Party, and was replaced by John Maynard Keynes.

gang who own the *Star* and worship Gladstone, and go mad for Ireland, forgetting England exists, and that men die of hunger underneath their noses in it, wanted to force him to prostitute his pen to attack John Burns. When he refused, they forced him to resign; and there he is, with his three years' work upon the *Star* all in their pockets. Nor is that all, in the reptile press of to-day, this sweating is carried on in every branch; reporters, printers, editor, and all are made to suffer to make the fortune of some gang of sweaters.

What is it that keeps the everlasting sham fighting going twixt Liberal and Tory. The press again; for it knows that in the strife of parties (meaning nothing, but rotation of the rascals in office) the working class can best be cheated from the contemplation of all true reforms.

As to be rich involves the fact of some-one else being poor - or else it is evident that riches have no value, being able to buy the services of no one when all are rich - so in the same way a Liberal to exist must have a Tory to expend his pious fury on, or else there is no fun, and the "infernal poor" begin to ask for Eight Hours Bills. This naturally creates a reptile Press for both sets of "rotating rascals." With Whigs and Tories we need to pay high for the services of clever venal knaves to keep the battle up by its everlasting Gladstone and Salisbury din, prevent the cry of the poor from being heard. What is lacking to the working class to-day is a definite policy, by means of which they can at once confound the Whigs and Tories - which really are but one - and at the same time enter into the enjoyment of their property, on which, at present, they are but sojourners, bond-slaves to the rich and cheated by Conservatives and Liberals alike.

What is that policy? Firstly, International relations with the workers of the Continent, destruction to the old-world war cries of race and creed.

The proletarian has no country, all are equally prisons to him alike. No matter if the Frenchman (without money) come to England and the Englishman cross to France, unless their purse is full, to the favour of the twelve hours day and subsistence wages in either country must they come. Lucky if they come to that, and not to swell the army of the unemployed.

Next, as a policy, the workers should endeavour to destroy the existing parties and extirpate the tyranny of capitalist or priest. Lastly, as a means to an end, reduce the hours of labour by a legislative enactment in order that there may be time to cultivate relations with the foreign workmen, and combine against the Whig and Tory thieves at home.

If this policy is the true one, and it is that enunciated by Karl Marx and Frederick Engels, endorsed by all the leaders of the Continental workmen; and at home, that one on which John Burns, Keir Hardie, Thorne, and all the leaders of the new Unionism are agreed. Is it to be wondered that the reptile press oppose it?

Think what would happen if it were followed out. That great thieves' kitchen - Parliament - instead of being manned by high-class gilt-edged magnolia-scented cooks of the upper classes - too fine to cook - would bear a different aspect and be filled with, say, 500 cooks drawn from the working classes - not there to thieve and to keep thieves in the enjoyment of their thieving, but each man ready to cook the national food and serve it up hot for those who make it.

What room would there be for a political press at all?

Therefore it is that the reptile Press ferments the ancient hatred betwixt the Englishman and foreigners, by talking of international competition and the trade of England - as if it mattered a farthing to the worker with wages at subsistence point - when shorter hours are talked of.

Thus it is in every strike, in every effort made by the working class, the Press must be against

them, as it fights in so doing for self-preservation.

In the past, no doubt, the Press has done us yeoman service, exposed abuses, made public deeds of oppression, helped men to check the power of kings, capitalists, and other rogues both great and small - not one word, therefore, against its freedom; on the contrary, our object still should be to make it free, and redeem it from its present (subservience) to capital.

A mighty lever is the Press. At present it is a dull chained reptile in the main pouring out its venom against all economic progress, and stabbing those in the back who criticise its patrons, the capitalists.

The working-classes, when they buy their paper so that it be neither the PEOPLE'S PRESS or *Reynolds*, should treat it as a news sheet, nothing more, and when they come to the lies and leading articles, exclaim with Lessing,[143] "Lie on, my friend, as only you can lie; your friends will not be taken in thereby; once only have they been deceived by you, that was when something that you said was true."

Reptile Press, one penny - and dear at the money!

~

Graham's attitude to those whose pay and conditions he had worked so hard to improve could be paradoxical to say the least. He was constantly frustrated by the worker's apparent inability to see to their own best interests; as liable to vote Tory as Liberal, let alone his new projected Labour Party. At a meeting in Dundee in September 1889, he stormed out after telling those assembled that they were only fit to be represented by capitalists, and offering a few epigrams on the stupidity of the working classes.[144]

Graham despised bourgeois aspirations, and was only too aware that once a working man had improved his position, he was just as liable to turn on his fellows, and betray his class. In this ironic piece, Graham puts the blame for these misguided ambitions on those cosy symbols of Victorian domesticity, the 'wally dugs'[145] that ornamented almost every Scottish mantle-shelf until at least the mid 1950s.

## CHINA DOGS
*The Labour Prophet: Organ of the Labour Church*, May 1892.

There have been many tyrants in history, from Dionysius of Syracuse down to Dr. Francia of Paraguay. Melted butter in English cookery has slain its thousands, tall hats have done fell execution on men's hair and morals, but none have, I firmly believe, worked as much destruction in the British mechanic's independence, as the harmless unnecessary china dog.

Some would say that the wooden dog is the best breed of dog ever pupped. The Spaniards have a proverb, "Alhaja que tiene boca nadie la toca."[146] This would seem to sustain the wooden dog theory; but before the china one it falls to the ground.

Granted that a wooden dog does not eat, does not growl, bites no children, gathers

---

[143] Gotthold Ephraim Lessing (1729-1781). German philosopher, dramatist, and critic.
[144] David Lowe, *Souvenirs of Scottish Labour* (W & R Holmes, 1919), p.36.
[145] Scots slang: Wally = China clay.
[146] Spanish: No one comes to buy a jewel with a mouth.

no fleas, and also that the same applies to the china canine, either plain or coloured, still the two are essentially different. The wooden dog is democratic, the china pup is mugwumpish. One is the outward visible sign of poverty, as exemplified in the penny toy; the other the counterfeit presentment of an inward and must unspiritual grace - the grace, I mean, of a hideous respectability. Let but a china dog, with his patches of yellow on the back, his goggle eyes, and chain round his neck, strong enough to restrain an elephant, but once appear upon a mechanic's chimneypiece, and ten to one but he is a lost (political) man.

Here I must pause, and thoroughly explain myself. I have no animus against the imitation of living things, either by painting or by plastic art, as the Mohammedans have. I do not think, as they do, that the creator of a statue or picture of a living creature will be called upon by the Creator of all things to put a soul into it, or else receive the greater condemnation. No! that is not my faith, and I am glad of it; for I fancy the china dog endowed with spirit would, indeed, be a terrible "wild-fowl," and I, for one, would almost as soon gnash my teeth in Hades as go bail for the behaviour of a pack of any pottery dogs.

My reason for viewing the dog I have referred to is not, as some might anticipate, because I have become possessed of a secret whereby I can turn out these faithful animalculæ a penny cheaper than the ones with which Staffordshire has enriched us. Not I.

My reason for disagreeing with these dogs is quite a moral one. Let them but appear, let them but only view the workman's family with a round and vitreous eye, and he is lost.

No matter if a Radical nurtured on "Reynolds,"[147] no matter even if a Socialist such is the power for evil of these china demons that the man begins to alter from the date of their appearance. As the "National Liberal Club" is to the Liberal politician, so to the workman is the presence of these chimney ornaments I write of. In both cases the man suffers a change, before, perhaps, he sees the real world with real eyes - sees it in its misery and dullness, in its drink, its lies - perceives it in its hideous reality a place for

---

[147] George W. M. Reynolds (1814-1879) a populist writer, publisher, and radical. Now mostly forgotten, during his lifetime he greatly outsold Dickens and Thackery, and on his death, he was described by the trade magazine *The Bookseller*, as: 'the most popular writer of our times.'

devils. Now, such the influence of the dog or club, all becomes changed. Not such a bad world, after all, my masters. Only lie a little, cheat a little, cringe a little, squirm a little, and, presto, the ladder's rungs slip underneath your feet, and you yourself, by imperceptible degrees, rise to the top. What if in the process you leave your friends and fellows in the mud, break your wife's heart, spavin [148] the horse that draws you - look but to the Scriptures, and you will find a hundred texts to justify your baseness.

"Whatever is, is right." That is so; for see, the china dog still views you from his post between the candlesticks and foreign shells upon your chimneypiece, and seems to smile.

What do I mean, do you say, with all this prate of china dog? Well, this. There is a tendency in England towards respectability. A man who is respectable is generally a man lost. To be respectable does not imply a moral change in a man. Respectability only attacks a man from the teeth outward. He may still cheat, and drink, and lie, and cringe, but, if he outwardly become respectable, the man is saved in this world. Of the next, if there should be one, I do not speak.

A man, we will say, has been a Socialist on a pound a week. Suddenly his wages rise to thirty shillings or two pounds. What happens? Well, too often, a change comes over the spirit of his life, and he turns "mugwump." Socialism is too vulgar and too common-place for his converting. Step by step the opinions of a lifetime leave him. Radical has not so desperate a sound in ears polite. Therefore he becomes a Radical, professing all the time that Socialists and Radicals have the same end in view, well knowing al the time that Radical and Socialist are just as wide apart as Christian and Mohammedan, as Catholic and Protestant, Siite or Sunnite, Wesleyan and Baptist; or, to make the matter plain, as Christians of a nearly similar but slightly different sect.

Then the black coat appears and all that implies. The men who worked with him declare that Jack or Jim has become a toff, the fact being really that he is a mixture of a skunk and fool. Perhaps, though, not his fault. England, the paradise of wealth, the hell of poverty, is built that way. Thus in every branch and section of mankind in England the taint exists. 'Tis snob writ large! The working man puts on the air and apes the way of the small tradesman, the tradesman of the wholesale man, the merchant of the

---

[148] Osteoarthritis of the lower hock joints.

country gentleman. He in his turn strives to be a lord. The lord monkeyfies the marquis, and the last the duke. So from the bottom to the top, and top to the bottom, the same thing goes on.

Thus every class plays unwittingly into the hands of the sweater, who pockets the pelf and laughs at all, till the dread moment comes when he becomes a knight, Sir Peter Purseproud, and English nature claims him for as big a fool as all the rest!

The wish to rise in one's class is the best arm the sweater has in England Would you condemn, then, every man to stay in exactly in the place that he was born in? roars the Radical. Not so, my friend. What I would say to every man is - rise to the top of the tree as soon as possible. Take good heed, though, that, in the process of your rise, you push no weaker brother in the mud. The man who from a workman becomes a capitalist is oftentimes the greatest enemy of his fellows.

How can a man become a moneybag in 1892? By sacrificing all thought of humanity in his heart. By toiling late and rising early, by passing through the world a stranger to all joy and to all pleasure.

Pleasure and joy! What do they mean in England? For the rich they mean, too often mere materialism and the expenditure of thousands to be bored. For the poor, too often, beer.

Why is it so? In my opinion, because this cursed competition leaves no time in life for innocent enjoyment. In the scheme of English life no place is left for joy. On the one side, great expense and infinite ennui, and on the other, work and work and work, with only time for beer when work is done.

Therefore, I hate the china dog, like as he were a fiend. I mean I hate the thing, be that thing what it may, that inclines a man to fold his arms upon his paunch and think the world is not so bad a place, and hope those agitators will all get "six months' hard."

Progress in the future will be - must be - in the mass, and not, as heretofore, by the unit. Suppose a thousand men - and that is much supposing - every year were to rise from the workers' ranks and become capitalists. What then? Would that affect in any way (for good) the thousands and the millions who still remained grubbing and grasping?

Therefore it is that the eight hours day is such a matter for all men to strive for. It sinks self, and self once sunk, a man becomes a man, and learns to realise a man can but

106

be saved by men, and men by man. Once grasp this fact and the whip falls from the sweater's hand. Competition itself loses its hold, and the first step is taken. On competition is the power of capital based. Weaken but once the hold it has on men, and show them that, in rising to the top, their duty is to take their brother with them, and the first step is taken.

Then can man, looking on his china dog, his hideous stovepipe hat, his knighthood, or whatever is a golden calf to him, value them for themselves, and not, as now, for the barrier they put betwixt him and his fellows. Till that time be come, I say devoutly,

"DAMN ALL CHINA DOGS !"

~

In 1888, a critic wrote of Graham: 'He labours under the settled conviction that civilisation is a failure.'[149] Malcolm Muggeridge believed that Graham's political ideology was similar to Morris's nostalgic utopianism,[150] but his political and literary stance is perhaps better described as 'Arcadian,' i.e., the longing for an idealised (but vanished) past, as in the anti-capitalist, dystopian fable below, written near the end of his Parliamentary career. Graham is not a dreamer of the future and its false god, Progress; the future holds no attractions as long as human nature remains unreformed. To him, progress, and the hand of capital, could only have a baleful effect on everything they touched, as in this much-reprinted piece:

## THE EVOLUTION of a VILLAGE [151]
*The Albemarle*, June 1892.

I knew a little village in the North of Ireland - call it what you please. A pretty, semi-ruinous, semi-thriving place. Men did not labour over much there. All went easy (*aisy* the people called it); no man troubling much about the sun and moon; still less bothering himself about the fixed stars or planets, or aught outside the village. All about the place there was an air of half-content, tempered by half-starvation. No man ran; few even hurried. Every hedge was shiny, half broken-down, cut, flat, free seats. All the population lounged against these; for they served to prop men up as they discussed for hours on nothing. Cows marched up and down the lanes: sometimes

149 T. G Bowles, 'Mr. Bontine Cunninghame-Graham, M.P.,"J.P., D.L.' in *Vanity Fair* (25 August 1888), p.145.
150 Malcolm Muggeridge, 'Cunninghame Graham,' *Time And Tide* (28 March 1936), p.440.
151 It first appeared in a booklet entitled *Economic Evolution*, published by The Deveron Press in 1891. It was also published by the Socialist Party of Ireland, as *An Irish Economic Revival* (no date), and collected in Graham's anthology *Success*, in 1902.

children led them by a string, or, seated on the ground, made to believe to watch them, as they ate, much in the same way, I suppose, that shepherds watched their flocks on a memorable occasion near Bethlehem, or as people do in Spain and the East to-day. Goats wandered freely in and out of the houses. Children raggeder, and happier, and cunninger than any others on the earth, absolutely swarmed. Herod (had he lived in those parts) could have made an awful *battue*[152] of them, and they would not have been missed. Children, black-haired, grey-eyed, wild-looking, sat at the doors, played with the pigs, climbed on the tops of cabins, and generally permeated space, as irresponsibly as flies.

Trees there were few. The people said the landlords cut them down. The landlords said the people never left the trees alone. However, let that pass. Creeds there were, two - Catholic and Protestant. Both sides claimed to have a clear majority of sheep. They hated one another; or they said so, which is not the same thing, by the way. Really, they furnished mutually much subject of entertainment and of talk, for in this village no one really hated very much, or very long. All took life quietly.

On the great lake[153] folk fished lazily, and took nothing save only store of midge-bites. The roads were like pre-Adamite tracks for cattle: nothing but the cow of the country could cope with them; and even that sometimes sustained defeat. Still, given enough potatoes, the people were not miserable; far from it. Wages were low - but yet they were not driven like slaves, as is the artisan of more progressive lands.

In the morning early, out into the fields they went, to while away the time and lounge against the miniature round towers that serve as gate-posts.

Those who did not go out remained at home, and, squatting by the fire at ease, looked after their domestic industries, and through the "jamb-wall hole" kept a keen eye on foreign competition, or on the passing girls and women, and criticised them freely as they passed. Still there was peace and plenty, of a relative degree. No factories, no industries at all, plenty of water power running to waste, as the Scotch agent said, and called on God to witness that if there were only a little capital in the town, it would become a paradise. What is a paradise? Surely it is a land in which there is sufficiency for all; in which man works as little as he can - that is to say, unless he likes to slave - which

---

152 The beating of bushes to flush out game.
153 Lough Neagh.

no one did, or he would have been looked on as a mad-man, in the village by the lake. Men reaped their corn with sickles, as their forefathers did, in lazy fashion, and then left the straw to rot. Agriculture was all it shouldn't have been. Sometimes a woman and an ass wrought in one plough - the husband at the stilts.

Men were strong, lazy, and comfortable; women, ragged as lazy, and, when children did not come too fast, not badly off. The owner of the soil never came near the place. Patriot lawyers talked of liberty, and oppressed all those they got within their toils; but still the place was happy, relatively. Those who did not like work (and they were not few) passed through their lives without doing a hand's turn, and were generally loved. Any one who tried to hurry work was soon dubbed a tyrant. Thus they lived their lives in their own happy way.

If they were proud of anything, it was because their village was the birthplace of a famous hound. In my lord's demesne his monument is reared - the glory of the place. Master Macgrath[154] - after the Pope, King William, Hugh Roe O'Neill,[155] or Mr. Parnell - he seemed the greatest personage who ever walked the earth. "Himself it is was that brought prosperity among us. Quality would come for miles to see him, and leave their money in the place. A simple little thing to see him: ye had never thought he had been so wonderful. The old Lord (a hard old naygur!) thought the world of him. 'Twas here he used to live, but did his business (winning the Waterloo Cup) over on the other side." England seemed as vague a term as China to them, and quite as far removed. Master Macgrath, the Mass, the Preaching, the price of cattle at the fairs, and whether little Tom O'Neil could bate big Pat Finucane - these were subjects of their daily talk, A peaceful, idle, sympathetic, fightingly-inclined generation of most prolific Celto-Angles or of Anglo-Celts.

Agiotage,[156] Prostitution, Respectability, Morality and Immorality, and all the other curses of progressive life, with them had little place.

Not that they were Arcadians; far removed from that. Apt at a bargain, ready to deceive in little things. In great things, on the whole, "dependable" enough. Had there been enough to eat, less rent to pay, one faith instead of two, milder whiskey, and if the

---

[154] A famous greyhound in the sport of hare-coursing (1866-1873). Buried at Lurgan, County Armagh.
[155] Hugh O'Neill (1540-1616), the 2nd Earl of Tyrone, is best known for leading the resistance during the Nine Years' War, the strongest threat to English authority in Ireland.
[156] The speculative buying or selling of stocks.

rain had cleared off now and then, the place had been about as happy as it is possible to be, here in this vale of tears. Little enough they recked[157] of what went on in Parliament, upon the stock exchange, or in the busy haunts of men.

Once in a way a Home Rule speaker spoke in the village hall. The folk turned out to cheer with all their might, and in a week or two an Orangeman came round, and if possible, the cheers were louder than before. In fact, they looked upon the rival Cheap Jacks as travelling entertainments sent by Providence on their behalf.

Except on Pitcairn's Island, Tristan d' Acunha [sic], or in some group of islets in the South Seas before the advent of the missionaries, I doubt if anywhere men fared better on the whole.

But still a change was floating in the air.

One day a traveller from Belfast came to the village, and it struck him - "What a place to build a mill! Here there is water running all to waste, the land is cheap, the people vigorous and poor; yes, we must have a mill.

The priest and minister, the local lawyer, and the Scotch land-agent, all approved the scheme. All they wanted was but capital.

The want of capital is, and always has been, so they said, the drawback of the land. Had we but capital, we should be rich, and all become as flourishing as over there in England, where, as all know, the streets are paved with gold.

Alas! they never thought that on the golden pavements rain down floods of tears that keep them always wet, hiding the gold from sight. They never dreamt how the world crushes and devours those who leave little villages like this, and launch the vessel of their lives upon its waves. They could not see children perished and half-starved; they did not know the smug sufficiency of commerce; and had never heard the harlot's ginny laugh. Therefore, the proposition seemed to them a revelation straight from God. Yes, build a mill, and all will turn to gold. The landlord will get his rents, the minister his dues, the priest his tithes, the working man, instead of being fed on buttermilk and filthy murphies,[158] will drink tea (they called it *tay*), feast upon bacon, and white bread, and in due course will come to be a gentleman. Wages will rise, of course; our wives and children, instead of running bare-foot or sitting idle at the doors, will wear both shoes

---

[157] Archaic: Cared about.
[158] Potatoes.

110

and stockings, and attend mass or preachment "dacent," carrying their parasols.

The syndicate of rogues, with due admixture of fools and dupes, was got together; the mill was built. The village suffered a great and grievous change. All day long the whirr and whiz of wheels was heard. A daybreak a long string of girls and men tramped along the dreary streets, and worked all day. Wealth certainly began to flow; but where? Into the pockets of the shareholders. The people, instead of sturdy, lazy rogues, became blear-eyed, consumptive weaklings, and the girls, who formerly were patterns of morality, now hardly reached eighteen without an "accident" or two. Close mewing up [159] of boys and girls in hot rooms brought its inevitable result. Wages did not rise, but on the contrary, rather inclined to fall; for people flocked from the country districts to get employment at the far-famed mill.

The economists would have thrown their hats into the air for joy had not their idea of thrift forbidden them to damage finished products, for which they had to pay. The goods made in the mill were quoted far and wide, and known for their inferior quality throughout two hemispheres.

Yet still content and peace were gone. The air of the whole place seemed changed. No longer did the population lounge about the roads. No longer did the cows parade the streets, or goats climb cabin-roofs to eat the hose leek. The people did not saunter through their lives as in the times when there was lack of capital, and therefore advancement, as they thought. They had the capital; but the advancement was still to seek. Capital had come - that capital which is the dream of every patriotic Irishman. It banished idleness, peace, beauty, and content; it made the people slaves. No more they breathed the scent of the fields and lanes, but stifled in the mill. There was a gain, for savages who did not need them purchased, at the bayonet's point, the goods the people made. The villagers gained little by the traffic, and became raggeder as their customers were clothed. Perhaps the thought that savages wore on their arms or round their necks the stockings they had made, consoled them for their lost peaceful lives. Perhaps they liked the change from being wakened by the lowing of the kine to the "steam hooter's" call to work in the dark winter mornings - calling them out to toil on pain of loss of work and bread, and seeming, indeed to say: *Work brother! Up and to work; it is more*

---

[159] Confinement

111

*blessed far to work than sleep. Up! leave your beds; rise up; get to your daily task of making wealth for others, or else starve; for Capital has come!'"*

~

Graham did not write for those he called 'the respectable': "Respectability is England's curse, and Scotland's bane"[160] – 'Respectability! I hate respectability [. . .] What did respectability mean? Why, when respectability shut the door of its snug villa it showed humanity out.'[161] But, what had begun as a spontaneous and eloquent outpouring of angry polemic, both on the public platform and the page, against what he saw as society's iniquities and hypocrisies, slowly developed into a form of art, and Graham turned more and more to the literary sketch as a means of conveying his message, as in the cynical commentary on Queen Victoria's funeral, below, a subtle indictment of Empire, and poverty.

Graham's works are either journalistic, or nostalgic, demonstrating an acute observational skill, which drew from an extraordinary visual and olfactory memory, and a steely eye for: "the trifling actions of which life is composed."[162] Hugh MacDiarmid described his work as being: "of exceptional brilliance,"[163] and Graham as "potentially the greatest Scotsman of his generation,"[164] while T. E. Lawrence (of Arabia) described his work as: "the best verbal snapshots ever taken I believe." [165]

## MIGHT MAJESTY AND DOMINION
*The Saturday Review*, 2nd of February 1901.

A Nation dressed in black, a city wreathed in purple hangings, woe upon every face and grief in every heart. A troop of horses in the street ridden by kings; a fleet of ships from every nation upon earth; all the world's business stilled for three long days to mourn the passing of her who was the mother of her people, even of the poorest of her people in the land. The newspapers all diapered in black, the clouds dark-grey and sullen and a hush upon the islands and upon all the vast dependencies throughout the world. Not only for the passing of the Queen, the virtuous woman, the good mother, the slave of duty; but because she was the mother of her people, even of the poorest of her people in the land. Sixty odd years of full prosperity; England administering to the good

[160] Cunninghame Graham, 'Ca' Canny,' *The People's Press* (29 November 1890), p.7.
[161] *The Edinburgh Evening News* (18 March 1887), p.3.
[162] Cunninghame Graham, 'At Dalmary,' *The Saturday Review* (4 December 1909), p.689.
[163] Hugh MacDiarmid, *The Company I've Kept*, (Hutchinson, 1966), p.75.
[164] C. M. Grieve (Hugh MacDiarmid), *Contemporary Scottish Studies* (Leonard Parsons, 1926), p.49.
[165] David Garnett, Ed., *The Selected Letters of T. E. Lawrence* (World Books, 1941), p.343.

of universal Empire; an advance in the material arts of progress such as the world has never known, and yet to-day she who was to most Englishmen the concentration of the national idea, borne on a gun-carriage through the same streets, which she had so often passed through in the full joy of life. Full sixty years of progress; wages at least thrice higher, when a girl, she mounted on her throne; England's dominions more than thrice extended; arts, sciences, and everything that tends to bridge space over a thousand times achieved and a new era brought about by steam and electricity, all in the lifetime of her who has passed so silently through the once well-known streets. The national wealth swollen beyond even the dreams of those who saw the beginning of her reign; churches innumerable built by the pious care of those who thought the gospel should be brought home to the poor. Great battleships, torpedo boats, submarine vessels, guns, rifles, stinkpot shells and all the contrivances of those who think that the material progress of the Anglo-Saxon race should enter into the policy of savage states, as Latin used to enter a schoolboy's minds, with blood. Again, a hum of factories in the land, wheels whizzing, bands revolving so rapidly that the eye of man can hardly follow them, making machinery a tangled mass of steel, heaving and jumping in its action, so that the unpractical on-looker fears that some bolt may break and straight destroy him, like a cannon ball.

All this, and coal mines, with blast furnaces, and smelting works with men half naked working by day and night before fires. Infinite and incredible contrivances to save all labour; aerial ships projected; speech practicable between continents without the aid of wires; charities such as the world had never known before; a very cacoëthes[166] of good doing; a sort of half-baked goodwill to all men, so that the charities came from superfluous wealth and the goodwill was of [a] platonic kind; all this and more during the brief dream of sixty years in which the ruler, she, who was mother of her people, trod the earth. All these material instances of the past change in human life, which in her reign had happened and which she suffered unresistingly, just as the meanest of her subjects suffered them, and as both she and they welcomed the sun from heaven as something quite outside of them and, as it were, ordained, her people in some dull faithful way had grown into the habit of connecting in some vague manner with herself.

---

166 Latin/Greek: An irresistible urge, often something inadvisable.

For sixty years, before the most of us now living had uttered our first cry, she held the orb and sceptre and appeared to us, a mother Atlas, to sustain the world. She left us, almost without a warning, and a nation mourned her, because she was the mother of her people, yes, even of the meanest of her people in the land.

So down the streets in the hard biting wind, right through the rows of dreary stuccoed houses, frowning like cliffs, respectably upon the assembled mass of men, her funeral procession passed. On housetops and on balconies her former subjects swarmed like bees; the trees held rookeries of men, and the keen wind swayed them about but still they kept their place, chilled to the bone but uncomplainingly, knowing their former ruler had been mother to them all.

Emperors and kings passed on, the martial pomp and majesty of glorious war clattering and clanking at their heels. The silent crowds stood reverently all dressed in black. At length, when the last soldier had ridden out of sight, the torrent if humanity broke into myriad scores, leaving upon the grass of down-trodden park its scum of sandwich papers, which, like the foam of some great ocean, clings to the railings, round the roots of trees, was driven fitfully before the wind over the boot-stained grass or trodden deep into the mud, swayed rhythmically to and fro as seaweed sways and moans in the slack water of a beach.

At length they all dispersed and a well-bred and well-fed dog or two, roamed to and fro sniffing disdainfully at the remains of rejected food which the fallen papers held.

Lastly a man grown old in the long reign of the much-mourned ruler whose funeral procession had just passed stumbled about stepping upon the muddy grass and taking up a paper from the mud fed ravenously on that which the two dogs had looked on with disdain.

His hunger satisfied he took up of the fragments that remained a pocketful, and then whistling a snatch from a forgotten opera, slouched away onward and was swallowed by the gloom.

~

## IN CHRISTMAS WEEK
*The Saturday Review*, 2nd of February 1907.

The roar of London slackened, and those pterodactyls of the streets, the motor-omnibuses, seemed to disport themselves like great Behemoth or Leviathan, reducing their creators to an inferior place, as if they lived upon the sufferance of the great whirring beasts.

The white-faced, hurrying, furtive-looking crowds, which throng the pavements for the most part of the year, have given place to multitudes of comfortable folk on shopping bent, who walked less warily than the work-driven slaves, who move about the streets seeming as if they felt that everybody's hand was armed against them, and that to halt a moment in the race exposed them to its blow. A biting frost clad hydrants in steel mail where water dropped from them, and spread white blotches on the wooden pavement at which the cab-horses, inured to petrol patches on the stones, to mud, even to blood after an accident, to paper blowing in their eyes, and all the myriad night noises of the town, shied as at something menacing, so far away had Nature gone out of their lives, as if no vision of green fields in which they played and raced beside their mothers, so stiltily upon their giraffe-looking legs, ever returned to haunt their labour deadened brains.

The electric light shone blue against the trunks of the trees, and the sharp cold almost dispelled the scent of horsedung which perfumes the air of London, as if to nullify our attempts to set a bar between ourselves and other animals, and bring us face to face with their and our common necessities and origin, laughing at the refinements of material progress, and showing us that the one way by which we can escape the horrors of the world lies through the portals of the mind.

Peace upon earth, goodwill towards all mankind, was the stock phrase in every church, as if to make the bitterness of life outside more manifest, reducing as it did the preachers' words to a mere froth of wormwood on the air, or at the most a counsel of perfection towards which it was not worth one's while to struggle, seeing it set so far out of reach.

Holiday-making crowds filled Piccadilly, which looked quite unfamiliar without its strings of crawling cabs and prostitutes, plying for hire upon its stones, as eventide drew near. One felt a sort of truce of God was in the air, and that the Stock Exchange, and sweating den, and the gigantic manufactory, in which a thousand toiled to make vast sums of money for some uninteresting and quite unnecessary man, were quiet, and that perhaps even the wretched negro in the indiarubber [sic] bush might have a day of rest.

115

The parks, under a canopy of white, turned fields again, and as the dusk came on, the sound of church bells in the air gave a false feeling of security, though one was well aware no tiger-hunted jungle held half the perils of the vast stucco solitude in which we live. Day followed day, cold, miserable and cheerless, and the town left deserted, by the myriads who make it look like an ant-hill, on which the ants all strive against each other, instead of helping one another after the fashion of their semi-reasonable prototypes, set one a-thinking on the Eastern legend, framed in a warm and sunny land, and therefore quite unfit for the chill north, which was the cause of such a change in life.

The frosty stars shone out, so cold and clear, they seemed but the reflections of some world extinct, which had preserved its light, but with the heat evaporated. The moon was more congenial to our northern blood, pale, passionless and with an air of infinite yearning after something unexpressed, whilst the full yellow beam of light of Jupiter recalled one to the plains where in far Nabothéa the three kings sat gazing on the stars - a kingly occupation, and one which nowadays all their descendants have allowed to fall into disuse. Perhaps unwisely, for if they followed it, who knows if some particular bright star might yet arise on their horizon to guide them upwards out of the realms of self?

It may be too that all of us are kings born blind, and that the guiding star is shining while we sit sightless with our dim orbits fixed upon the mud. Or it may chance that motor-cars, arriving at the stable where the lowly Saviour babe was laid, would have affrighted all the humble company, for the gulf that yawns between the millionaire's fur coat, and poverty, is wider far than that between the watchers by the ass and oxen's stall, and the three sheiks who lighted down from off their horses to adore.

Nor was the gulf between the sheikhs, the watchers, and the animals stabled so snugly, with their warm breath making an aureole about the sleeping baby's head, or, folded on the plain beneath the stars, so deep as that which yawns between the modern dweller in our stucco Babylon and his selected breeds of animals rendered so bestial by improvement as scarce to move the pity of their owners for all their various pains.

At any rate, in that old cosmos, with its simple and unreasoning life, so like the life of plants and trees, as fixed and as immutable as are the seasons or the tides, there was a sympathy, unthought of, but all the same at hand, which though it did not spend itself in theories, redeemed mankind from many of its sins. Justice, one hears, is but a modern growth; but in its action on the lives of men it toils a thousand leagues behind the old brutality, which though it certainly denied all rights, admitted kinship, or at least was conscious of a link between all sentient things, just as some city who had created man in his own image might feel ashamed when called upon to punish and destroy beings so like himself, though for all that he could not hold his hand.

So in the Christmas week, with its fierce cold and misery to thousands mocked by false protestations of the brotherhood of man, and pinched with hunger in the midst of wealth, it must have seemed that all the legend was but another of the corpse-candles lighted to set them running after its thin flame.

Then came a thaw, and all the iron-bound streets became Sloughs of Despond, in which a million horses turned to machines, chained in their stables, and taken out but to pound ceaselessly upon the cruel stones till it was time to be led back again and chained up for the night, toiled wretchedly, not comprehending that they were agents in the progress of the world. But all the time the church bells pealed, and all the time the planets shone out soft and mellow, making one think involuntarily upon some old bright world which perhaps never existed save in dreams, but which we now and then have to imagine for ourselves or else go mad at seeing ugliness revered as beauty, and wealth adored as wisdom, with all the meanest qualities of man enthroned as virtues, like a tin sky-sign setting forth some trash with its full-bodied lies. But frost or thaw, silence or traffic, all was the same to the vast vulgar town, the hugest monument to Philistinism that the world has ever seen.

The blackened muddy snow, reminding one somehow of something pure defiled, then scorned and cast upon the mire, lay piled up in heaps in the chief squares, left there by accident or design long after it was cleared from off the streets, as if to give the magnates in their shapeless palaces the mumps, and render them as hideous as the great cubes of masonry in which they lived. Misery seems to reign triumphant in the wilderness of bricks, where dullness strove with a smug hypocrisy to make life unendurable, whilst slowly the great city seemed to take up its usual course as the drear week drew out. Ladies in motor-cars, with the hard, uninviting air that wealth imparts so often even to youth and beauty, flitted past, scattering the mud on those whose toil paid for each article of dress they wore, as if they had conferred a favour on the world by deigning to exist. The chill and penetrating damp which rises from the London clay after a thaw, makes its way into the bones and soul, to them was but another stimulus to life and aid to appetite. Neither the look of wretchedness of men or animals seemed to say anything to them, although no doubt their minds were all alive with charitable schemes; for never in the history of the human race has charity, that most unhumanising virtue which has ever made mankind think itself better than its fellows, walked in our midst so blatantly, or justice hid itself more timidly, than at the present day.

Boys, cold and pinched, with voices rendered harsh by all the gin their parents had imbibed, ran shouting out the names of newspapers, flourishing broadsheets on which the headings told of murders, adulteries, cheating and robbery; and smug-faced citizens and prurient-minded girls, their pink-and-white complexions, strangely at variance with the twinkle in their eyes, eagerly stopped and bought them, jostling the men as if by accident, pleased at the contact with them as they passed, and yet taking offence at once if but a word was said, saving their conscience in the national way, which finds all things permissible if but due silence is preserved.

So dull and strenuous was the life that it appeared impossible that in other lands the sun was shining, and that the brown-faced men and merry black-haired women had time to love and be beloved.

But that naught might be wanting to set forth the kindlier aspects of our pomp and state, in a small narrow street well strewn with offal from the stalls of coster-mongers' barrows, under the flaming light of naphtha lamps, a line of men stood waiting at the door of a soup kitchen at which some charitable soul or council had provided refreshment for the body - that body which, we know, matters so little in a transitory life.

The mud had eaten holes in their clothes, and their pinched faces under the electric light, drink-swollen and blotched, looked corpse-like as they stood shivering in the snow, which, falling down like feathers on their hats, gave them a look as if they had been supers[167] at the pantomime of life, and at some signal from the wing would break into a dance.

The stream of passers-by watched them unmoved, thinking no doubt that idleness

---

[167] A supernumerary actor. A non-speaking performer.

or drink had brought them to their present situation; and as they waited for their turn some coughed and others scratched themselves, or muttered it was "'ellish cold" shuffled and stamped as the snow melted on their hair and filtered through the rags.

On every side the strenuous current of the world flowed past them, leaving them stranded in the mud, with the safe shores of progress and of wealth slipping away from them, as a spent swimmer, struggling for his life, watches the banks of a swift-running stream race past before his eyes.

Sometimes the line of men swayed like a wounded snake upon the road as one of them passed through the door, and as the others waited for their turn, one muttered to a chum, "Blime me, cheer up! it'll be better under Socialism," and spat upon the stones.

~

## SET FREE
*The Saturday Review*, 7th of January 1911.

A fine, persistent rain had filled the streets with mud. It lay so thickly that it seemed as if black snow had fallen, and from the pools which had collected here and there upon its surface the passing carriages were reflected, as by a mirage, distorted in the glare of the electric light. The passers-by all had a look of ghosts in the thick foggy air. Rain trickled from the hats and umbrellas, and mud and water oozed beneath their tread. The thoroughfare was blocked in places with cabs all full of people going off upon their holidays, for it was Christmas week. Bells were heard fitfully, calling the faithful to the churches to prepare to celebrate the birth of Him who died upon a Cross to bring peace to the earth.

The trees which overhang the roadway by the park dropped inky showers upon the tramps sleeping or talking on the seats. The drops splashed on the stones and on the cross-board of the rest of porters' burdens which still survives, a relic of the past, between the cast-iron lamp-posts with their bright globes of light. Here and there at the corners of the streets that lead down to the artery between the parks stood women dressed fashionably, wearing large hats with ostrich feathers. True that their numbers were diminished, for an orgasm of virtue had recently swept over those who rule, and had decreed Vice should pay homage to her twin-sister Virtue, but only on the sly. Still they were there, to show how much had been achieved for women by our faith in the last thousand years. Policemen stood about upon their beats, stout and well fed, looking with scorn if a taxpayer in a threadbare coat passed by them, and ever ready, after the fashion of the world, to aid the rich, the strong, and those who did not need their help.

During the week the churches had been thronged with worshippers. Some went to pray, others resorted to the fane from custom, and again, some from a vague feeling that religion was a bulwark reared in defence of property in seasons of unrest, though this of course had not been reasoned out, but felt instinctively, just as a man fears the dangers of the night. Hymns had been sung and sermons preached inculcating goodwill, peace, charity and forbearance to the weak. Yet London was as pitiless as ever, and the strong pushed the weak down into the gutter, actually and in the moral sphere. Women were downtrodden, except they happened to be rich, though men talked chivalry whilst not refraining for an instant to take advantage of the power that law and nature placed within their reach. The animal creation seemed to have been devised by God to bring to all that was most base in man. If they were tame and looked to him as man, in theory, looks towards his God, he worked them pitilessly. Their loves, their preferences, their simple joys, attachments to the places where they had first seen the light and frisked beside their mothers in the fields, were all uncared for, even were subjects for derision and mirth. If, on the other hand, they were of those, winged or four-footed, who had never bowed the knee or drooped the wing to man's dominion, their treatment was still worse. They had no rights, except of being killed at proper seasons, which were contrived so artfully that a bear three months of the whole year was left unstained by blood. Woods in their thickest depths witnessed their agony. Deep in the corries of the hills, in fields, in rivers, on the land, the sea, and in the bowels of the earth they left their fellows, dumb, stricken, wretched, and died silently, wondering perhaps what crime they had committed in their lives so innocent and pure. No one commiserated them, for they were clearly sent into the world as living targets to improve man's power of shooting, or to be chased and then to pieces in order to draw out the higher feelings of his self-esteem and give him the opportunity to say, as their eyes glazed with death, There is one flesh of man, and yet another of the beasts.

Through the soft rain the roar of the great city rose, though dulled and deadened, still menacing and terrible, as if the worst of human passions, as always happens in a crowd, had got the upper hand, and were astir to wreak themselves on any object ready at hand. Machines ran to and fro, noisy and sending forth mephitic[168] fumes, and seeming somehow as if they were the masters and the pale men who drove them only slaves of the great forces they had brought into their lives. They swerved and skated, bearing their fill of trembling passengers, and making every living thing give them the road on pain of mutilated limbs or death as horrible as by the car of some great idol of the East. No car of Juggernaut was half so terrible, as they took their passage through the streets men shrank into the second place and seemed but to exist on sufferance, as tenders of machines.

Still, it was Christmas week, and the glad tidings preached so long ago, so fitted for the quiet ways and pastoral existence of those who had heard them first, so strangely incongruous with us of modern times, were still supposed to animate men's minds. The night wore on, and through the sordid rows of stuccoed houses the interminable file of cabs, of carriages, and motor omnibuses, still took its course, and trains of market cats drawn by puffing engines began to pass along the street. In them, high in the air, lying upon the heaped-up vegetables or seated on the backboard clinging by one arm to the chain, boys slumbered, their heads swaying and wagging to and fro as the carts rumbled on the stones. Then the carts disappeared, and the remaining traffic increased its speed in the half-empty streets, the drivers, anxious to get home, shaving each other's wheels in haste or carelessness. Round coffee-stalls stood groups of people in the flaring light of naphtha lamps - soldiers, a man in evening dress, a street-walker or two, and some of those strange, hardly human-looking hags who only seem to rise from the recesses of the night, and with the dawn retreat into some Malebolge[169] of the slums. The time and placed broken down all barriers of caste, and they stood laughing at obscenities, primitive and crude, such as have drawn the laughter of mankind since the beginning of the world.

In the great open space between the junction of the parks, where on one side the hospital frowns on the paltry Græco-Cockney sham triumphal arch,[170] just underneath the monolith from which the bronze, Iron Duke looks down upon statues of the men

---

168 Noxious.
169 The eighth circle of Hell in Dante's *Inferno*.
170 The Wellington Arch to the South of Hyde Park. An equestrian statue of the Duke of Wellington stands nearby.

he qualified as "blackguards" in his life, a little crowd surrounded something lying on the ground. A covered van, battered and shabby, stood, with a broken shaft. Under the wheels the mud as stained with a dark patch already turning black, and the smashed shaft was spotted here and there with blood. A heap of broken harness lay in a pile, and near it on its side a horse with a leg broken by a motor omnibus. His coat was dank with sweat, and his lean sides were raw in places with the harness that he would wear no more. His neck was galled with the wet collar which was thrown upon the pile ion harnesses, its flannel lining stained with the matter of sores which scarcely healed before work opened them again. The horse's yellow teeth, which his lips, open in his agony, disclosed, showing he was old and that his martyrdom was not yesterday. His breath came painfully and his thin flanks heaved like a wheezy bellows in a smithy, and now and then one of his legs contracted and was drawn up to his belly and then extended slowly till the shoe clanked upon the ground. The broken leg, limp and bedaubed with mud, looked like a sausage badly filled, and the protruding splinter of the bone showed whitely through the skin.

The little crowd stood gazing at him as he lay not without sympathy but dully, as if they too were over-driven in their lives.

Then came a policeman who, taking a book, wrote briskly in it, after taking down the deposition of the owner of the horse.

The electric lamps flared the scene. In the deserted park the wind amongst the trees murmured a threnody, and on the road the dying horse lay as a rock sticks up, just in the tideway of a harbour, thin, dirty, overworked, castrated, underfed, familiar from its youth with blows and with ill-treatment, but now about to be set free.

# THE LABOUR ACTIVIST

In late 1888 Graham wrote the following Introduction to 'A Labour Programme' by J. Lincoln Mahon, who had contributed to 'A Plea For the Chainmakers,' and who at the time was often in Graham's company. E. P. Thompson described Mahon as 'a floating agitator.'[171]

This slim, hard-bound volume is inscribed 'The House of Commons, Nov. 1888', and is considered by Thompson to be 'a clear blue-print of the I.L.P.'[172] The contrast however with 'A Plea For the Chainmakers' could hardly be greater; Graham's style is measured and consensual, languid almost, moderated perhaps to facilitate Mahon's reasoned, but potentially incendiary proposals for the reorganisation of society. The journalist and socialist, Henry Champion, criticised it for being impractical,[173] but of Graham he says: 'he contrives to write some true and pointed sentences but, as is his wont [. . .] to wrap them up in sayings which, to adopt his own trick of Shakespearian quotation will be 'caviar to the general." [174]

---

171 E. P. Thompson, *William Morris: Romantic to Revolutionary* (Pantheon Books, New York, 1996), p.351.
172 Ibid. p.525.
173 *The Labour Elector*, (12 January 1889), p.8.
174 Hamlet, Act II, Scene II. (Too sophisticated for those who read it).

# INTRODUCTION TO A LABOUR PROGRAMME
The London Press Agency (1888).

A man who writes an Introduction to a book should be prepared, I suppose, to go bail for its opinions. This I find an easy task as I have been advocating the tenets of its author for the last two years. It has always seemed to me that out of the fluid condition of lava-like heat in which men's brains are at present, a solid state must eventually ensue.

Then as to how this state must be brought about. Nature, in all her operations, is slow, cruelly slow; and I suppose will proceed in the same merciless manner with the evolution of society as she has proceeded with the evolution of mankind hitherto.

The majority of Englishmen have always been, and, I believe, always will be, somewhat slow of intellect, somewhat attached to old customs; to those old customs that the practice of our fathers has proved to be suitable to our condition. They have always been impatient with those who would change anything, even for good, if they advocated the change in a violent manner. For theory, the national intellect has always been rather inclined to show contempt; for practice, the most entire confidence.

But, as all are agreed that it is not absolute perfection to have the unemployed always with us, as almost all will allow that the accumulation of population in large towns tends to degeneration of both mortality and physique, it remains to someone to gather up the threads of public opinion and bind them together in order to turn them to political account. Hamlet, though he was prince of Denmark, was a complete Englishman when he complained of sweet religion being made a complete rhapsody of words. Had he been a Frenchman he would not have cared, if only the words were beautiful.

Now, I take it, the average Englishman dislikes to have politics a mere rhapsody of words. He turns with impatience from the construction of perspective [sic] Arcadias to the practical proposer of something that will do himself and his generation good. I do not mean to say that he refuses all credit to Kossuths [175] and Garibaldis of other countries, but he believes that there is no room for such characters in England. Nevertheless, he is impatient of the fact that profits and rents are falling. It galls him to

---

[175] Lajos Kossuth (1802-1894). Political reformer who inspired and led Hungary's struggle for independence from Austria.

hear of the increasing badness of English manufactures. The revelations of the Sweating Commission have appalled him. He finds that it is no longer possible for him to lay his hand upon his waistcoat and not perceive that it is shoddy. Being an honest fellow in the main, he would change this if he could only see how to do so. Few Englishmen like to see their fellows suffer. An increasing proportion are clearly aware of the prevailing misery but distrust those who propose too sweeping remedies. They want better security than Bardolph's,[176] and are more inclined to accept the plan of a workman than the theory of a man of letters. The author is a working-man, and, as such, should be better able to speak for his class than the writer of this introduction. If I comprehend his argument thoroughly, he starts from the proposition that parliamentary institutions are an integral part of our national life, that if a sponge were passed over the present generation, the first thing that the next generation would do would be to resort to some modification of the same system. This, I think, is the political idea contained in this book; with the social aspect of the question I will deal later on. He sees that parliament is not fulfilling the object for which it was created, and he proposes by the introduction of new blood to put new life into our body politic.

What object he proposes to himself and to the public I think I understand. He would have a closer connection between the constituent and the member; a connection not only, as at present, of duty, but also of self-interest. It may be said, I know, that hitherto workmen in the House of Commons have represented Trade Unions and not poverty. This, I imagine, he would rectify by showing that Labour representatives might be something more than mere party politicians. He sees what has become of the factory acts, and would endeavour to extend their principle to all ages and conditions of workers. Seeing that the state is mainly composed of workers and that in the words of *Ecclesiasticus*, "by their labour is every state maintained," he would endeavour to make plain to working-men, that the man who is afraid of the influence of a State in which his class is the dominant one, is as he who is afraid of his own shadow.

Contemning all ideas of force and revolution, certain to repel many and to attract few - and those few the most unstable - he sets himself to solve the social problem by natural and not supernatural agency. I mean he does not seek to fill empty stomachs

---

176 A drunken character in Shakespeare's Henry IV, Parts 1 & 2, and The Merry Wives of Windsor.

through the medium of broken heads, or to waft us to prosperity with a whiff of melenite[177] [sic] ("whiff of grapeshot" has been used by conservative politicians), but by exercising the constitutional pressure of those who have the power and will not use it.

Send to parliament not only representatives of the prosperous and organised artisan, but of that starving residuum, the effort to support which is rapidly turning our Trade Unions from fighting to charity organisations. Granted that politicians are corrupt; granted that they would crawl through a common sewer to place and position! This proves the argument to the writer. In proportion as politicians are weak, so do they less overshadow the people.

What would we think of he who on a desert island refused to take the first chance that presented itself of escape by raft or plank, but preferred to wait the coming of a ship or the arrival of some tall ammiral?[178] Surely, it were better that we should set about now, in honest practical fashion, to try to show how the average Englishman may participate in the riches around him; may participate in the leisure at present unknown to him; may make the machine his servant and not his master.

Columbus was fifty-four years old when he left the port of Palos; but he left his name upon the page of history; he gave his new world to Castile and Leon before he was sixty. The time to act is now, whilst the present generation is young; in order that the lives of the workers may not be consumed in fruitless agitation. What a wild, unknown Western world, not less difficult to access, I allow, but not less glorious in acquisition, is there open to the man who will discover the means whereby the working-classes may possess their America, nay, even will take them with him and plant them on it - without a journey. The America is here, richer far than the wildest imagination of the bold adventurers of the 16th century painted Eldorado. The treasure is here, too, richer far than Potosí.[179] But a legion of demons guard it - demons of prejudice and bigotry, of class hatred and all uncharitableness.

But I hold that not only are the rich not wise, that a mask of gold does not hide all deformities, but that they are not even happy. How can a man be happy who sees his fellows suffer? How can a man help but feel ashamed even of his admiration of Andrea

---

[177] Melanite. A powerful explosive.

[178] An archaic form of 'admiral,' or a ship; "some tall ammiral" is a quotation from Chapter XIV of Thackeray's 'The Newcomes.'

[179] A city in Bolivia, which produced fabulous wealth for the Spanish Conquistadors.

126

Mantegna,[180] when he reflects that the majority of his fellows soar no higher than the woodcuts of the *Police News*.

I believe that the doctrines contained in this work are calculated to attract rather than repel the thoughtful. I think that there is nothing to frighten any sensible man, "or nimble squib to make afraid the gentle woman."[181] No, but a serious and thoughtful attempt to shew that Dives and Lazarus are of one common flesh in the very nature of their sores. Should dogs lick them both? Far better than that the wolves of revolution should involve both in one common destruction.

I can understand that the mere denunciation of capitalists tends to disgust many even of those who are averse to the present system. I can hear them say that they want something practical. Here they have a practicable scheme. I need not attempt to describe it in detail; suffice it to say that it is easy of comprehension, that its action would be gradual, that it would not at first be of necessity antagonistic to capitalism, but would rather tend to supplant it by degrees. As it is outside the spree of ordinary commercialism and creates a market of its own in the wants of its producers, it avoids many of the elements of failure that have foredoomed kindred schemes.

It would seem vain to expect, though it were well to at least hope, that the great quarrels of rich and poor should be settled without some sharp collisions. But this scheme seems to me to present a method of solution which will neither degrade the workers to mere stone-breakers nor drive the capitalists into a corner. The purpose of my author seems to be that the State should step in and (create) a reorganisation of industry by taking some of the workers who cannot find employment, placing them upon some of the land that is not properly used and giving them the use of some of the redundant capital. Here is a scheme which the most conservative might wish to see put to the test. I leave to its author the responsibility for its details. But I would commend it, as a practicable proposal for dealing with a burning question, to the careful reader, to the politician, to all who would help to lessen the load of misery which hangs like a millstone round the neck of our nation.

I never have believed that salvation would come from above, I mean from the study. I believe that the people themselves will work out their own emancipation,

---

[180] Andrea Mantegna (1431-1506). An Italian painter.
[181] A misquotation from the 'Prologue' to Ben Jonson's 'Every Man In His Humour.'

kicking off here a bolt, there a bar, loosening their chains link by link. As a horse let out of a dark stable door does not run at first but stares blindly about him, so do the people on emerging from their dark stable of ignorance. They will run in good time, and what I want to see is a fair open field for them to exercise their efforts on.

This book, unlike many others, is wanted. Something is wanted to join the scattered threads of democracy. Liberals, Radicals, Positivists, Socialists, Co-operators, Trade Unionists - all are Democrats. They all strive for the elevation of humanity. Why not strive together?

Meanwhile, let me say that the subject of this book should be the subject of every man's thoughts. The good ship civilisation sails smoothly along; the passengers on deck enjoy themselves. But how of those in the stoke-hole of poverty who "grunt, sweat, and fardels bear"?[182] How else may we hope to understand their feelings but by getting a party of true representatives of Labour? Who but the poor can speak for the poor? Already they have the vote. It lies with them alone to say when they shall actually wield the power.

And so I take my leave of the readers of this book to moralise, like the fool in Shakespeare, on what it contains, but believing, unlike him, that more is to achieved by earnest and hopeful effort than by merely railing at Lady Fortune in the settest of set terms contained in the language.

~

Keir Hardie and Graham had both worked to create a labour pressure group within the Liberal fold, but Hardie clung to this forlorn hope much longer.[183] Since July 1887, Graham had been promoting his friend as the first true representative of the working class in Parliament, but the concept of 'class politics' was anathema to the Liberals, and, being rejected as a Liberal candidate, Hardie stood as a 'Labour' candidate for Mid-Lanark on the 27th of April 1888, but against concerted Liberal opposition, he was badly defeated. It was now obvious to all, even to Hardie, that they could not work with the Liberals, and that a new party was needed. Robert Smillie, the secretary of the Larkhall Miners' Association, and a close colleague of Hardie's, was the only member present at its birth who wrote a first-hand account, and tells us of Graham's inspiration:

---

[182] Hamlet: Act III, Scene I.
[183] Labour M.P., Emanuel 'Manny' Shinwell, described Hardie as: "essentially not a socialist but a temperance reformer."

On the day after this historic election a number of Keir Hardie's supporters met in Hamilton to mingle their tears together. It could not be said that that the gathering was a joyful one - although, looking back on it after all these years, I do not think that we were absolutely downhearted. In fact, my opinion is that the result of this election acted as a stimulus to many of us to go forward. Mr. R. B. Cunninghame Graham was present at this meeting, but he was not downcast. Instead he took the view that we should go on with the forming of a new and independent party. The meeting adopted this view, and it was decided that we should start out on a new line independent of the other two political parties.[184]

A meeting was held on 19th of May, and the motion was passed unanimously: 'In the opinion of this meeting it is desirable that a Parliamentary Labour Party should be formed in Scotland, and we hereby appoint the following as a committee to arrange for a conference to be held at the earliest possible date.' That conference was held on 25 August, with Graham in the chair. He was elected President, and Hardie, Secretary. At this first conference, the new party passed resolutions on: full adult suffrage; triennial parliaments; payment of M.P.s and expenses; home rule all round; abolition of the House of Lords; state insurance; opposition to state control of the hours of labour; the abolition of primogeniture and entail, and the 'Georgist' programme of taxing land (not nationalisation). All of these were policies that Graham and others had campaigned on, and we can only conjecture to what extent his influence directed these initial proposals.

~

**RALLY IN HYDE PARK:**
EXTRAORDINARY SPEECH by MR. CUNNINGHAME GRAHAM.
*The Coatbridge Express*, 14th of November 1888.

*A demonstration was held on Sunday afternoon* [11 November] *in Hyde Park, London, to commemorate the riots that took place in November of last year, and to express sympathy with the Americans in their struggle against the capitalist class. Contingents were present from all the more prominent Radical clubs, accompanied by bands accompanied by flags and numerous bannerets. One flag bore the inscription "Remember Chicago November 1887. There may come a time when our silence will be more powerful than the voice you are now strangling." There were about 4,000 people present; and the chief speakers were Mrs. Parsons, Chicago;*[185] *Mr. William Morris, and Cunninghame Graham M.P. The first resolution, moved by Mr Tachatti, condemned the exploitation of labour by capital. Mr. Cunninghame Graham MP seconded the motion:*
I do not intend to address you on the principles of Socialism, but to set before you

---

[184] Robert Smillie, *My Life For Labour* (Mills & Boon, 1924), p.293.
[185] Lucy Eldine Gonzalez Parsons (1853-1942). An American labour organiser, and revolutionary socialist. Probably born into slavery to parents of Native American, African American, and Mexican ancestry. She was wife of the newspaper editor Albert Parsons who was hanged with three others in 1887 by the state of Illinois on charges that he had conspired in the Haymarket Riot in Chicago.

certain definite facts, and certain duties that you, as Englishmen, are interested in and ought to follow. I want to tell you that there was at least one member of the House of Commons who is inclined to protest against the legal murder of the working classes whether in Chicago or in Trafalgar Square. (*Cheers.*) There are many amongst you who are ignorant of the facts that did Sir Charles Warren order his police to disperse that meeting the result might be fatal to many, and you would know that men killed thereby would render the others liable to what is called constructive murder. John Burns and I had been tried for constructive riot, and were found guilty. The Chicago men were tried and found guilty of constructive murder though they were innocent in fact.

I have myself often sat at the Quarter Sessions, and knew that the evidence which convicted men was such as would not condemn a poacher for having shot a rabbit. (*Laughter.*) Yet they were shouting for law and order, and wanted to bolster up their kings and queens, and a House of Lords that is useless and draining the country of huge salaries. This is also true of the House of Commons, which is made up of capitalists who grind down the people. It was to keep this law and order in England that they killed two men who were guilty of no crime against anyone in Trafalgar Square. It is surprising that men who did this should go unpunished and their deeds un-revenged. (*Cheers.*) The Liberal and Tory parties have both been silent on these murders, but they have been talking about Irish outrages and singing the praises of Gladstone *gloria in excelsis* - (*Laughter.*) - but have forgotten that there was such a place as London existing on the face of the earth.

If there are any members of the shopkeeping class here, I wish that they would interest themselves in the working classes, for the interests of both are identical. I wish to see a great revolution amongst the shopkeepers, I want to begin a revolution with them, a plan of campaign in order to bring the wooden headed Tories to their senses. It has often been remarked that it takes fifty years to drive an idea into the head of an Englishman, but I would add that when it was once there, it took 500 years to drive it out again. I declare that Home Secretary Matthews and Sir Charles Warren must be dismissed. (*Prolonged cheers.*) I would like to see a meeting of the lazy and idle aristocrats in Belgravia or Grosvenor Square - they are the real unemployed - singing "God Save the Queen," but I would also like to see the real workers there too furnishing a strophe for the starving poor of the country. I hate society (thereby meaning the wealthy and the titled classes). I have a standing dislike for society; it is a society which gave us the House of Lords - (*groans*) - it is a society which is responsible for poverty and distress, the misery of the city of London, and it is answerable to the crimes of the city, and of those committed by "Jack the Ripper."[186] It is society which is vilifying and paralysing the community, and driving the starving poor to desperation, whose cries are ascending to Heaven against it. The murders of men in Trafalgar Square[187] went unpunished and un-revenged, but I do not believe in the blood for blood and eye for eye doctrine which some Christians believe, who sit in their wealthy churches on Sunday, but I am glad to see that a breath still lived in the democracy of London, and I defy Sir Charles Warren to hold a public meeting in an open space in the Metropolis. I believe that ere long the human race who toiled would acquire that measure of social freedom and comfort which it has already been enabled to gain in the political world. (*Cheers.*)

~

1889 was a relatively quiet year for Graham in Parliamentary terms. However, his political journalism was now in full swing,[188] and his round of speeches throughout the country in support of the miners, and dock and tram workers, and promoting a Labour party, continued unabated, sometimes reaching ten a week. It is Hardie who is credited with founding the Labour party, but in these formative years, it was Graham who raised the profile, although he remained a controversial figure. Their new party also faced strong opposition from within the trade union movement, which, at the time, was closely allied to the Liberals. At a stormy Trades Union Congress in Dundee in September 1889, a beleaguered Hardie was forced to defend his friend against very outspoken opposition: "If you got out on the streets and ask the first hundred men you meet who is the leader of the Labour party in Parliament, what name would be mentioned in answer? (*Voices, "Broadhurst" and "Keir Hardie," and laughter.*) − not Keir Hardie − (*laughter.*) − but a man who was in this hall, and not even honoured with a place on the platform − Mr Cunninghame Graham. (*Slight applause, and loud cries of "No, no".*) There is not a man in the House of Commons who is recognised as the leader of the Labour party apart from the man I have named." (*Hear, hear, and "No, no."*)[189] The

---

186 What turned out to be the last of the five 'Ripper' murders occurred two days earlier, on the 9th of November 1888, in an already tense city. It was not Warren's alleged handling to the Trafalgar Square riot that ended his career as Commissioner of Police, he resigned after largely unfair attacks by the press over his handling of the Ripper investigations.

187 These alleged deaths occurred in a separate incident, not related to Graham's action.

188 Graham's foreign adventures also continued, and along with his promotion of worker's rights, and his attacks on Parliament, his 'Foreign Notes' became a regular feature in H. H. Champion's *The Labour Elector*.

189 Transcribed into the first person from *The Scotsman* (5 September 1889), p.6.

Fabian, Beatrice Webb, who was present at the Congress, regarded the Labour rebels as having: 'filthy personalities full of envy and malice,' and the socialist speakers as 'a crew of wretched reputation [. . .] beardless enthusiasts and dreamers of all ages.' She noted the antagonism - almost hatred, among the TUC leaders, who were trying to keep out 'wolves in sheep's clothing.'[190] *The Scotsman* was jubilant:

> Both Mr Hardie and Mr Graham [. . .] were denounced, and sneered at, and ridiculed in the most merciless manner. Mr Hardie [. . .] holds the opinion that the present labour members so-called are useless – he regards them, or some of them, as being hand in glove with capitalists. They do not approve his "labour party," and they do not in the Congress even ask to the platform Mr Cunninghame Graham, who has done more for labour than any of them. [. . .] The truth is, that Mr Hardie and Mr Cunninghame Graham represent the Socialist movement, which has little or no faith in Trade Unionism, and looks to the State for everything. The Trade Union leaders are not Socialists.[191]

The real extent of the new party's support, and its activities, are difficult to unearth, as newspapers did not report their meetings. David Lowe, a journalist colleague of Hardie's wrote of it: 'The origins of an unpopular movement are not easily collected. Early events of importance passed unrecorded, and successes which gave heart to the pioneers were received in silence by the newspapers press.' [192] It was rumoured, however, that the executive was careful not to appear together, in case they were photographed as representing the party's full strength.[193]

## SPEECH GIVEN AT THE ODDFELLOWS' HALL, EDINBURGH
Under the auspices of the Scottish Parliamentary Labour Party.
10th of June 1889.[194]

I contrast the boasted greatness of the Empire with the fact that last evening I attended a meeting of Glasgow tramway men to protest against a working day of sixteen or seventeen hours and ask for the boon of a twelve hour day! I agree with the previous speaker that an eight hours' bill would not settle the labour question, I do not go about advocating a universal pill; but I maintain that in dealing with practical people such as the Scottish and the English, one has to take them step by step on the way to

---

[190] Norman Mackenzie, Ed., *The Letters of Sidney and Beatrice Webb* (Cambridge University Press, 1978), pp.69-70. Webb converted to socialism in the following year.
[191] *The Scotsman*, 5 September 1889, p.6.
[192] David Lowe, *Souvenirs of Scottish Labour* (Glasgow, 1919), p.v.
[193] William Martin Haddow, *My Seventy Years* (Robert Gibson & Sons, 1943), p.34.
[194] Reconstructed from *The Scotsman* (11 June 1889), p.6.

132

emancipation, and the first step appears to me, on the road to emancipation, is a general reduction in the hours of labour. I advocate a general reduction in the hours of labour, in the first place, because I think it would relieve the pressure at present, and, in the second place, because after a period of years it would necessitate another reduction in the hours of labour, which would inevitably, in my opinion, strike a death blow at the capitalist system.

*Mr. Cunninghame Graham then spoke on the question of affecting this reduction through the medium of the two great political parties in the State.*

Whatever differences might separate these parties upon other matters, there is no difference between them when it comes to a question of the breeches pocket, and that is the way I present it to you. Speaking man to man, I would say that the people of this country have been the Christ crucified betwixt the two thieves - of the Liberal Party and the Tory. (*Applause.*)

I believe that to carry into effect such measures as an eight hours bill, it will be impossible to get measures for the emancipation of labour from the Imperial Parliament, as we know it at present. If, however, we had a Parliament for Scotland we might be able to carry into effect a good many of the measures that it would be completely impossible to carry in the Imperial Parliament. (*Applause.*) There are men who assume to be our representatives in Parliament, who, if men were starving on the High Street of Edinburgh, would hesitate to embark rashly in any scheme for their amelioration until Mr. Gladstone had given his consent on the matter. But with all due respect and admiration for Mr. Gladstone, there are questions before which Mr. Gladstone paled, and before which no man should hesitate for a fraction of a second in making up his own mind, even if Mr. Gladstone never gave it his consent. (*Applause.*) One of these questions is the institution of a Scottish Parliament, because without it we should experience the very greatest difficulty in introducing labour legislation for Scotland. Owing to this question not having been put foreword at election times, members of the present House of Commons can turn round and say that they had no mandate from their constituents to advance labour legislation.

*The Scotsman* told us the other day that there was no need for a labour party, but I assert there is. In Parliament we have 670 members, out of whom 9 are working class members, and some moderately invertebrate. (*Laughter.*) It can scarcely be said there was enough leaven to leaven and move such an inert mass as the House of Commons. And yet we are told in effect that all we have to do is go on voting Tory and Liberal; to open our moths and shut our eyes, and see wages gradually decreasing and hours of labour gradually increasing; and thank God for it every five-and twenty-minutes. (*Laughter*) Why is it that men go on working sixteen or seventeen hours a day when they must prefer eight or ten hours? The reason is to be found in the unemployed labour that is always ready to undersell them; and so it has always been my endeavour to restrict the number of those who are not in receipt of employment. If, with the passing of a general eight hours bill we could give employment to even 200,000 persons additional, a much greater social result would be obtained than by any political measure such as the abolition of perpetual pensions, the passing of Home Rule for Ireland, or any other movement of the same kind. I believe that the movement for a general reduction of the hours of labour is becoming an international one, and I deny that I am seeking to legislate in advance of public opinion. It is for the working classes of this country to disregard party cries, and send men to Parliament pledged to emancipate labour, pledged to do away with the state of things in which all the work and labour were on one side and all the pleasure and enjoyment were on the other; pledged to do away with a system under which the working classes have to give at least two or three turns of work to various kinds of thieves before they put a penny in their pocket. (*Applause.*)

*The resolution was put to the meeting and declared by the chairman to be carried unanimously. A second resolution was then put, and seconded: "That this meeting recognises the necessity for the formation of a distinct labour party in Parliament, and accordingly pledges itself to afford all the assistance in its power to Mr. Cunninghame Graham, M.P. in his efforts to form such a party, and believes that the best method of assistance is to form a branch of the Labour Party in Edinburgh." Mr. J. Keir Hardie supported the resolution . . . The resolution was then put to the meeting, and declared carried.*

~

# SPEECH AT THE TEMPERANCE HALL, SHETTLESTON

30th of October 1889.[195]

There are two schemes of salvation well known to us – one is salvation by good works, and the other, justification by faith. I can tell you straight that I am one of those men who believe in salvation by good works; and one of the reasons I have for believing in that particular scheme of salvation politically is this, that I have always noticed that the school of theologians who believe in salvation by good works looked after the condition of the poor in their congregations, whereas the theologians who believed in justification by faith apparently considered this life so trifling and so unworthy of consideration that they did not take any trouble in the material welfare of their congregations.

As I consider that the aim and object of all politics is to ameliorate the condition of the poor, to get men better wages and better education, to remove women from disgraceful and discreditable ways of gaining their livelihood, to diffuse a higher standard of comfort throughout the nation, and things of that sort, I do not care a single farthing for those who believe in justification by faith scheme of political salvation (*Cheers.*) When I hear speeches delivered by eminent statesmen on the very great progress made by the working classes in the last fifty years I am always a little doubtful. I believe that a select aristocracy, if I might call it so, of skilled labour in Great Britain has made great progress in the last fifty years, but I do not consider the vast body of unskilled working class is in a much better position than they were fifty years ago. The condition of the great residuum of unskilled labour in London, in Glasgow, and in the Black Country, as well as the condition of the crofters in the Highlands, and of the large proportion of the whole population of British India, calls for our earnest attention, because this condition does no credit to our civilisation. It is a disgrace to both political parties, and is only to be put right by the actions of working men – the ruling class, if they only knew it, of this great Empire.

These are not the words that ordinary politicians utter, because in a great measure, they are carried off their mental legs at the sight of the immense wealth of the aristocracy, and still more of the plutocracy, and by the statistics that were carefully

---

[195] Reconstructed from *The Scotsman*, 31st of October 1889.

cooked up by such men as Goschen[196] and Giffen.[197] No doubt ordinary politicians believed what they said. Yet they were as much deceived as the men who prepared the long columns of figures (*Cheers.*) If, therefore, in the richest country in the world, the vast bulk of the population was poor, and if even the unskilled working population was not three or four weeks from actual destitution, surely it was incumbent on them, as units of the vast working population, to ask themselves wherefore this state of affairs existed; whether it always had always existed, and whether they were contented that it should go on existing for future generations.

I hate the poor in the sense that I hate to see so many of them about when there is no necessity for it (*Cheers.*) I hold that this state of things could be remedied. I dissent entirely from those who say it s God's will. They could abolish the poor out of this nation by legislation. (*Loud cheers.*) Is anyone going to stand up who is in possession of his five senses and sustain to him, by clear and well-argued reasoning, that there was not enough wealth for all in this country? Is it not notorious that they produce more wealth than any other nation? (*Hear, hear.*) What, therefore is the reason that there was so much misery, degradation, starvation, and so much of what there should not be in these kingdoms? In my opinion, it is not from the faults of production, but rather from the faults of distribution. But a politician, if he intended to do good, should not only be able and willing to point to blemishes in existing social circumstances, but he should be ready with remedies by which in his opinion they might be altered for the better. Is there any good in looking to the Liberal party for reforms in these social matters? Will they step forward and pass an Eight Hours Bill, or take any definite steps towards the nationalisation of the land, or the raising of the social condition of the working classes generally? For, if not, it is time for the working classes to weigh them in the balance, and if they find them wanting, to kick them out, and to get onto the scales themselves. (*Cheers.*)

Mr. Labouchère[198] has stated at Glasgow that social legislation has been retarded in the past by the Whiggish element in the Liberal party, and has expressed the hope that in the next Parliament there would be such a Radical element introduced that social

---

[196] George Joachim Goschen, British Chancellor of the Exchequer 1887-1892.
[197] Robert Giffen, a Scottish economist. Head of the Statistical Department of The Board of Trade (1876-1897).
[198] Henry Du Pré Labouchère, Liberal Member of Parliament for Northampton.

reforms would be certain. It is just those Radicals that I distrust quite as much as the Whigs. What working men must strive for is not merely to increase wages and shorten hours, but also to obtain the control of the land and the capital of the community. By these means you will get rid of some of the evils I have been speaking of – evils in the knowledge of which men belonging to both the Liberal and the Conservative party has grown old, but have not exerted the smallest atom of brain power to remedy. (*Cheers*.)

~

## EDITORIAL: THE PEOPLE'S MP
*The People's Press*, 26th of April 1890.

R. B. CUNINGHAME GRAHAM, M.P.
(*From a photograph by Bassano, specially taken for the PEOPLE'S PRESS.*)

Mr. Bassano has succeeded in taking an excellent likeness of the best friend the workers have in the House of Commons, as our readers can see for themselves. Mr. Cunninghame Graham looks just as we have seen him on a hundred platforms pleading the case of the Docker, the Gas-worker, the Railway Man, the Shop assistant, or any other worker that needs his help, with that native eloquence and evident sincerity that has won the hearts of the "unskilled labourers." Though he himself is a member of the capitalist - or rather landowning - classes he has done more for the workers than most of the "Labour Members," some of whom have turned out downright Reactionaries under the capitalist influence of the House of Commons. He did his utmost to get the Eight Hours Question discussed by the English delegates to the International Labour Conference, and has lately been turning his attention to the insertion of a clause in railway bills establishing an Eight Hours Day, but being prevented from moving that by the rules of the House, he is going to bring forward the question on a separate motion.

We do not think Mr. Cunninghame Graham finds the atmosphere of the House of Commons very congenial. At any rate, he does not refer to that important part of our "glorious constitution" in terms of very great respect, having come to the conclusion that most honest men come to after a practical experience of politics, that the majority of politicians of both parties are on the whole average humbugs. He longs, he says, at times to be back in South America, away from the depressing influence of British middle-class respectability, which is perhaps worse in Parliament than anywhere else. Mr. Graham belongs to an old Scotch family, the Grahams of Gartmore, a place in the Highlands of Scotland, 500 miles from Westminster. His mother, Mrs. Bontine, is a very clever woman, and from her he inherits his literary taste. He has seen a great deal of the world, was educated at Harrow - not, like his fellow countryman Robert Burns, at the plough - and for some years was engaged in cattle farming in South America, from which he returned with a wife, the daughter of M. Francisco José de Labalmondiére,[199] of Chilli. Mrs. Graham is an ardent Socialist, and is to be seen sometimes on the platform at Kelmscott House,[200] Hammersmith – and other Socialist meeting places."

~

To say that Graham found the atmosphere of the House of Commons less than congenial was an understatement, he regarded it with contempt: 'Parliament is about to meet once more. At the Theatre Royal, Westminster, clown, pantaloon, and harlequin (especially harlequin), comic policemen, and all the well know characters of the farce, are about to meet and greet us, at the pantomime, with "Here we are again, just going to do nothing.'[201] His whole Parliamentary experience was one of the utmost frustration, as expressed in the following extract from 1889:

No, not a word has been said, as usual, about the poorer classes, not a syllable has been breathed about the hours of labour, not a moment has been devoted to ascertaining under what conditions two-thirds of the population of London live and move and have their being . . . True, Parliament is the People's but the people don't

---

[199] It emerged many years after their deaths, that she was Caroline Horsfall, the daughter of a Yorkshire doctor, a fact which they had kept secret, probably because his mother did not approve of her. Graham's biographer, Anne Taylor, goes as far as to suggest that their relationship may have been the source for George Bernard Shaw's *Pygmalion*, which in turn was the source for *My Fair Lady*. Taylor, *The People's Laird*, p.287.
[200] The home of William Morris overlooking the River Thames. It was a centre of socialist activity in London.
[201] Joined To Their Idols, *The People's Press* (23 November 1890,) p.7.

know it. They are so deluded that they never realize that the stout, bald-headed, middle-aged, wealthy gentlemen, who form the great bulk of both Parties are really their own creatures and servants, and that newspapers do not chronicle the sayings and doings of these wind-bags for their own intrinsic merit, but because these windy mouthings are supposed (oh, the pity of it!) to be an expression of the feelings and wishes of the electorate. God pity the electorate, if this be the case; for the majority of the electorate is poor, is hard-working, is concerned with its daily struggle for bread, and how the rot (yes, I must call it rot), with which Parliament generally occupies itself can interest poor hard-working men is beyond my understanding [. . .] "There is one hole in this Parliament."[202] I almost wish the hole were big enough to let some working-class members through it or that the people would make haste and take the whole roof off the building.[203]

~

Prior to leaving Parliament, however, in one final, frustrated outburst, on the 4th of May 1892, Graham interrupted his old acquaintance Herbert Asquith,[204] the future Liberal Prime Minister, who was speaking in favour of the Purchase of Land Bill, which was an early proposal for compulsory purchase. Graham called out: "Perhaps the hon. Member will explain how shareholders in swindling companies (Order!) Oh, I am not going to be put down. (Order! and Name!) It is a matter of no importance to me whether I am named or not." Following further requests by the Speaker for order, Cunninghame Graham resumed - "What I want to know is, how do swindling shareholders in a company derive their funds?" (Order! and Name!) The Speaker then named and suspended him, to which Graham replied: "Suspend away!," then turning to Sir John Lubbock who had tried to reason with him, said - "Oh, leave me alone; I do not care a damn."[205] Like the previous occasion, he apologised to the speaker for any personal discourtesy, but added - "but I wish also to say that I consider I am suspended for standing up for Socialism," and in words that indicated his final exasperation with the House of Commons, he effectively ended his parliamentary career with the words - "I shall be glad to argue that question in the Park with 100,000 men; but this house is a swindle on them."

Despite his belief that only working men should stand as labour candidates, Graham stood as an 'Independent Labour Party' candidate for Camlachie at the General

---

[202] Paraphrased from the words of the infant King James VI at the opening of the Scottish Parliament at Stirling in 1671.
[203] The People's Parliament, The Labour Elector (24 August 1889), pp.118-119.
[204] Asquith, a lacklustre barrister, had been Graham's defence at his trial following 'Bloody Sunday.' He was Prime Minister from 1908 until 1916, and took the country into the First World War.
[205] This was a word that he was fond of using, in those polite times. In January 1890, the following rebuke appeared in an article for The Labour Elector. "When I write "damn," Mr. EDITOR, it is because I mean "damn." Therefore, in God's name damn me no damns with Ds and hyphens. It is a practice hideous in itself from an aesthetic point of view, and from a Socialist one it is Bourgeois and not to be endured.'

Election of 1892, and lost, badly, when the Irish vote cleaved to the Liberals after Parnell's disgrace. This did not however end his political activism, and a year later he was instrumental in founding the ILP with Hardie. Slowly, however, he was becoming disillusioned with those he referred to as 'piss-pot socialists.'[206] As Caroline Benn wrote - "The cloth cap man, once derided, was now exalted; Hyndman, the wealthy Oxbridge graduate, became a villain."[207] MacDiarmid names some men with whom Graham might have worked - "but the future of the Labour and Socialist Movement lay with a very different type with whom he could not have worked and from whom he could not have disguised his contempt," adding: "He was soon to throw himself more and more actively into the Scottish National Movement."[208] David Lowe, a journalist colleague of Hardie's, wrote that Graham had stood aloof from the cabals and dissensions, pettiness, and arguments, that plagued Scottish Labour, but that his real reason for resigning from the presidency and membership, was the failure of Hardie to support his demand for an apology from two party officials who had grossly insulted him.[209] However, by at least 1905, he was openly criticizing it: "Had the party been called a Socialist party I would gladly have come forward, but so long as "Labour" is attached to the question it made a farce of the whole proceedings."[210]

~

A general cynicism and frustration is more than obvious in the following piece, but it is not without affection, and a wry, touching humour.

### AN IDEALIST
*The Saturday Review*, 25th of August 1906.

The comrade who had lectured having sat down amidst applause, the chairman asked for questions on the Speech. In the long narrow hall the audience sat like sardines in a box, so thickly packed that they had hardly room to shout. The greater part were workmen, but workmen of the London type, sallow and slight and dressed in cheap slop clothes. Some foreigners gave colour to the gathering, and showed up curiously against a sprinkling of middle-class enquirers after truth. The latter, mostly mere callow-looking earnest young men from various provincial universities, dressed in grey flannel suits with green and yellow neck-ties, their fluffy hair looking like as it never had been

[206] A. F. Tschiffely, *Don Roberto: R. B. Cunninghame Graham 1852 - 1936*, (Heinemann, 1937), p.260.
[207] Caroline Benn, *Keir Hardie* (Hutchinson, 1992), p.xvii.
[208] Hugh MacDiarmid, *Cunninghame Graham: A Centenary Study* (The Caledonian Press, 1952), pp.9-10.
[209] David Lowe 'The First Time It Has Been Told: Why Cunninghame Graham Left the Labour Party,' *The Glasgow Evening Times* (11 Feb 1938), p.3.
[210] *The Scotsman* (23 December 1905), p.10.

brushed, and their long scraggy throats so thin, one wondered they contained the enormous Adam's apple which protruded over the low-cut collar of their shirts. One or two ladies, chiefly dressed in stuffs from Liberty's, sat half-constrainedly, and jotted down either impressions of the scene or notes of the more salient portions of the lecturers remarks. Three or four comrades, of the kind whose daily life is Socialism, that is of course talking about it, and laying off what the world will be like at its glad event, sat in front places, and now and then during the progress of the lecture had injected an "Ear, 'ear" or "Let 'em 'ave it", meaning of course the Bourgeois, who certainly that evening must have trembled in their shoes, to hear his vices publicly unveiled. They had the kind of likeness to the men who in the Quartier Latin remain art-students all their lives, wearing wide peg-top trousers, flat-brimmed hats, and flapping neckties of black crêpe de Chine, and who in cafés spout continually of art, and in their way are comrades, thinking that everlasting talk is the best way to paint a picture or to revolutionise the world. In front at a deal table sat one or two reporters, dull and uninterested, and to whom all creeds and faiths seem equal, and any kind of lecture or of speech, so many hours of tedious work, which they, bound to work out their purgatory here on earth, lived by reporting at so much the column or the thousand words.

Over the hall there hung an odour of hot people, and stale scent, mixed with fumes of coarse tobacco in the clothes, which is the true particular flavour of all meetings, Tory and Socialist alike, just as in times gone by extract of orange peel and sawdust marked a circus, or as in Catholic countries incense tones down the various smells which rise from all the faithful in a church.

No one responding to the chairman's call, he just had risen up to thank "our comrade for his eloquent, well thought out and delivered lecture, which all who 'eard it must allow was miles a'ead of all the frothy utterances of members of the two parties of boss frauds between 'oom laybour 'angs, as 'e might say upon the cross, the Liberals and the Tories, 'ypocrites and Pharisees . . . if ever there was 'umbugs . . . " when a man arose and said "Excuse me, Mr. Chayrman, I 'aven't got a question, but seeing that you're arsting for one, I'd like to say a word."

Boys seated in the gallery, to whom according to their philosophic state of boydom all meetings and all speeches simply were chances for diversion, shouted our "Ear, 'ear,

I saay let Betterton 'ave a word or two."

The chairman half-constrainedly resumed his seat, baulked like a fiery horse at yeomanry manœuvres in full charge, and toying with the water-bottle, on which great drops of moisture had condensed, called upon Comrade Betterton, with a request he would be brief. A little withered looking man of about seventy, stood up, yellow in colour as old parchment, and with some still remaining wisps of yellowish hair hanging about his head, like seaweed on a rock. His clothes were rusty black, and neatly brushed, his faded eyes of porcelain blue were set in rims of red, his knees were shaky and his whole being was pervaded by an air of great benevolence. Clearing his throat and looking around the hall with the assurance of a practiced speaker, he broke into a breathless sentence, fluent, unpunctuated, and evidently well known to the admiring boys, who cheered him to the fray.

"I've 'eard the speech," he said, "of the comrade who has addressed us at some length, I've heard and think it's 'umbug. As Shakespeare says, while the grass grows, the 'orse is starving." At this quotation a boy shouted "Why the 'ell don't he eat it then?" the ladies coloured, fearing the social revolution had actually begun, and from the chairman came the hope that the audience would keep to parliamentary language seein' that there were lydies in the 'all. Then having called upon our comrade to resume and not to take up too much time, and order being once again established, Betterton took up his interrupted speech, just as a phonograph cuts off, begins again exactly at the place where it was stopped. "What do I find? Nothing but all the means of livelihood monopolized, means of production in the 'ands of one set, land in the other, even the raw material all taken up by the capitalists. Things I say comrades is gettin' daily worse, nothin' being left on which a man can exercise his lybour, without a tax to pay to somebody for doin' it. What is a man to do? Sometimes I think all I can do is to go out and throw a bomb of dynamite involvin' in the sayme destruction all the bloodsuckin' sweaters and land monopolists . . . ." What more the speaker might have said, Providence only and the boys seated in the gallery knew, for a voice emanating from the body of the hall was heard to say in a sarcastic tone, "Why don't you go and throw it?" and in the shouts of laughter that ensued, the speaker discomfited, but still benevolent for all his fiery words, subsided in his seat, and with the usual compliments and the collection, without which no meeting, Socialist, Anarchist, Liberal, religious or

Conservative can ever end, the hall was emptied in a trice, the audience passing swiftly, with their eyes fixed on vacancy, before the comrades who at the door sat selling "literatoor."

This was the first occasion that Betterton revealed himself to my unworthy eyes. As time went on I knew him better, and became so to speak one of his intimates, for there are many kind [sic] of intimates, besides the sort you eat and drink with and stand with in the club window, and criticise the ladies' ankles as they pass. In the first place, he lived on bread and milk, thinking it wrong to take the life of anything (except of course a Bourgeois), so that the pleasures of the table were not exactly in his way.

The work of his profession, that of bill-sticker, took him far from my haunts, and caused him now and then some qualms of conscience, as when he had to cover hoardings, thick with announcements of some stuff or other which he knew was made with sweated work. An atheist by choice and by conviction, he yet had texts of Scripture always in his mouth, and used to say "Only I know you see the laybourer is worthy of his 'ire, or now and then I should just chuck it, it 'urts me to be covering up an 'oarding with a great picture of some 'arlot, for the advertisement of some blood-sucker's soap. An' badly drawn too, bad art" (for he was great on art) "and sweated stuff, not that I've anything to say against the 'arlot in herself, the most of them is driven to it by the rich."

As to why this should be, or how, he did not condescend to explanation, but still believed it firmly, holding as the chief axiom of his faith the wickedness of peers, who he apparently considered had as much power, for evil, as the French aristocracy before the revolution, or as Beelzebub. But notwithstanding poverty and the whole hive of bees he carried in his bonnet, his life was happy, and his faith so great it might have moved the House of Commons from its foundations in the mud, could he have found a lever ready to his hand. As it was, at his lodgings in a slum in Drury Lane, he used to issue broadsheets, printed and set up by himself, on yellow packing paper. The one in which he prided himself most was headed "Messalina,"[211] under which style and title he typified the Queen.

"Pause, brutal and licentious old queen, " it opened, "and think, if you have time to think, in the wild orgies of your bestial career." It finished with an adjuration to the

---

211 The promiscuous third wife of the Roman emperor, Claudius.

proletariat to unite, and the last line was "Blood, Blood, Blood, Heads off, Freedom and Liberty for all."

No larger than a sheet of notepaper, the little periodical was stuffed, so he averred, as full of facts as an egg is stuffed with meat, and naturally was never paid for, but placed by him upon his daily round in letter-boxes of houses of the rich. One of his pleasures (and they were few and innocent enough) was to depict the feelings of the lord into whose letter-box he had deposited his squib.[212] "When he sits after dinner, drinking his port wine, with his boots off before the fire, it will go through him like a smooth-tooth comb, and tremble may he," he would say; "Perhaps touch up his 'eart – who knows? – sometimes those chaps are is not all bad, only they eats and drinks too much, and 'as no time to think."

Not a dull day could Comrade Betterton remember in his whole life.

"Talk of the Greeks and the Romans," he would say, "of course the Romans most was bourgwaw, like ourselves, but the Greeks certainly 'ad opportunities. I mean in art and such like, and seeing people go about without their clothes, thus getting' rid of all 'ypocrisy and that, but then as to an ideal for hewmanity, they was deficient. All art was for a class. Now we live in a glorious time, I wouldn't 'a missed it for a lot. But as to art, exceptin' poor old Morris, most o' your painters and litteratoors and such is middle-class in their ideas, thinks that their kind of stuff is only for the cultivated classes, . . . and see your cultivated class, always at races and shootin' pheasants . . . care as much about the arts as dockers down in Canning Town. What I mean is, a man like me 'as 'is ideal nowadays, and can look forward to a time, when all these Bastilles is pulled down . . . its figuratively I use the word. You needn't larf . . . It does a man's 'eart good to look forward to a time when all your middle-class ideals shall be swept away, and mankind let alone, to grow up beautiful, 'ealthy, artistic and as unmoral as the Greeks. That 'ere morality has been the curse of men of my class, making us 'ypocrites and driving us to drink."

So he went on bill-sticking for his daily bread and moralizing always, both in and out of season, and testifying to his faith, with all the unction of a martyr at the stake, as once, when at a public meeting, packed to the ceiling with religious folk, someone

---

[212] A satirical attack.

averred he spoke "as he hoped in the spirit of his master, Christ," Betterton, rising from his seat, remarked, " 'E aint my master, Sir."

Benevolent and yet ridiculous, kindly, half mad and shrewd in all his speculations upon life, on things on motives and on men, most likely years ago his bills are covered over an inch thick with others, his pot of paste turned mouldy, his brushes worn down to the wood, and he himself safely enfeoffed[213] in the possession of the inheritance to which he had been born, a pauper's funeral, and grave.

Still when I sometimes look on his life's work in literature, the pamphlet "Messalina," in which poor Queen Victoria is so roundly and unjustly vilified, and think upon the pleasure that no doubt the writer had in its production in his one stuffy room in Drury Lane, it is not always easy to be sure if one should laugh or cry.

~

Despite his growing misgivings, during an apparent rapprochement with his Labour colleagues, Graham chaired "a great socialist demonstration," in late 1906, promoted by the Independent Labour Party, during which "A resolution was passed sending fraternal greetings to their Russian comrades, condemning the inhuman atrocities being perpetrated upon them." Robert Smillie then "moved a resolution congratulating the Labour Party in Parliament on the work accomplished in the House, and while recognizing the great good done by the trade unions among the workers, declaring that nothing short of an industrial commonwealth could solve the social problem." Graham who was the first speaker, in front of Keir Hardie, did not entirely agree:

## SPEECH AT THE ST ANDREW'S HALLS, GLASGOW
2nd of November 1906.[214]

Twenty years ago in this hall that we stood at the parting of the waters [. . .] it seems to me that every that the young and enthusiastic politician of twenty years ago in Scotland and England has been condemned more or less to see his dream shattered. . . It seems to me that a young that the young and enthusiastic politician of twenty yeas ago in England and Scotland to see his ideal, and see England and Scotland more delivered over, bound hand and foot to the power of money, than we have known throughout our national history. As I view the matter, national ideals have never been so low than it

---

[213] A property given to a peasant by a feudal landlord, for their allegiance and service.
[214] Transposed into the first person, from *The Glasgow Herald*, (3 November 1906), p.7.

is to-day there is little aspiration; there is little sympathy for freedom with the efforts of other countries to be free. Formerly the name of England was a lamp of liberty to those struggling for independence in other countries. Under the great Liberal Government and of the largest Liberal majority ever known we have disgraced ourselves and dipped our hands in blood, in the executions and the floggings and torturings of the men in Egypt,[215] which were not one whit better or more to be excused than were the torturings and the murderings and the inhumanities which are at present going on in Russia. But there is one bright spark of hope to-day which twenty years ago did not exist, and that is the rise of the Labour party. It is because I think that through the agency of the Labour party we are going to emerge from the bonds of inequality and going to strike hands of fellowship. With the men of foreign nations, imbued with the same aspirations of themselves, and I think that the inception of the Labour party and its rise on the political horizon marks an epoch in the history of our country, the most memorable since the great revolution that drove the Stuarts from the throne and placed the Republican party in power.[216]

*CRITICISM of LABOURISTS*

But there are certain aspects of the rise of the Labour party that I would like to criticise even in the presence of Mr. Keir Hardie. I do not wish to see the Labour party assume the same attitude in front of the Liberal party that undoubtedly the Liberal party has assumed hitherto in front of the Conservative party. I want it to strut forward boldly (*Applause*) knowing that behind it stands all the youth and all the thinking power of all the men of Great Britain. Above all, I look to the Labour party to raise politics out of the slough into which sixty or seventy years of Liberalism and Conservatism has plunged us. I look to the Labour party to raise our ideals, to remove materialism, to stand up for the weak, to say a word for those in Russia, who were today almost condemned by the so-called Liberal press of Europe and statesman who have largely got into power, promising things they had never intended to perform, and conveniently forgetting them when they enjoyed the fruits of office. I look to the Labour party to say a word for women. (*Applause*) I look to it to espouse the cause of

---

[215] 'The Denshawai Incident.' See passim, p.80.
[216] Ironically, Graham was a direct descendant of Robert II, the first Stuart king.

those ladies so disgracefully treated by the Magistrate in London – (*Applause*) - who were at present in Holloway Jail. Neither in the Liberal nor in the Conservative party will anything real be done for women's suffrage, but the men who stood behind Mr. Keir Hardie in the House of Commons are pledged to do something to uplift the political situation of women. We know how essential is that that there should be granted to the mothers of the population the franchise, which is refused to them, and freely given to the drunkard and the thief; the job-stocker, and the knave. (*Applause*) I look over the reading of history that is presented to us by the leaders of Liberal thought. It appears to me that that it has been presented falsely to us from its inception. It is my earnest hope that the good seed sown by Mr. Keir Hardie and his party in Parliament will bear fruit a hundredfold, that eventually they will become the dominant party in power. I believe that when this is so, it would be impossible for any party such as the Liberal party, to go to the electorate and say to them, "We appeal to you, because we have been faithful to the shedding of blood"; because the slaughter of miners at Featherstone, which has never been apologised for (*applause*) for which one word has never been said in extenuation by the leaders of the Liberal party, was the one tangible result of our administration. If a great reforming party has nothing to show further than the blood of a few of its fellow subjects on which to appeal to the suffrage of its fellow mortals, it was time that that party was cut down and cast into the oven, because it cumbereth the ground.[217]

~

## SPEECH IN MANCHESTER: MR GRAHAM'S DISAPPOINTMENTS
6th of December 1908.[218]

*A series of meetings arranged by the Right-to-Work Committee to discuss the question of unemployment was [sic] held yesterday in Manchester and Salford. [. . .] Mr. Ben Tillett[219] moved a resolution demanding that the Government should bring forward legislation which would provide healthy maintenance for those in work and work for the unemployed. Mr. Tillet said it seemed many years since he and Mr. Graham had last stood together in the fighting line, and it was disheartening that, looking back over a quarter of a century, they were still engaged on the same problem. It looked as if something*

---

217 Luke 13:7. The parable of the barren fig tree.
218 Transposed into the first person, from *The Manchester Guardian* (7 December 1908), p.9.
219 Benjamin Tillet (1860-1943) An English socialist and trade union leader.

*were lacking, and that their mission had failed* [. . .] *Mr. Graham spoke in support of the resolution, which was carried unanimously:*

I disagree with Mr. Tillet's views as to our position at the present time as compared to 22 years ago. Our efforts have been wasted in no degree whatever. In those early days our audiences were small, and people thought us mad. The workman was pathetically attached to the Liberal party, but now our views and adherents have not only spread throughout the kingdom, but are to be found in every part of the world. Still, at the present time we are faced by the fact that although we are living in the richest and most prosperous country in the world, hundreds and thousands of men and women are crying for bread, and are imploring Parliament to pass some legislation to keep the wolf from the door. We have in power what has been termed the most democratic Government of modern times. But this Government, after three years' consideration and study, has failed to take any practical steps to alleviate the vast amount of misery prevalent, and for this failure it stands arraigned and condemned in the opinion of every civilised man. (*Applause.*)

What has the Government done? Mr. Asquith has spoken of drastically dealing with the subject of unemployment. His scheme included the employment of men to deal with the erosion of lands on tidal rivers and afforestation, but these matters would necessitate concentration camps, which the Liberals so strongly opposed in South Africa. Afforestation would require twenty years to be remunerative. As a matter of fact, the Government are [sic] not in earnest. They are riding for a fall, and the last thing they have in their minds is to do anything of practical use.

I turn from the Government to the wild, mad, and frantic Socialists like Victor Grayson.[220] (*Applause.*) (You have to think now when you have to name these Socialists). There are Hyndman and Quelch,[221] and a few more, but a good many whose names were so familiar are in high places.[222] I enunciated a scheme to deal with unemployment and laid it before Glasgow Corporation, but they laughed it out of court. It was for the

---

[220] Albert Victor Grayson (1881-1920) An English socialist, and briefly an M.P. He disappeared in mysterious circumstances in 1920, after making charges of corruption against Lloyd George's Government for the selling of honours. See: Andrew Cook 'Cash for Honours: The Story of Maundy Gregory.' (The History Press, 2013).
[221] Henry 'Harry' Quelch (1858-1913). An English socialist, activist, and trade unionist.
[222] Dead.

construction of motor-roads. Such roads are now absolutely necessary, and they would come under the control of various county councils. Their construction would keep the unemployed at work for fifteen years at trade union wages, and the money could be easily borrowed by the councils. It is curious, however, that two months after Glasgow's refusal, General Booth[223] spoke in favour of such a scheme, and at a meeting of delegates of all countries held in Paris a resolution was unanimously passed urging upon all Governments the necessity of such roads.

In conclusion, I have something to say about the Labour representatives in the House of Commons, premising it with the remark that I dislike the words "Labour politics or Labour Party," as they are merely red herrings drawn across the trail. With the very best intentions, these forty men placed in their position in the House of Commons by the self-sacrifice of their brothers in the mines, in the factory, and at the forge have failed in their missions, perhaps by no fault of their own. For three years there has been no direct line of cleavage between them and the other classes. The inert mass of the House of Commons has been too strong for them. Why is that? There is an old proverb that you can't touch pitch without being defiled, and it has proved true again. They have become, perhaps unwittingly, statesmen, not revolutionaries. I stand for Socialism. I want a direct line of cleavage. (*Applause.*) In the next Parliament we shall have a small Socialist party, with members of the type of Victor Grayson (*Applause.*), but at least it will be able to take up the cause of the unemployed. (*Applause.*)

This new honeymoon with the Labour Party had been short-lived. In 1908, the poet and adventurer, Wifrid Scawn Blunt asked for Graham's help to get Labour M.P.s to act over the Moroccan crisis and recorded Graham's response: "[. . .] but he tells me they are a useless lot. When they get into Parliament they are at once bitten with the absurd idea that they are no longer working men, but statesmen, and they try too behave as such [. . .] they would do more good if they came to the House in a body drunk and tumbling about on the floor."[224] On the 11th December, 1919, in a letter to the English dramatist Henry Arthur Jones, Graham wrote: "I had hoped in Socialism to find a gradual demise of selfishness and a better feeling between man and man [. . .] You will admit, I think, that my ambition was not a low ambition. That I was deceived, and that all the golden dreams of Morris have vanished in nine bestial and inarticulate years [. . .] has not been my fault." Several years later, in a letter to R. E. Muirhead,

---

[223] William Booth (1829-1912). An English Methodist preacher, and founder of the Salvation Army.
[224] Wilfred Scawen Blunt, *My Diaries*, Vol.II (Alfred A Knopf, 1921), pp.196-197.

Graham wrote of the Labour Party in Scotland: "They bear the stigma of North Britons, and secondly of Labour men, the most blatant piece of hypocrisy ever invented. Socialist is a good word and represents a great idea, why hide it under the meaningless alias of "Labour." That joined to North Briton makes a fool of anyone who uses it. Let us have done with all this hypocrisy."[225] Despite invitations to do so, he constantly turned down the chance to re-enter Parliament. Such an invitation came from South Aberdeen in 1910, to which he replied in a telegram: "Many thanks for the honour done me, but I decline. Would not re-enter gas-works for £5000 a year."[226]

During this period, Graham's socialism and anti-imperialism took on a more militant, revolutionary hue, having long ago lost faith in Parliamentary democracy, and now, the ability of the Labour Party to provide effective solutions to social problems. The use of violence was excused, and, in the cause of national liberation, even political assassination. (see Graham's speech at the 'Nationalities and Subject Races Conference' in 1910, below). Friedrich Engels had initially believed him: 'a Communist, Marxian, advocating the nationalisation of all means of production,'[227] but later changed his mind, describing him to Karl Marx's daughter as 'an English Blanquist.'[228] Certainly, while in South America, he had been caught up in revolutionary turmoil, and was described as being among 'the apostles of violence,'[229] and his advice to striking Broxburn miners in 1887, was seen in some quarters as encouraging law-breaking.[230] In his Preface to a book entitled 'Revolutionary Types,' Graham writes: 'He who wishes to see Christ's kingdom upon earth, the Rule of the Saints, the Fifth Monarchy in operation, or what not, is almost certain to be an anarchist [. . .] Still, take them for all in all, undoubtedly they were worth a whole wilderness of Liberal politicians, and their worst vices were virtues compared to the best qualities of those they strove against.'[231] G. K. Chesterton recalls a speech by Graham in which he said: "I have never been able to feel myself that tyrannicide, in certain circumstances, is intrinsically and inevitably indefensible.'[232]

Graham had been an associate of the Russian assassin and Nihilist, Sergey Stepnyak,[233] and for a time, had joined the Marxist, British Socialist Party.[234] In 1908, in the depth of

---

[225] Cunninghame Graham, letter to R. E. Muirhead (12 March, 1932), NLS.

[226] *The Scotsman* (7 January, 1910), p.9.

[227] Wilhelm Liebknecht, *Briefwechsel mit Karl Marx und Friedrich Engels*, ed. George Eckert, (Mouton, The Hague, 1963), p.304.

[228] Engels, p.183. Blanquism: Attributed to Louis August Blanqui (1805-1881), who proposed violent insurgency, carried out by a small group of dedicated, professional, revolutionaries, not the working classes.

[229] *The Scots Observer* (29 June 1889), p.146.

[230] *The Scotsman*, (8 October 1887), p.8.

[231] Ida Ashworth Taylor, *Revolutionary Types* (Duckworth, London, 1904), pp.vii-xiv.

[232] G. K. Chesterton, *Autobiography* (Hutchinson & Co, 1936), p.271.

[233] One of William Morris's circle, Sergey Stepnyak-Kravchinsky (1851-1895), was the assassin of General Nikolai Mezentsov, Chief of the Tsar's secret police. Stepnyak was killed by a train at a railway crossing at Woodstock Road, Chiswick, London, while apparently day-dreaming.

an economic depression, and following an impashioned speech on behalf of the unemployed, in George Square, Glasgow, *The Scotsman* accused Graham ('a fanatical philanthropist') of encouraging violence and crime: 'The meaning of such language is perfectly unmistakable. Mr. Graham protests his sense of responsibility; but nobody who recalls his career would attach any high value to that [. . .] his speech is calculated to promote a resort to crime by people who are not habitual criminals.'[235] The Great War and events in Russia, however, seem to have cured Graham of these revolutionary impulses. At a speech in Plean in 1918, when asked if he would vote for the recognition of Soviet Russia, he replied: '[. . .] the only recognition I would give the miserable blood-stained wretches, Lenin and Trotsky, would be at the end of a piece of hard rope on the gallows.' (*Laughter and applause.*)[236]

~

Despite his disillusionments, Graham's campaigns, speeches, and his letter-writing, remained undiminished, and he continued to attack what he saw as the cant and humbug of the major political parties. At the snap General Election called in January 1910 in the midst of a constitutional crisis caused by the rejection of the 'People's Budget' by the House of Lords, Graham picked up his pen again:

**PATRIOTISM?** - Letter to the Editor,
*The Saturday Review*, 29th of January 1910.

Sir,

Now that the alarums and excursions[237] are over, and each side has secured a great moral victory, on the plea of patriotism, it may be worth while to inquire into the right that either wing of the Capitalist Party, the Tory-Liberals or the Liberal-Tories, have to the use of the word that heads this letter. Dr. Johnson defined patriotism as the last refuge of a scoundrel. Well, we have progressed (we are told) since his time, and it may now be defined as the first blast on the tin trumpet of the politician.

They are all patriots. Tory-Liberals and Liberal-Tories alike. Yet the country will inevitably be ruined if either section of the great party gets into power; both sections

---

[234] In all likelihood, he resigned in 1916 when the partys' anti-war faction gained decisive control. (*The Manchester Guardian*, 22 April 1916), p.7.
[235] *The Scotsman*, Editorial (25 September 1908), p.4.
[236] *The Stirling Observer* (2 December 1918), pp.2-3.

[237] An Elizabethan stage-direction used by Shakespeare and others to indicate frantic activity. *All'arme!* = To arms!

say so, and affirm it with posters. During the recent election, which resembled nothing so much as the discharge of a gigantic sewer into a vast and mephitic cesspool, so rank was the abuse, so vile the imputation of dishonourable motives, and so open, naked, and unashamed the scramble for the loaves and fishes, every lie was uttered, every personality belched forth, and every dishonourable trick resorted to in the name and under the style of patriotism.

Sir Thomas More, looking round the world in the person of one of the characters in his Utopia, discerned nothing but a certain conspiracy of rich men seeking their own commodities under the style and title of the Commonwealth. If we have progressed politically since the days of Dr. Johnson, it is certain that we have made little economic progress since those of Sir Thomas More. All that we seem to have gained is the loss of shame, and that is the greatest gain that can happen to a politician of the calibre of the "patriots" who have just put up the British Empire to Dutch auction. That is really what a General Election amounts to. The pity of it is that the prize is usually knocked down to such low bidders. "Free Trade and cheap bread", cries the Liberal. "Protection and high wages", the Tories roar. You will observe, it is all with the pretence of the public good, just as it was in the days of Sir Thomas More.

The speeches of Ministers and even of unsalaried candidates never revealed the smallest real interest in the lot of the poor. Yet the question of the unemployed is the only question that is worth any study to a serious politician. Mr. Balfour confesses that Protection would not be a remedy. He could hardly do otherwise with the examples of Germany and the United States before his eyes. Mr. Asquith cannot pretend that Free Trade is a solvent. If he does, he had better walk down the Thames Embankment some night. Neither can escape the dilemma by averring all the unemployed are unemployable, for the question at once arises, If that is the case, did they not become so under the alternate rule of the Liberal and Tory parties?

How, then, are the rival mud-slingers of the Liberal and Tory gang entitled to the title of patriot which they so fully claim for themselves and so utterly deny to the opposite wing of their party? Surely the idea of pay rather takes the gilt off the patriotic gingerbread? Yet the first action of whichever section is victor in the sham fight they call an election, is to appoint a Cabinet. This Cabinet, containing some twenty members, will adjudge itself salaries out of the national purse, ranging from ten thousand a year to the head swagman, down to, say, one thousand to the sub-secretary of useless affairs. If the thing stopped there, it might not be so obvious, for even patriots must live, though the necessity of their doing so requires a very achromatic microscope to disclose it. Their uncles, nephews, relations will each have his little bit out of the plunder of the Empire when once the swag is shared. What of the best information about stocks and shares?

Lastly, what of the contracts? Remember the brown-paper boots in the Boer war; do not forget the putrid beef. Yet these commodities were furnished by the purest-souled of patriots. It might be well to keep in mind the half-tamed "redomones"[238] (for this word ask your Argentine tipster in the City) furnished as well-broken troop-horses, and given to our men to ride upon to catch the Boers.

Before I pass from this, as patriots say, how does it happen that the framer of the telegram, "Send no mounted men," has never yet been tarred and feathered, as he ought to be?

Patriots, eh? I thought a patriot was one who served his country without the thought of a reward. Well, we have changed all that, and both wings of the great Tory-Liberal party, first and foremost, have gone out for the swag. After all, what is a Dreadnought but a swag-ship, whether in England or in Germany? Swag[239] in the contract, swag in the steel of which the ship is built, in every link of the chain cable – swag from truck to keel. Build eight, build ten, build twenty Dreadnoughts, whether at Portsmouth or Kiel; the object of their building will be swag, for as Sir Thomas More said, now three hundred years ago, nothing is to be seen but a conspiracy of certain rich men (patriots) seeking their own commodities under the style and title of the Commonwealth.

R. B. CUNNINGHAME GRAHAM

~

As late as February 1914, *The Manchester Guardian* reported: "He is a well known figure in the West End of London, not only in the clubs, but also in Trafalgar Square, where

---

[238] Wild horses.
[239] Money or goods taken by a thief or a burglar.

153

he has probably made more speeches than any other living man [. . .] and is always in the middle of any revolutionary movement. He does not favour the moderate groups of Socialists, but is generally to be found associated with the extremists."[240] However, World War I would change everything, and split the socialist movement asunder. On the 2nd of August, two days before Britain declared war on Germany, Graham addressed a huge rally in Trafalgar Square with Hardie, and other socialist leaders. According to Hardie's biographer, William Stewart: 'the latter gentleman's speech [Graham] was said to have made the most profound impression, and to have been [. . .] the best he had ever delivered, which was saying a great deal. "Do not," he implored, "let us do this crime, or be parties to the misery of millions who have never done us harm."[241]

However, in November 1914, *The Glasgow Herald* reported that Graham had been given a commission by the War Office (at the age of 62),[242] and by December, he was in Montevideo buying horses for the soldiers at the Western Front.

[240] 'Miscellany,' *The Manchester Guardian* (23 February 1914), p.7.
[241] J. William Stewart, *Keir Hardie: A Biography* (Cassell & Company, 1921), p.344.
[242] *The Glasgow Herald* (4 November, 1914), p.6. Graham stated that he was offered the grade of Colonel, which he refused: 'thinking it ridiculous for a private citizen not a military man to hold such a title.' *The Stirling Observer* (2 December 1918), p.3.

# SOCIAL FREEDOMS and WOMEN'S RIGHTS

Graham's radicalism extended well beyond his views on the plight of the poor and indigenous peoples, but into the whole of Victorian society. He was particularly exercised by the status of women, and early in his political career, addressing an audience in Glasgow (while under heavy bail after Trafalgar Square), he gave expression to sympathies rarely heard on political platforms of the time:

I know it is not the custom in this country for a woman to speak on a public platform, particularly in Scotland, but the times are so critical, and the disposition of the ruling classes is so tyrannical, that I hope I may be pardoned if I venture - as it has always been woman's mission to speak for the friendless, and to alleviate as much as possible the wrongs and miseries of humanity. I know that there are some who say that in Great Britain that there are practically no wrongs to liberty, and that the law is equal to all, and that all we have to do is obey it. (*Hear, hear, and laughter.*) If this is so, surely there is something wrong in the present condition of the laws in the Highlands - in the Highlands! [. . .] Do not women bear to the full every hardship of the crofter's lot? Do they not suffer - aye, and in silence, not in action, which makes suffering so much keener - (*Cheers.*) - so infinitely more heart-breaking? Do they not suffer when their fathers and their husbands are driven out by the pangs of hunger to the bare hillside to hunt for deer? And may it not be that the knowledge that one woman has had the courage to face an audience to express, or endeavour to express the interest she feels in their lot, and the deep sympathy she feels for them, may stir the heart of some poor crofter's wife when the meal is running low - when in the long winter nights she sits crouching by the embers listening to the howling of the wild wind down the glen, her heart burning with the bitter sense of injustice and wrong, and her children crying to her for bread which she cannot give them. (*Great cheering.*)[243]

Graham also held a consistently sympathetic view on the position of prostitutes,[244] and regarded the marriage markets of the upper classes in Victorian and Edwardian Britain, where young beauties without a dowry offered themselves in marriage to rich old men,

---

[243] *The Coatbridge Express* (28 December 1887), p.1.
[244] Paul Bloomfield writes that this sympathy offended Edwardian taste, and led to his books being neglected.

155

and many other society marriages, as "a clerical-absolved prostitution." He was also a stern critic of what he saw as prudishness and double standards in public and private life among the elite, repressive rules for women, and sexual freedom for men - as long as it remained uncovered.

A case in point was that of his friend Charles Stewart Parnell (1846 - 1891), one of the most charismatic and significant figures in 19th century British politics. Like Graham, Parnell was a Protestant landlord, and a land reform agitator (like Graham), and the founder and leader of the Irish Parliamentary Party. He was sometimes referred to as 'The Un-crowned King of Ireland' (Andrew Lang described Graham as 'The Un-crowned King of Scotland'). Parnell's party split in 1890, following revelations about his private life, which created a huge public scandal. Graham, however, was quick to defend him against hypocrisy, and blatant political opportunism, even though Parnell was directly, and then indirectly, responsible for Graham's two election defeats:

**PARNELL**: An Open Letter to *The Labour Elector.*
25th of January 1890.

Yes, I know. 'Thou shalt not commit adultery.' That is to say: Thou shalt not be found out committing adultery. Now, I do not express any opinion on the Parnell - O'Shea case. I have no opinion to express, and if I had one, should not express it. I neither know nor care whether Mrs. O'Shea was Parnell's mistress or not. What can it matter to me? Still less, what can it matter to the case of Home Rule for Ireland? I hear among the ranks of the 'unco guid,'[245] an attempt will be made to damage his political reputation through the aspersion of his private character.

Is this as it should be? Perhaps Mr. Stead will say 'yes.' Perhaps the great Nonconformist Party will say 'yes.' I say: 'no.' Do I mean, therefore, that the private character of a politician is not to be taken into account when we consider his public actions? Do I mean that adultery is not a venial crime, and to be made light of? Certainly not. There are crimes that warrant the public in withdrawing all confidence from the man who commits them. There are actions - actions considered, I am well aware, perfectly legitimate in the Stock Exchange and in the office - that should be sufficient to hunt a man from public life. Is this one of them? I say, 'no.' It seems to me that the offence charged against Mr. Parnell is merely the offence of being found out.

---

[245] A hypocrite. Robert Burns, 'Address To The Unco Guid [Uncommonly, or exceptionally good], Or The Rigidly Righteous.' (1786).

That is to say, if he has been found out, for of that we know nothing yet. Look around the House of Commons, look at the well-fed, idle, rich men in it, and then ask me to believe they are all earnest practisers of social purity. If this is so, and if the public knows that even St. Stephen's[246] harbours a fair proportion of offenders against the Seventh Commandment, and knowing, tolerates scandal; why, therefore, this tone amongst so many Liberal papers of affecting to treat Mr. Parnell as a criminal? Had he been an obscure member of the Irish Party, some McHafferty, or O'Rafferty, or some member for Ballyshaughuttery, is one to suppose anyone would have cared a farthing? It is because on the Liberal posterior the imprint of the Parnellite boot is so clearly to be traced, even without the aid of smoked glass, that this freezing tone has come over so many of his quondam[247] allies, assuming for the sake of argument the O'Shea thesis. Has, therefore, Mr. Parnell altered his political convictions? Are the funds of the Irish National League likely to be less justly administered? Are the paid members of the Party the less likely to receive £2 a week, or whatever it is, with less punctuality? Had the offence with which Mr. Parnell is charged been of a different nature, had he been accused of taking shares in a company which paid a dividend of 25 per cent; then I can well understand the feeling of repugnance that must inevitably have crept into the hearts of the allies. Is it not well-ascertained fact that the Liberals are men of principle, and that the Tories are hounds? Is it not a matter of public notoriety that no good Gladstonian Liberal ever accepts more than two and a half per cent return on his money? I should think so; for if not, what do their public mouthings mean? If a man commits a crime that disposes people to think that on account of it he is unreliable in his dealings with them; then, if he is a public man, we are right to take our oyster shell and write quickly on it: 'Banish him.' If on the other hand the offence is one that the vast majority of men take pleasure in committing as long as there is no danger of being found out - is one which two-thirds of the House of Commons are in the habit of doing - why then, I say, let him who is without sin, put out his well-gloved hand, and rushing in front of the steam-roller, let him seize a jagged flint and hurl it at the Liberator's head. If then he feels qualms of conscience, let him rather retire in haste to the Liberal meeting and spout there on Freedom of Contract.

---

[246] A general nickname for The Houses of Parliament.
[247] Former.

This whole affair is evidently the specious plot of some knaves calculating to play upon the well-known hypocrisy of the British nation. Taking into consideration moreover, the help that they will receive from Tories of the baser sort, and not forgetting the delight that will be caused in the Liberal camp if the strong man who has rubbed their weak noses in the first can be brought to confusion. I have referred to Sir Charles Dilke.[248] Now I am not concerned in the least to defend him. All that I say is, that Sir Charles Dilke was not treated with justice.

Does anyone believe that the political principles of the man are altered? It is because a set was made against Sir Charles Dilke by men and women who were likely enough no better than himself, that I am constrained to write these few words on the Parnell - O'Shea incident. If we push this mania to its logical sequence, we must assure ourselves that the Judge before whom the case comes for trial is a man of absolutely pure private life. If he be not - why, how is he any more fitted for the Bench than is Parnell to be the associate of Brunner, Balfour, Gladstone, Churchill, myself and other wealthy men who live on the labour of others? In no other country in the world but England would it, I believe be possible to get up a cry against such a public man on such a question. This is, as I understand it, no question of seduction of a young child; no case of unnatural perversion of appetite such as that of the so-called West-End Scandals. [249] The Bible applies another and plainer word, if I remember rightly, to the offence. This is simply a case of the natural affection of two grown-up people, for I understand Mrs. O'Shea has also arrived at years of discretion. Now what I contend is, that in no other country in the world would it be possible to ruin a public man on such a question. Should it be possible in England?

Yes, if - if all our people were pure themselves - if such a thing as a Divorce Case was unknown in the land.

However, when I take up a newspaper (which I confess I do as seldom as I can), I find whole columns and columns are devoted to divorce. When I look up lives of statesmen who have been honoured in this land, I find that some of them were

---

[248] An English Liberal, and Radical politician. Touted as a future Prime Minister, his aspirations to higher political office were effectively terminated in 1885, after a notorious and well-publicised divorce case.
[249] Also known as 'The Cleveland Street Scandal' (1889), where police discovered a homosexual male brothel in Fitzrovia, London. The government was accused of covering up the scandal to protect the names of aristocratic, and other prominent patrons.

notorious offenders in this respect, and that no one thought of doubting their political principles on that account. Are we, then, so much better than our fathers? Well then, I say, that it is impolitic, unjust, and thoroughly hypocritical to try to raise a cry against a man for an offence which, if it hurts anyone, assuredly does not produce a tithe of the misery, poverty and ruin that a single morning's speculation on the Stock Exchange often entails on humanity.

What! hunt an adulterer from public life, and take a sweater[250] to your chaste arms? The thing is ridiculous in a state of society in which marriage itself is too often a clerical-absolved prostitution - in a society in which we see a Prince marry his daughter to a boon-companion in his adventures, and no one raise a voice of disgust and contempt - a society in which every day we see mothers eager to marry their youngest and fairest to old, painted, padded, lecherous baboons, simply because they have rank and wealth. If the Liberals are to banish, and the Tories to persecute Mr. Parnell for his alleged connection to Mrs. O'Shea, what are we to do with H ———, and S———, and Z———, and all the others whom we know to be guilty of similar offences? Let us form a huge Vigilance Committee, and whilst the bulk of the population are delivered over to long hours and low wages, let us leave the consideration of such matters to fools, and let us, as practical men and women, turn our attention to practical matters - such as the one I have been writing about.

~

Making comparisons between Graham and Oscar Wilde might at first appear unlikely, but the parallels are there. Both came from privileged backgrounds, both had strong, politically active mothers, both were outsiders, and at the time, both were equally well known. Both were dilettante socialists and supporters of Irish independence, both were rebels against social conventions, both had served prison terms, and both were, although by very different means, critics of Victorian society, particularly over the position of women. It was thus appropriate that *The Saturday Review* commissioned Graham to write a review of Wilde's tragic masterwork *De Profundis*, which first appeared in print on the 11th of February 1905, over four years after Wilde's death, but even then, it was a brave defence of his friend. Graham makes no reference to the nature of Wilde's conviction and imprisonment for 'gross indecency,' but takes a broad-minded view of Wilde's sexuality. In a letter to W. H. Nevinson on the 27th of

---

[250] One who employs sweated labour.

November 1927, Graham discusses Wilde's compatriot Sir Roger Casement, who had been hanged for treason in 1916:

> The abnormality of his private life [his alleged homosexuality], which I hear from Conrad, from Englishmen who had known him in Paranagua and Rio de Janeiro, did not weigh with me in the least. As you say, we cannot hang all who have Casement's vice, and after all it is not a disease that is catching in the least.

## VOX CLAMANTIS [251]

*The Saturday Review*, 4th of March 1905.

I knew him and admired his gifts. Most people now recall his wit, his humour, his brilliancy, his poetry, his prose, his errors, triumphs, and his fall. I most remember his great kindliness. It is the greatest quality in man. Without it, all the talents, all the virtues, lack somewhat; with it all errors, even crimes, can be condoned. Few books in any language, treating of prisons and of prison life, are comparable with this. Generally (and this your doctor knows) a man in prison is sustained either by consciousness of innocence, by pride, indifference, or by the thought that on emerging from his malebolge,[252] he has a home in which to hide himself.

He had none of these to help him as he picked the oakum, paced round and round the yard, stood in the prison chapel bawling the hymns, or worst of all sat idle in the cell in the long winter afternoons before they light the gas, or perform the dreary round of duties which only those who have performed them estimate. Some men have tamed a mouse. Others wait as a youth waits for his sweetheart, till a robin comes to a window-sill to peck at crumbs.

Nothing (to prisoners) can ever make the prison flower ridiculous, or hackneyed, in spite of sentimental books.

He had no mouse or robin, only his soul to tame, so sitting down he has depicted for us how it itself against the bars, until at last it fought no more, and he and it had peace. But the peace he had was not of the kind those have who throw themselves into the arms of some religion, which till then they have refused. Only the peace that comes to all men when they have learned as he did that sun and moon and stars, the seasons, tides, the equinoxes, the flowers and trees and Nature will be as much theirs

---

[251] Latin: The Voice of One Crying Out.
[252] See passim, p.121.

even in sorrow, as they ever were in joy. So by degrees he learned to bear it all, even though from the outside world nothing but sorrow came to heap the mass of sorrow growing in his heart. His mother's death moves him to such abasement that but to read it makes oneself ashamed to be a man.

Hardly in any literature does such a great and bitter cry pierce the heart, as does this anguish of the poor soul, dressed like a zany[253] as he says himself, ridiculous in grief, a clown of sorrows, as miserable as is the plaint of an old woman outraged by drunkards and then scorned. Well does he say, that in most martyrdoms, to those who heaped logs or lit the straw, the sufferer must have appeared a fool, and without dignity or style. Had Cranmer[254] written in his cell after his great refusal, and before the fire had purified, his outpourings would surely have been akin to Wilde's. But he redeemed himself, whereas the writer of the book had no such luck. Therefore, the charitable man, if there be such in this age of self-sufficiency, must take this book for expiation and in it find his martyrdom, and read it as a thing that might have happened to himself. This done it is a scripture for our learning. Written of course in gall, with a pen made of hyssop[255], but truly written and as such more valuable than all the books of all the moralists. Each man can see what he likes in it, and to some it may seem mystic, to others philosophic, and again to certain minds, a reconciliation, but to me what most attracts is that the point of view is still unchanged.

There was about the man a curious courage, rarer perhaps than that of those who rush on death (with a side-glance at glory as they run), or those who do their duty all their lives from temperament or fear. This as it seems to me is shown in every line of the whole book, and most of all when he dwells on his fits of weeping in his cell, in such a way that though he sees his weakness, at the same time you feel his strength. He has a sort of absence of what the French call "respect humain", such as one sees in Arabs, and withal a certain dignity, like a fallen angel to whom at times celestial music echoes still, but distantly.

Surely he is right to say that punishment wipes out the offence, for, if it does not, those who punish cannot be judges, but mere torturers?

---

253 French/Italian: A clown.
254 Thomas Cranmer (1489-1556). Archbishop of Canterbury. Burnt at the stake for treason and heresy.
255 An herbaceous plant with a supposed purifying qualities. Psalm 51: 'Thou shalt purge me with hyssop, and I shall be clean.'

Right through the book reflections such as this must make the Philistine, whom as he rightly says is the sworn foe of all repentance, wince not a little beneath his armour of self-righteousness.

Scattered about the book are flashes of his old humour, as when he calls "La Vie de Jésus" a gospel by S. Thomas, or talks about an order to be founded for all those who have no faith, and this I fain would hope sustained him, for when all is lost, even to honour, it is the only stay. Perhaps it is philosophy made manifest to those brought low, and to whom consolation is denied.

No degradation seems to have killed his love of beauty for itself, and it is brave of him to say that he does not regret his previous life.

All his reflections upon Christ remind one of an educated pagan, who admired whilst not believing, but yet are true and just, so just, one wonders why one never thought them for oneself. Who but himself writing in anguish in his cell could have written "To turn an interesting thief into a tedious honest man was not his [Christ's] aim". And yet how true it is, for God could not deny imagination to his Son. In the letter which his faithful friend and editor[256] prefixes to the book, the writer says that "prison life makes me see people and things as they really are." That is true to some extent as when he dwells upon the frank contempt of Christ for mere material success, but that the saying is but true in part he gives the proof himself. The mystical in art, in life, and nature was what he says on his re-entrance to the world shall be his goal. Now mysticism is a temperament born in a man as are his hair or eyes, no one can cultivate it, like faith it is a quality which must grow alone, and he had neither. Thus it may be by straining after what he had not, that he lost what he had, and his expression, which was everything, never returned to him.

The book is beautiful in all its misery, and worth a million of the dishonest self-revelations of the men who write about their souls as if their bodies were mere pillow-cases. One reads with indication how he stood soaking in the rain, handcuffed and dressed in prison clothes, whilst a mob jeered him at a railway station. Had he been twice as guilty as he was and of a serious crime as cheating or the like, or cruelty, human respect should not have been thus outraged, for the man condemned by law is

---

[256] Robert Baldwin 'Robbie' Ross. In 1950, Ross's ashes were placed inside Wilde's grave in Paris.

surely sacred, as we have taken from him all means of defence. Judges and postmen and all public servants ought to understand that whilst we pay them and place our correspondence and our property, more or less in their hands, they should execute their offices with due discretion, and not allow a letter or a soul to fall in the mud, for fools to stamp upon, for on them may be written things more sacred than themselves. With the exception of Morris and of Parnell, when he was alive, no one bulked greater in the public eye than Wilde, and when the paltry politician, even though he rest his boots upon the table of the House from the green benches of the salaried crew that forms a Government, is long forgotten, the unhonoured poet in his dishonoured grave will be remembered, and his works read by every man of taste. Reading the beautiful but miserable book, some things console one, first that he had a friend who both in evil and good repute stood by him to the last. When the poor wretch, condemned to hell before his time, records with his tears how it consoled him only to have received a brief salute in passing, one thinks better of mankind, as if rewards were ever given to desert, the faithful friend has his. He who brings comfort to the soul in pain is better far than he who, himself sinless, dies without sympathy, for by that sin devils have fallen to a lower depth.

All through the book there is a vein of tenderness, not that false tenderness which sorrow sometimes gives, but real and innate. The love of flowers, of children, of the trees, the sun and moon and the stars in their courses, call to us from this crying voice, for pardon. His joy of life, and all the sufferings which to such a man those two fell years must have entailed, speak for him to us, asking us now, after his death to pardon, and when we speak of him, to call him by his name, to make no mystery of his fall, and to regard him as a star which looking at its own reflection in some dank marsh, fell down and smitched itself, and then became extinct ere it had time to soar aloft again.

There was a tragic but revealing postscript to Graham's friendship with Wilde, as related by Graham's biographer (some would say amanuensis), Aimé Tschiffely: [257]

---

[257] A Swiss-born, Argentine professor, writer, and adventurer. Tschiffely (1895-1954) wrote a number of books, most famously *Tschiffely's Ride* (1933) in which he recounts his solo journey on horseback from Argentina to New York City, an epic adventure that still marks one of the greatest horse rides of all time.

When Oscar Wilde was in sore trouble and most of his friends ignored him, he stopped Don Roberto who happened to be out riding early one morning. Wilde had been sitting alone on a bench near Rotten Row, and when he rose and the rider recognised him, he brought his horse to a standstill, and leapt off to grasp Wilde's hand.

"What am I to do?" Wilde asked after having explained his serious troubles to his sympathetic friend who had listened patiently to his tale of woe. For once Don Roberto's Spanish mannerisms led him to make a *gaffe* which he regretted to his dying day, for on several occasions he told me how, without realising it, he raised his arm, and pointing to his temple with the first finger, made a noise similising a revolver shot, by flicking the middle finger over the thumb. Before Don Roberto was aware of what he had done, Wilde, sobbing like a child, said: "I know it's the only way out, but I haven't the courage." [258]

~

Votes for Women was a political topic that dominated the late 19th and early 20th centuries, creating a mass movement that encompassed women of all classes, who were increasingly driven to greater militancy and violence in the face of Parliamentary resistance. This was a political cause and strategy that Graham whole-heartedly supported. In an interview in 1909 he said the following:

The success of any individual system of tactics can never be ascertained until the end of the war. It is too late to deplore, even if one should like to do so, the aggressive tactics of the more advanced section of political women, because they are too deeply committed to draw back. [. . .] Ever since I entered Parliament in 1886, I have seen an increasing band of M.P.s pledged to grant a suffrage to women. An unredeemed pledge is as useful to an M.P. as it is to a pawnbroker. Personally, I have never seen Parliament move except under pressure of the boot applied *a tergo*. [259] It may have been that the 300 members who are pledged to female suffrage would have sat quietly as a row of hulks on a mudflat had they not been stimulated a little by the tactics of the Suffragettes.[260]

---

[258] Tschiffely p.349.
[259] Latin: 'To the rear.'
[260] Robert Birkmyre, 'An Appreciation of Cunninghame Graham,' *The Idler*, (February 1909), pp.479-480.

# WOMEN'S SUFFRAGE: SPEECH AT THE ST ANDREW'S HALLS, GLASGOW

*The Glasgow Herald*, 4th of October 1907.[261]

*The cause of women's suffrage has obviously a considerable following in Glasgow. St Andrew's Hall was almost crowded last night when four of the most eloquent leaders in the movement pleaded on behalf of the unfranchised sisterhood. The ladies are not without sympathisers among the sterner sex, and although ladies predominated in the audience and the platform there was also a large number of men. It was significant also that the demonstration was under the auspices of "The Men's League of Women's Suffrage." The fact that Mr. R. B. Cunninghame Graham was in the chair doubtless accounted in some measure for the dimensions of the audience.[262] But the fair agitators themselves are also interesting personalities. The fact also that such notable champions of the cause as Mrs Despard,[263] Mrs Billington-Grieg, Mrs Philip Snowden,[264] and Miss Christabel Pankhurst[265] appeared on the same platform disproved the rumour that had been current that there are dissensions among the leaders.*

The movement has reached almost a crisis in its history. People have almost ceased jeering, and have begun to persecute. All movements go though on or two phases. First they are laughed out of court, then comes persecution. In this case the persecution has not been entirely from the one side. (*Laughter*) One thing is evident; the great and good, the opulent, and the democratic Liberal party has been drawn blank (Laughter). Our pawky Prime Minister[266] – (*Laughter, applause, and hisses*) – has proved a somewhat broken reed, and the letter which appeared in the "Glasgow Herald" the other day pinned him like a well fed moth to the paper. The other members of the party had been sleeping, or peradventure, on a journey to Denshawai[267] in order to pic-nic perhaps upon the scene of the action which undoubtedly would entitle them to their cruel place in history. It was strange that three consecutive Liberal parties had celebrated their advent to power by a baptism of blood. In regard to the question of women's suffrage, we have had no

---

261 Transposed into the first person, from *The Glasgow Herald*, (5 October 1907), p.8.
262 In fact, Graham had been elected Vice-President of the Scottish Women's Liberal Association in 1889.
263 Charlotte Despard (1844-1939) was an Edinburgh-born Anglo-Irish suffragist, novelist, and Sinn Féin activist. In 1930 she joined the Communist Party. She was the sister of Sir John French, a hero of the Second Boer War, and Commander-in-Chief of the British Expeditionary Force during the first year of World War I.
264 Ethel, later Viscountess Snowden (1881-1951), a socialist and human rights activist. She was the wife of the prominent Labour politician, and future Chancellor of the Exchequer, Philip Snowden.
265 Later, 'Dame' Christabel Pankhurst (1880-1958), daughter of Emmeline Pankhurst, leader of the women's suffrage movement in Britain. During World War I, she toured the country making recruiting speeches, and her supporters handed a white feather (of cowardice) to every young man they met, wearing civilian dress.
266 Sir Henry Campbell-Bannerman (1836-1908).
267 See passim.

expression of opinion from responsible Minister, except an adverse one; and Mr Asquith,[268] dear Mr Asquith (*Laughter*) – ran out of the back door – though history did not state whether he left his coat in the hands of any of the ladies, like another Minister in olden times in somewhat similar circumstances. (*Laughter.*)[269]

Personally, I always look upon the question as one of economics, and indubitably and absolutely soldered together with the rest of the great economic problems of the age. If we consider the question dispassionately we will see that every question affecting women, even the question of the custody of children after divorce, was merely an economic question. War, diplomacy, marriage, divorce, the alliance of this country with other countries, each and every question, political and social, which comes before the nation for solution is almost entirely a question of economics, of bread and butter, if we come to basic principles. It is not as inartistic and unliterary people said, degrading to this question to argue upon a commonsense basis. Truth can never be degraded. Did Velasquez, when he painted Philip IV with bleary huge eyes and pendulous cheeks, degrade him? To have painted him other than he was would have been degrading to both monarch and painter. Afterwards, the same Philip was painted upon the well-known white-faced proud bay horse. What did the bleary eyes and pendulous cheeks matter? The truth has been achieved, and it did not detract one iota from the fact that Philip was absolutely the best horseman in the kingdom. (*Applause*)

I approach the question from the point of view of adult suffrage. (*Applause*) To approach it from any other point of view would, in my opinion, be to degrade it, and to accept brief measures would be to detract from its importance. Half a loaf in politics was always worse than no bread. (*Laughter and applause*) Who would wish to possess himself of half a bicycle upon a journey? (*Laughter*) It was the same in politics. That was the cause of the failure of the Irish party. Irish Home rule has been put off for a whole generation; and that is why the Labour party, the eminently respectable Labour party (*Applause*) were so insignificant in the House of Commons. Lions roaring in the desert. Heroes on the platforms when there is no danger, and dumb dogs – with a few honourable exceptions – in the House of Commons (*Applause*) Women in that House would at least not sit tamely there: they would not cling to the benches like a lot of

---

[268] See passim.
[269] Asquith by this time had gained a reputation for lecherous behaviour.

mandrakes, afraid to be uprooted as ever the mandrakes of the Scripture. (*Laughter*)

Let me take an example from the sweated industries. It has always appeared to me that the lot of the sweated female match maker was such as to attach herself and make her sympathise far more frequently with the sweated tailor than she did with the wife of the opulent sweater nodding her Aigrette plumes[270] - in spite of all that has been written on the question – in her motor car, neatly painted in order to be in harmony with her summer frock. (*Laughter*) If that proposition does not commend itself to women then it is impossible to argue the question on economic grounds.

It is said that the brain of woman was inferior on the whole to that of man. If the brain of the average woman was inferior to the brain to be observed upon the benches of the House of Commons then the brain of the average woman could not be remarkable for much specific density. (*Laughter.*) If Parliament was composed entirely of women, it could not possibly be more foolish than the present Parliament composed entirely of men. (*Laughter.*) If there had been women in that august sphere, there might not have been laid the blot upon their national escutcheon,[271] the miserable massacre of those helpless Arabs at Denshawai, to go down to the national discredit without at least a protest. I do not know a word in the whole English dictionary that raises my gall like the word 'statesmanlike.' (*Laughter.*) So eminently statesmanlike and cowardly was the behaviour of this Parliament that there was not a single man – the same as in Sodom and Gomorrah – to stand up in defence of that hideous and unnecessary cruelty and most undiplomatic measure. (*Applause.*)

No one man nor woman should be debarred from voting. The pauper and the prostitute should have the right as well as the millionaire and the matron. (*Applause.*) No single individual in the nation escaped taxation, and that should be a cogent argument in favour of extending the suffrage. (*Loud applause.*)

~

Graham's bruising experience in the House of Commons had convinced him that voting changed nothing, but as a committed supporter of equal rights for women, not

---

[270] A once-fashionable headdress consisting of white egret feathers.
[271] Dishonour the reputation of one's family.

simply votes, proposed more radical changes in the following piece. He is silent on how these changes might easily be achieved, and thus it remains a manifesto, but a far-reaching one for its time. Watts and Davies describe it as: 'in some ways a remarkably far-sighted discussion of feminine emancipation. Attempting to be two jumps ahead - ahead of the Pankhursts' campaign for the vote [. . .] Graham almost leapfrogs into Women's Lib campaigns of the 1960s and 1970s.'[272]

## THE REAL EQUALITY OF THE SEXES
*The New Age*, July 1908.

In the actual struggle for the franchise now going on, I am but little interested. It is certainly a great movement and a just one, but the franchise, to men, has proved but a broken reed as far as social freedom is concerned, and there is no apparent reason why it should prove more potent in the hands of women.

My real sympathy is with their social and economic freedom. Almost every institution, economic, social, political, and religious (especially religious) is designed, or has become without designing a means to keep women dependent on men.

Now men nowadays have a hard enough struggle to keep themselves, and it is to their manifest advantage that women should be able to maintain and fend for themselves in life.

As to the servitude that our present political system brings on women, have not a thousand eloquent feminine tongues set it forth, throughout the length and breadth of the land?

No man can add anything to what they have said, except in the particularly masculine realm of humour. It would appear that wit is a feminine and humour a masculine quality, and it is doubtful if even adult suffrage will ever remedy this state of things. It has, however, often struck me that a convention of the most foolish women in Great Britain, chosen with the greatest care by the most incompetent of the female electorate, could not well be foolisher than is the British House of Commons, elected as it is at present entirely by men.

That the present political system is a potent engine for the subjection of women, anyone who has ever been at an election can at once understand.

We know that Englishmen are free and equal before the law, yet no country

---

[272] Watts & Davies, p.226.

exists where there is greater decision of classes except perhaps the United States. One man is a bounder, another a barbarian, a third a sanguinary Jew, a fourth a snuffling Nonconformist, a fifth a bigoted Catholic, a sixth a stuck-up Churchman. A soldier is said to be narrow, a tradesman mean, a politician a shuffler, a stockbroker a cheat, a lawyer a deceiver, a doctor a fee-hunter, and "to lie like a vivisector" has become a proverb. Yet, in the mass we are all "God's Englishmen," and at election time we are assured that the Lord himself being but imperfectly equipped for the task of creation, left the world unfinished for us to correct its shortcomings. But below all these divisions, and ticketed persons, there yet exists a lower abyss. The working classes, before whom we all truckle, but whom we heartily despise in our hearts, are the real objects of our scorn. You make a fool of the working-man, says the Tory to the Liberal, and then the speaker sneaks out to see what he can do to secure the vote of the Helot at the next election.

Needless to say, both Tory and Radical amongst their friends speak patronisingly but disparagingly of the class on whose backs they climb into front seats at the national hog-trough. There comes an election, and both parties drag themselves on their bellies before the class they despise, and each professes his admiration of the virtues, the sobriety, the perseverance, the uncomplainingness of the class of whose thriftlessness, unreasonableness, insolence, and incapacity they have no words hard enough to stigmatise. And so with women; all their frivolity, their love of change, their want of grasp of a political situation, and their other mental and moral failings about which we hear so much nowadays when two or three (men) are gathered together, would all be overlooked when their votes were required for some great "cause" or another. Women should not forget that a "cause" is the means whereby a politician is put into the position of being able to plunder the nation; and they should not forget that if on the whole our politicians are honest over the counter, that in the "jug and bottle" department of contracts, making use of knowledge acquired on the Stock Exchange and the like, that when the south wind blows they can tell a hawk from a hernshaw.[273] So that the first step to political consideration is obviously the vote, though it would do little enough    towards

---

[273] Hamlet, Act II, Scene II.

complete emancipation, which, of course, is an economic and a sexual affair, for them.

It is conceivable that every political disability now relating to women might be swept away and that wages become equal for equal quantity and quality of work done by men and women, and yet the position of women be but little really altered unless the existing social and religious institutions and the views incident to the prevalence of these institutions were radically changed.

That way alone leads to emancipation, although the franchise may do some little good, if only at election time. Women's emancipation is first an economic and then a sexual and religious matter after all. Once alter all the laws which set up property above mere human beings, and women will be free, and man also, for women agitators always forget (just as men do) that to free one sex and leave the other slaves is quite impossible. In the old days in Carolina the negro and the master both were slaves. The Christian religion has been too readily assumed to have been the only faith which has raised women in the social scale.

Only repeat what is false long enough, loud enough, and with a sanctimonious air, and people will believe you, although you know it is a lie. In point of fact, it has taken nineteen hundred years for women to gain the same quality before the law as they enjoyed in the time of Hadrian. The Romans had a married woman's property act at least as much in woman's favour as in our own.

During those nineteen hundred years the Church, whether Greek, Roman, Anglican, or Nonconformist, has fought against all efforts to place men and women on an equality before the law. All know the mediæval Church's attitude towards women as a sex. She was unclean, a snare, the undoer of mankind. Virginity was placed above the maternal state, thus showing that the Church thought she knew better what was good for us than did the power she knew as God. Only when priests were feed and Latin mumbled was commerce between the sexes ought but a deadly sin.

Thus did the Church degrade both sexes, and constitute itself the universal brothel-keeper of mankind. Its sacramental marriage, which at first was but a means of regulating natural affection for the priests' benefit, become in the lawyer's hands an instrument for the protection of property, and women, being weaker, bore the full brunt of any step aside when once the fees were paid and the indecent service

170

duly mumbled out.

Man had his children and his money protected, and his wife became his slave, and has remained so to the present day. She will remain so until the marriage laws are changed; divorce (charter of liberty to women) made easy, and the dual contract made soluble at the will of both or either party to it, instead of being, as it too often is, a life-long chain. By these means, and by legitimisation of all children and the abolition of the degrading custom of making breach of promise an actionable thing, woman's true freedom will be attained.

What can be more unjust than that a man who has run his course like twenty thousand bridegrooms rolled up into one should insist on marrying what he calls "a pure girl"?

His wife should be a hardened prostitute, that is, if prostitution hardens more than does enforced celibacy. Thus, then, it seems to me, emancipation lies in ways more difficult to follow than the mere agitation for the vote. When some of these things that I have indicated have been achieved, women will really be emancipated; and, standing on her feet, look a man squarely in his eyes and say, "I have done this or that because it was my pleasure," and the man, looking back at her, will see she is an equal, for in freedom of the will lies true equality.'

~

Partly demonstrated in 'Parnell' (1890), below, and 'The Reptile Press' (1891), Graham's views on the cant and hypocrisy surrounding private and public morality stand in sharp contrast to the social norms of his time. These radical views, however, find no better expression than in the following article, which is startling in its modern relevance.

## THE ENEMY
*Justice: The Organ of Social Democracy*, 13th of May 1913.

Sometimes I think the fight for liberty is harder here with us than it is elsewhere. In Russia, for example, there exists a social liberty such as we Englishmen have no idea of, or can understand; but freedom as we know it is quite unknown in things political.

People who write of life in Moscow or St. Petersburg describe a state of things, especially in questions which only touch the individual, which the British Philistine has never contemplated, even in his dreams.

Women and men elect to live together, dissolve their union and make other ties, and no one even criticises, thinking such matters purely personal and of no interest to the outside world. Here, as we know, such matters form cheap and nasty talk of everyone. In fact, they have become the staple dish, and pruriently minded men and women seem always to be prowling round trying to find out filth. Such and such a book is banned because it tries to speak the truth. A play raises a shout of execration only because some situation of which the whole world is perfectly aware often arises in men's daily lives is touched upon. That is to say, is touched on seriously, for only let the presentation of it raise a laugh and all is well – dirt is not dirt if only you laugh at it. Thus a man when he steps into a pool of liquid road-scrapings does not soil his boots provided he has the grace to laugh.

With us, except the crimes of murder and of poverty, scarcely a crime is left but sexual irregularity. That is to say, when it happens to be found out.

It ruins politicians who, had they cheated on the exchange, swindled a friend, or sold a blind man a lame horse, would have found plenty to excuse them. Breaches of good faith and integrity hardly or ever ruin public men; but breaches of the marriage laws ruin absolutely, and their damnation s eternal, both in the present world and in the next.

In Russia, whilst nothing of the above has any bearing on the public life of any man, all the world knows the state of tyranny under the Government of the Czar. One thing is certain: that in Russia the fight is not obscured as it is here with us. Tyranny and cruelty come out into the open, and all who face them do so at the peril of their lives.

This makes the Russian Radical or Socialist an enemy not only both of Church and State, but of religion as it is taught, and consequently of the morality that religion inculcates.

No English Radical that I have ever met comprehends this attitude, and too few Socialists.

You cannot both serve God and Mammon, say the Scriptures, or, as the proverb hath it, honour and profit cannot go in the same bag.

Enemies of the present state of things must be enemies not only of the State and all its works, political and economical, but of the Churches and their moralities and faiths.

There is no other halting-place for Socialists: either they must reject the whole, or swallow all – or not be honest.

How miserable it is to see a man who calls himself a rebel run to church to save his soul.

First let him satisfy himself he really has a soul to save, and then if he is so anxious on the matter let him save it by good works.

To bring morality back to its real meaning, or, if you like it better, to evolve a new and reasonable morality, that is the problem for us all.

Which of us has not heard of small-souled man, a crafty bargainer, hard to the weak and cringing to the strong, described as a good man, only because no woman ever tempted him?

Yet to call such a creature virtuous is to misuse the word, to tamper with first principles, and erect a vicious standard by means of which all the most vicious attributes of man are overlooked.

Such men swarm thick as flies amongst the Liberals, and the fact that such false standards are accepted, often by Socialists themselves, renders the fight for Liberty as hard, or harder, with ourselves as it is to any country in the world.

When once Goliath stalks into the field, no matter how huge be his shield, how vast his strength, or what the weight and sharpness of his lance, David can match him with a sling.

In England, the giant has the cunning of the serpent, in addition to his strength, David, with us, may smite him all over with his smoothest pebble from the brook, not that he slings over-much, though, for English David is a prudent youth; but none of all his missiles find their mark. The fact is, there is no particular mark to aim at.

The armour is so cunningly contrived that it is quite invisible; but at the same time, equally impenetrable to attack.

The sweater cries out, "Hit the landlord. St. Smug for Liberalism!"

The landlord yells, "Down with the sweater!"

Both of them cry, "St. George for Merry England!"

Thus the Reformer, Socialist, Radical, Anarchist, or what not, stands like a bull in the arena, pawing the sand and bellowing with fury, but impotent to strike.

The attempt to hold at one and the same time Socialist views on economics, and Christo-bourgeois views of what the bourgeois Liberal calls "morality," is the chief difficulty that the reformer finds athwart the path.

Each system of society must have a system of morality suitable to its needs. The remains of feudalism that till a short ten years ago lingered in rural England, were like germs of a disease. So with the system of morality that holds a sexual offence more serious than the most miserable crime against mankind.

No thinking man or woman preaches universal license. Not that they think that it would be a crime against religion, still less because they think such matters have any real concern with what is called society; but they all now that were it general it would be a crime against the race.

Drunkenness, gluttony, cruelty to children and to animals, cheating and sweating, suppression of the truth and defamation, all are far worse offences against mankind than is the overstepping of the line of conduct that Liberal politicians call "the moral code."

Let us see, now, how it works out. In my own recollection I have known three or four public men, men honourable and true, reformers, honest in money matters, and above reproach in all their dealings with their fellow-men in most respects, stuck down and howled at for errors in a matter which their accusers were exempt from, perhaps from lack of opportunity, or of iron in their blood.[274]

No doubt they would have said (patting their paunches): "Our lives at least are clean!"

Strange that the men who heard them should not have perceived that usurers, oppressors of their fellows, gluttons, and money-grubbers do not live pure lives.

The reason no one saw the fallacy of what they said was because so many advanced thinkers on economics, sociology, and the likes are still slaves to the ethics of a bygone age.

This comes from Puritanism, and Puritanism in its very essence is rank tyranny. Moreover, a mean, spying, prurient-minded tyranny. They say that many multi-millionaires, those who endow towns with a public lavatory (but without funds to keep

---

[274] Obviously, one such was Parnell.

it up), that oil and iron lords, compared to whom our richest dukes are just as poor as is our Chancellor, are churchgoers, deeply religious and the husbands of one wife.

What if it is so? Those private virtues have nothing in the world to do with public life. As well when a man sings out of tune and people hiss, exclaim: "He is a Wesleyan!" as to bring forth the private virtues of a sweater as an excuse for him if he shoots down his workmen in a strike.

This strange inversion of the importance of public and of private actions, derived from Puritanism, and still prevailing in the United States, where men call actions "smart" that would make devils grin, is, above all things, the chief reason for the low ideals of all public life.

Get rich, by all means that you can, only get rich, and all the rest will be forgiven to you. That is our practice, no matter what the motto that we use.

Be pure in private; but in public intrigue, suppress the truth, condone oppression of the weak (as at Denshawai, Casa Blanca, or in Tripoli), break every pledge, attribute every low-souled motive to opponents, bully small nationalities, blow wretched negro huts to pieces with shells of melinite [sic], cringe to the knout[275] Czar; it is all right so that you never have fallen into the only sin that damns a Liberal plutocrat − that is to say, if he is caught, and has no time to pay.

As well attempt to console a man whose wife has run off with a friend, by saying that the seducer in his capacity as secretary to the local golf club was an honourable man, and in the House of Commons voted Liberal.

I see the enemy in what is called the Cocoa Press, just as a Frenchman or a Spaniard sees him in the Church.

We all distrust those who put on an air of being better than mankind.

If angels were volplaned suddenly to earth, the chances are that we should loathe them for their superior virtue. How much more shall we loathe those who see all there is to see in modern life − its littleness, or infinite meanness, lack of all ideal, its cruelty, oppression of the weak, its gloom and ugliness, and, standing in their pulpits, bless their Lord that it is good, fair, honourable, improving every day, and that all wrongs will shortly be redressed.

---

[275] A whip.

The enemy is he who knows all this but seeks to stop others knowing it; the man who, always anxious to spy out the private faults of private men, condones the public shortcomings of those of his own party, when the first should be looked at with charity as perhaps incidental to our nature, the others scourged with chains.

□□□□□□

# IRELAND

From the beginning of his political career, Graham had been a vociferous supporter of Irish Home Rule, on the hustings, in print, and at meetings up and down the country, and it had been the support of recently enfranchised Irish voters that had won him his Parliamentary seat. All this had brought him into contact with the leading Irish politicians of the day, and it had been in support of freedom of speech in Ireland, that he had been beaten on 'Bloody Sunday,' and imprisoned.

However, Graham rarely mentioned Ireland in Parliament, as there were: "[. . .] many more able speakers than myself to deal exclusively with that question and were returned exclusively by Irish electors for that purpose."[276] In fact, filibustering by Irish M.P.s, under Parnell's direction, was grinding Parliament to a halt, and in Graham's eyes, holding back legislation on pressing social issues. He soon came to believe, moreover, that Ireland had become a convenient political football for both the Tories and the Liberals to slow down change, and, that the Irish themselves, particularly in Britain, should be fighting for social justice as well as Home Rule.

## HOME RULE
*The People's Press*, 20th of December 1890.

If the working classes had ever asked themselves the question, why the way in which a small fraction of the empire (Ireland) was to be governed, was called a question of such import that all else must be stopped for it, perhaps they would answer as I do, that the reason was because the Whigs and the Tories had found a buffer between them and social questions, and that the tacit understanding had been come to that Home Rule should always be a question.

It was convenient, very to be able to close the mouths of those who asked for labour legislation, with the Home Rule plug. Had they been forced to admit they positively detested the mere idea of labour legislation the people might have found them out . . . If the Irish nation want political rather than social freedom, if they want the Pope to rule their country, if they want to protect their industries, to set up a Republic, if they want all or none of these things, they should have to power to choose them. At present they may be said to be a race apart, caring for naught but national affairs. It may

---

[276] *The Airdrie Express* (25 November 1889) p.5.

be, when they have weighed their "patriots" up and found them merely bourgeois after all, they will tire of them, and try something better.

To the Englishman, Home Rule (for Ireland) is less than nothing. He owes justice to Ireland as he does to Yorkshire and other provinces of the Empire . . . to see the poor Irish cheated and betrayed by both our parties haunts my mind.

It looks as if the Irish and the chiefs of both sections of their party and the Liberal leaders held very different ideas of what Home Rule may be . . . Home Rule to Irishmen seems to have meant a Parliament to settle Irish business, the Land, control the police, appoint the judges, and put on or take off tariffs. To the English party, however, it seems to have meant a sort of select Vestry, sitting on College Green, subservient to the ship of fools in Westminster in all respects.

Thus we have wasted five years of our lives to try to bring about that which no man seems to be able to put in words.

It is pretty fooling enough to say "I am in favour of Home Rule for Ireland," and not say what that means.

Home Rule is not worth having if it does not imply the power to settle the Irish question that is the control of land in Ireland . . .

The right to govern oneself seems a great deal on paper. In real life the right often remains a right but not a power, in consequence of economic conditions. Green flag (with harp) might wave on Dublin Castle. St Andrew's lion (with thistle and bagpipe music) over Edinburgh; and on Carnarvon Tower the national ensign of the Welsh, and still in all these countries sweaters might rule the roost . . . if the Irish want Home Rule (even to separation), why, let them have it, a' God's name. Only let it be understood that here in England (and in Scotland) we are at a bigger job, and that, like ancient Pistol, we shall not fall foul for toys.[277]

~

Fifteen years after Parnell's death, Graham's memories of him were published. He had already developed his impressionistic sketches and portraits that he excelled in, were perfect mediums to convey poignancy and personality, often through his evocation of the ordinary. His reports on the funeral of William Morris - 'With the North-West

---

[277] Henry IV, Part II.

Wind'[278] and of Keir Hardie - 'With the North East-Wind'[279] stand testament to his depth of feeling, and "an eye intil him like a hawk"[280] for the details that others miss. His wisdom, and his disarming honesty, combined with a style that has been described as: 'rhapsodic and metamorphic'[281] to recreate men of flesh and blood, but are also an uncompromising and damning indictment of the British political system.

## An TIGHEARNA:[282] A MEMORY of PARNELL
*Dana* (Dublin), November 1904.[283]

He always seemed to me a creature from another world, or a survival of some older type of man. Not that in ordinary respects he differed from the usual race of all mankind, having their passions, weaknesses, and all the rest developed to the full, together with an incapacity to get his stirrup-leathers the same length, on horseback, when he rode. His strangeness was, as is the strangeness of a faun or hamadryad,[284] beings we all know did exist and have their being, so strongly has their personality been drawn for us and petrified in stone.

Occasionally we feel that characters in poems and in pictures are far more real than the sham human beings who go about in millions, pretending to be men.

The subject of my recollection, and how sad it is to rack the half-sealed chambers of my mind for the impressions of dead friends left on it, as the sun leaves pictures, so some think, indelible on every stone, was one of those whose death strikes us as an injustice and in some way a mistake.

Crossing St. James's Street I well remember seeing the bill, "Death of the Irish Leader," and thinking that it was some error of the press.

Your politician dies, and it appears quite natural. Last week he had his knighthood; a month ago became the last of all the peers, received the garter at the last royal birthday, and now resumes the sleep which was but three parts broken during the whole course

---

278 *The Saturday Review* (10 October 1896) p.389. The day after Morris's death, Frank Harris, the owner and editor of *The Saturday Review*, approached Arthur Symons and G. B. Shaw about writing articles - Symons on Morris's poetry, and Shaw on his Socialism. Harris warned each to "stretch yourself," as Graham's 'stuff' would be hard to beat, whereby he believes that Shaw acknowledged Graham as 'a Master.'
279 *The Nation* (23 October 1915) pp.147-148.
280 Cunninghame Graham: 'Loose and Broken Men,' *The Scottish Historical Review* (January 1913), p.113.
281 William E. Fredeman: 'William Morris's Funeral,' in *The Journal of William Morris Studies* (Spring 1966), p.29.
282 Irish Gaelic: The Lord, or The Chief.
283 Reprinted in 'His People' (1906).
284 A Greek mythological being that lives in trees.

of his life. One pauses, recollects his small peculiarities, his tricks of speech and manner, and then forgets him, half-pitying, half with contempt, thinking an ill-graced actor has passed through the wings, into the freedom of the streets, and left behind him nothing but the remembrance of his faults, when once the electro-plated glamour of the daily press had been rubbed off, leaving the tin all bare.

But when a man, such as was Parnell passes, all the infinities of life fall off, and only his originality and greatness stay. Then it becomes a marvel that the multitude of rats has seen the undoing of a lion. One tries to cipher out in what his influence lay, then gives it up, and is content to say, "I knew him, may he rest well at last.

In the dull, drab and common world of English life where everything is done upon the lowest level that the intellect of man can compass, in which our Gladdies and our Dizzies, with Pam and Bright and Buckshot Foster [285] and the rest, appear like vestrymen unglorified, a figure such as his seemed almost insolent.

It is too soon perhaps to try to mark his place in history, but since Old Noll[286] (hero in England, and in Ireland devil), perhaps no stronger character has played its part upon the boards of the great theatre at Westminster. He had not eloquence as generally appraised, although at times the intensity of hate he bore us and our twaddling institutions gave him a glacial fire, which scorched even the dull wet-blankets of the House, where all is commonplace.

He was not deeply read, not even in the history of the land for which he fought. He was not humorous, nor had he wit, but now and then inflections came into his voice, which stirred one more than all the spurred-up cape rings of orators, as when he finished up a phrase with "This is going on today in Ireland," in which he put such force and venom that the word Ireland seemed to die upon his lips in froth.

I cannot think of him as popular even at home on his own estate, nor yet at school, still less with his own followers, especially with those of them who sold their Lord, and quite omitted to make sure the thirty pieces should be paid; and when they lost them did not have the grace to hang themselves.

Not popular, in the hail-fellow-well-met and loudly cheered conception of the word, but yet with an attraction for all women whom he came across, who were drawn to him

---

[285] William Edward Foster (1818-1886). A Liberal politician.
[286] Oliver Cromwell.

by his careless treatment of them, and by the wish that nature had implanted in their sex, to be the rulers of all men who stand above their kind.

Straying about the House of Commons after the fashion of a new boy at school, I chanced to sit down quite unthinkingly upon a bench. An Irish legislator edged up and whispered, "You're sitting in his seat."

To this I answered something about the seats being free unless they had a name attached to them, and I fear bade my interlocutor fare to Gehenna by the shortest route.[287] A gentle voice behind me almost whispered in my ear, "Quite right, the seats are free."

This laid the first stone to the building of a desultory friendship which lasted till his death.

Occasionally we dined together, not talking very much, as we had nothing very much in common, except the love of horses.

Of them Parnell knew little, and the little that I knew was almost absolutely from the colonial point of view, so that our theories did not conflict, as often happens between friends. On politics we never talked, as upon almost every point we disagreed, he leading a great party, I being a mere unit of an amorphous crowd of Nonconformists, Temperance Reformers, Deceased Wife's Sisters Monomaniacs,[288] and Single Taxers, with all the faddists and the dried fruit of outworn Liberal politics which at that time the tide of Liberalism had left like jelly-fish and seaweed, stranded and dying on the beach.

And what a beach it was, strewn with dead remains of Leagues and Foundations and Societies, mostly composed of Treasurer and Secretary, long-haired and stammering speakers, all with their theories of prompt regeneration for the body politic, and a collecting box to shove beneath the public's nose.

We raved, we ranted, and we called on Englishmen to rise, to embrace the movement and ourselves, and comprehended that social and political emancipation was at hand and that we were men.

Amongst this herd of addle-brained and sometimes generous, sometimes self-interested reformers (but in all instances belated), which the late lowering of the

---

[287] Go to hell.
[288] A reference to the repeated attempts to legalise such marriages, previously ruled incestuous. Such an Act was passed in 1907.

franchise had let loose upon the world, and most of whom had not sufficient wit to run a coffee-stall, the figure of Parnell stood out, like the Old Man of Hoy[289] stands out against the sea. The little waves of the above referred to muddletonians, who with their iteration damnable and advocacy of reforms long dead, surged round him, almost unnoticed and unnoticeable.

The larger scum of Liberal and Conservative, each again occupied with questions which had long been superannuated, left him unmoved.

The party leaders feared and hated him, for he despised them, and his outlook upon politics seemed but to point out all their lack of strength and capacity.

Gladstone, who though in talk for fifty years, never contrived to say a single thing either original or worth remembering, was overbalanced by him,[290] and Salisbury looked on him as a Turk looks at a native Christian who rebels, whilst Morley, from the dreary, arid heights of Mount Philosophus admired and wondered but supported loyally, although perhaps feeling a little hurt at having to play the second violin to one who knew no Greek. Balfour, by virtue of his æstheticism, was repelled, and did not hesitate to shoot out of mildly philosophic lips. Churchill admired, and perhaps intrigued with him whom without doubt he thought a rebel, but in politics and love all that succeeds is fair. Chamberlain very likely dreamed of some municipal Home Rule, with Parnell as a county councilor glorified, a parliament for gas and sewage, existing by his will in Dublin, and all the Irish Nationalists, appareled in frieze coats and battered hats stuck with dudheens[291] and shillelaghs in their hands, dancing round and singing "Long Live Birmingham."

No one else counted, and in this motley crew of dreamers and of dullards, with here and there an able man upon the make, to give consistency, the Irish Leader jostled for a place.

Whatever were his faults, and I suppose that being human, he had many of them, one thing was clear to me, that above all he hated England and her ways. With what a setting coldness, as of ice upon the edges of a crater, he would say "your country" or "your Queen." Even the House of Commons, stupid as it was, would shiver, and red-

---

[289] A sea-stack on Orkney.
[290] Graham had said that Parnell had been: 'done to death by party factions and by the hypocrisy of Gladstone.' *The Glasgow Evening News* (4 July 1892), p.5.
[291] A clay pipe with a short stem.

faced Tory Squires, and Nonconformists reared on seed-cake and lemonade, rise in their seats, shaking their mottled or their plebeian fists at his calm smiling face.

It did us good to hear him stammer through a speech, misquoting all his notes, halting and trying back, and pouring all the vitriol of his contempt upon us as we sat.

It seemed as if some sort of incoherent Daniel had come to judgment and was about to pass sentence on us all.

The British Parliament for generations had listened to the tirades of all kinds of Irishmen, but they had all been of another sort and different magnitude.

In them, the Saxon was a tyrant and a brute, a sort of Juggernaut, feared and yet envied, who had laid waste the land. But now he figured as an ass, and was ridiculous, whilst all the Irishry, taking their cue from their chief's speeches, publicly thanked their gods that they were Irish, and professed to think that the word English, applied with reference to themselves, was more than infidel, and quite as bad as Protestant, or thief. Thus did the Chief make it impossible for British ministers to take up the "poor Patrick" attitude, which in the past had always been a trump.

No one, I think, was ever hated by the House as was Parnell, and he returned its hate a hundredfold, taking delight in gibing at it, and making it absurd.

Nothing offended him as much as when some hypocritical "Noncon," whom he and Gladstone had kicked round into Home Rule, would walk about the "union of the hearts," and the prophecy that soon all difference of race would be obliterated. Then as he ground his teeth, and his pale cheek grew white with rage, he sometimes muttered "Damn them," with so much unction and such fervency, that one felt sure his prayer, if not immediately vouchsafed would be taken up *ad avizandum*[292]– as the lawyers say, and perhaps be of no avail. But whether it was answered, or fell harmless on the unwholesome air of parliament, it had the effect somehow of setting one a-thinking of how great a fraud the British Empire was, and rousing one out of the feeling of sublime contentment with ourselves, with which we of the Celto-Saxon race are prone to look at things here below, knowing that we enjoy a place apart and specially reserved for us in mansions in the skies with all repairs performed for us, by the Creator of the World.

When we debated with such circumstance, and with citation of innumerable

---

[292] Medieval Latin: In Scots Law, time taken for further consideration of a judgment.

unnecessary figures (the ever-present refuge of a dullard in a speech), some weighty matter of a railroad in the Midland Counties, it was a sight to see the Irish Leader lounge into the House, stroking his beard and pulling his moustache with long white fingers, on which dull sparkled his historic sapphire ring. He would remark half-confidentially to his lieutenant, "Biggar, I think that this debate ought not to finish before twelve o'clock." To which Sancho Panza would reply, "It's quite impossible; I've let the boys away." Then, absently, as if he had never seen the man, or at that instant suddenly became aware that he persisted still in living, Parnell would say, "Tell Gallagher to speak." "Gallagher, sir, the only thing he knows is butter." "Well, let him speak on butter."

And in an instant, Gallagher would rise, quite unprepared, and speaking, maybe, for the first time in that august assembly, which, as a general rule, strikes us of the predominant partnership stark dumb and curdles all our brains.

With figures and with facts, which all looked feasible, the string-pulled member-marionette would thunder forth on the injustice done to Irish industries in general, and that to Irish butter in particular, be the abominable Bill before the House. After an hour, with perspiration running down his face, he would begin to talk about the Irish question as a whole, be pulled up by the Speaker, engage in wrangles with the Tories, and speak and speak, with illustrations of his theme, with so much vigour and aptness, that you began to think a hideous wrong was going to be done. Just about midnight Parnell might saunter in and either say "I think I will not speak," or "Biggar, tell that fool to stop, I wish to say a word." Then word would somehow be conveyed to the rapt orator, who would subside, perhaps in the very middle of the phrase, and Parnell, rising, would proceed, apparently quite coldly but with shut fists, and a light foam about the corners of his mouth, to distil vitriol, drop by drop, into the very should of Englishmen, till Gladstone, putting on his hat, would leave the House, and comfortable Liberals, who had been cultivating a Cork or Limerick brogue, by means of which to show good will to Ireland, would shiver in their broadcloth coats, and curse the day they made him their ally.

No one, I think, since Oliver the Great and Good (I write for the mere Englishry) has made the House of Commons tremble to its cowardly depths, as did Parnell, and never Irishman before or since his time, if we except Hugh Roe O'Neill, has ever

184

treated, upon equal terms, with the old English foe.

Undoubtedly, he both despised and hated Gladstone, who on his part showed plainly that he was in the presence of a stronger man, and though after his death he damned him with faint praise, could not have been much disappointed when, after his nine days' waiting, the Nonconformist cat jumped when it did, and shut Home Rule off for a hundred years.

Not that I think Gladstone did not believe in Ireland's wrongs, but that he did not want to see an Irish parliament led by a man far stronger than himself.

During the days of *sturm und drang*[293] when he was fighting for his soul, I now and then saw him now and then as one sees a figure in a dream.

Once seated in an old-fashioned eating house off the Strand, he wandered in, and seeing me, sat down and talked during the dinner which he could not eat. We spoke of horses, of which, as I have said, he knew but little, and I not overmuch, and then sauntered down to the House, to find it counted out.

Then came his death and funeral, with as it seemed, no one ashamed in Ireland, and everybody secretly pleased in London, as if they felt an enemy of England was gone, as in fact was the case, for he who lets a Briton see he does not reverence him and his country, commits the crime against the British Holy Ghost, a spirit plethoric and heavy, generous but overbearing, and as well stuffed with pride as is an airship or a fire-balloon with gas.

Let him sleep well, a Protestant among the serried graves of those who lie looking towards Rome, whilst they wait the Trumpet's call. A Saxon leader of a Celtic race, a man who, though no orator, yet held enthralled a parliament that lives on talk. Well may his spirit hover hesitatingly between the towers of Westminster, where he enforced respect, and the grey columns of College Green, the unfaithful Mecca, which he never lived to reach.

---

[293] German: Storm and stress.

□□□□□□

# BRITISH IMPERIALISM

The Labour Party's loss was to be literature's gain, as slowly Graham turned his energies to writing for literary magazines, his "favourite exhibition ground"[294] being *The Saturday Review*, the redoubtable owner and editor, Frank Harris having recruited him in 1895.[295] Up until the early 1930s there followed a constant stream of articles, histories, sketches, and reviews, on the subjects closest to his heart - South America, Morocco, and Scotland, many critical of what others regarded as progress, which to him was destroying social cohesion at home, and indigenous peoples and environments abroad:

> His will be accomplished who, having made the earth a paradise, gave it to us to turn into a purgatory for ourselves and all the dwellers in it.[296]

Many of his sketches set in foreign climes have an implicit anti-racist and anti-capitalist message, but he poured his greatest scorn on British imperial ambitions in pamphlets and newspaper articles, at a time when, with Victoria's Diamond Jubilee approaching, fevered imperial jingoism was nearing its height, reaching its blaring crescendo during the Second Boer War, and, the relief of Mafeking in 1900.

There was, however, growing unease and doubt among certain sections of British society over the future and aims of the Empire, while some were concerned that Britain's seeming rush to amass territories, to offset growing challenges to its predominance, was casting it in the role of villain, particularly when the imperatives of empire were laid bare in a white-on-white war. A key event that exacerbated British moral qualms, and international condemnation, was the botched Jameson Raid of 1895 to 1896, which had been aimed at provoking conflict with the Boers. Following this debacle, Rudyard Kipling (whom Graham and his friends regarded as '*the* enemy'[297]) published an extraordinary rallying cry - *Hymn Before Action* (1896), which attempted to consolidate the imperial task, while dismissing foreign anger. It was perhaps no coincidence, then, that Graham published four notable anti-imperialist tracts in 1896 and 1897.

Surprisingly, it was the 'Tory' *Saturday Review* that published Graham's first major anti-imperialist articles, since they were a direct attack on Frank Harris's friend Cecil Rhodes

---

[294] Watts & Davies, p.108.
[295] Never shy of self-congratulation, Harris wrote: 'What a crew of talent to get together on one paper before they were appreciated elsewhere – [H.G.] Wells and [Bernard] Shaw, Chalmers Mitchell, D.S. McColl, and Cunninghame Graham.' Frank Harris, *Contemporary Portraits* (New York, 1920), pp.47-54.
[296] Cunninghame Graham, 'Un Angelito,' *The Saturday Review* (1 January, 1896), p.17.
[297] Edward Garnett, letter to Cunninghame Graham, 26 January 1899. The Manuscript Collection of Admiral Sir Angus Cunninghame Graham, National Library of Scotland.

(whom elsewhere Graham had called 'The Bulawayo Burglar'[298]), and on British intrigues in southern Africa against the Boers, as a means of gaining access to the goldfields and diamond mines.

## FRAUDESIA MAGNA I
*The Saturday Review*, 21st of March 1896.

It is stated that the hatred (almost Biblical in its intensity) entertained by the citizens of the United States towards the inhabitants of these islands is largely due to the virulence and malignity of the views set forth about us in their school-books.

As to whether children are really so much influenced, or not, in early life by the folly of their elders is not within the scope of this article to inquire. We are (perhaps influenced by our school-books) accustomed to declaim against the villainy of Cortes and Pizarro, and generally to say hard things about the Spanish conquest of America. The practice is in some respects a salutary one, for it distracts our attention from the contemplation of our own misdoings and develops a spirit of criticism which has made us beloved by nations.

It is but reasonable to suppose that three centuries of progress and contemplation of our own morality have conduced to a different spirit amongst the "conquerors" of Africa to that which animated the "conquistadores" of America.

We need not look for a Bernal Diaz,[299] nor for a Cortez among them, as, according to Bernal Diaz, Cortez "knew Latin," and even made verses, having been at Salamanca? It is not laid to the account of Oxford that Mr. Cecil Rhodes is not a poet, for "Quod natura non dat, Salamanca non præstat."[300]

In his "History of Paraguay" Father Charlevoix asks if the conquest of America can be held to be lawful, if it can be justified from Scripture, and if the inhabitants of America had been gainers thereby. The first two questions he disposes of in a manner which my lack of acquaintanceship with the rules of theological controversy renders it difficult for me to follow. As to the third he opines that, though the Indians were decreasing rapidly even in his time (1750 *circa*), any temporary inconvenience they might

---

[298] Cunninghame Graham, 'The Dirge of the North Wind,' *The Labour Leader* (7 October, 1896), p.361.
[299] A conquistador in the army of Cortés, who later wrote an account of the conquest of Mexico.
[300] "What nature does not give, Salamanca does not lend." Motto of The University of Salamanca.

feel on that account would be amply compensated for by the introduction amongst them of the true faith. I do not purpose to inquire if the introduction of the hut tax, and the other branches of the numerous true faiths that English, Dutch, Jews, and Portuguese have introduced into South Africa, have compensated the Bushmen, the Hottentots, and others for extinction, or the Matabele, Zulus, and Swazis for subjection. All these matters I leave to theologians, and am content to recognise that it is a glorious fate for any savage to be removed from his sphere of unusefullness by the hand, or through the agency, of an Englishman. What I am concerned with is that, as it is our mission to spread truth, religion, and morality over the world, a cursory examination of some recent events should justify our pretensions.

I am also anxious to make plain that our national characteristics, as truthfulness, modesty, fair dealing, and international generosity, stand as high to-day as when we first perceived that we were the sole depositories of the above-mentioned qualities.

In order more readily to focus the question I will select Johannesburg as the best instance of a town in which our national characteristics have had free play without the somewhat narrowing influence of an inquisitorial public opinion. In order to make plain my meaning, I may perhaps be allowed a short exordium to try to trace the manner in which that city came into existence. First, then, a wide expanse of plain, clothed after rain and grass, and dotted with flowers like the south "camps" of Buenos Ayres in the spring-time, broken into vales by rocky hills, cut into cañon by watercourses, roamed over by countless herds of zebras and hartebeest, by springbok and other antelope after their kind, haunted by lions: a veritable paradise of noble beasts all ready placed there by an all-wise Providence on purpose to make sport for his most favoured nation.

The natives, artless and bloodthirsty barbarians (to the full as void of interest as if they had been all created by Mr. Rider Haggard), passed Arcadian lives without the aid of gin or missionaries, or the necessity to prove that they had worked so many days a year for the white man.

All was content tempered by murder. In the kraals the chiefs exercised a tyranny almost as complete as if they had been British capitalists.

Knobkerries and assegais were relatively so insufficient that, had they not be replaced by British and more moral modern weapons, the game in the Transvaal had been to-day almost as plentiful as game in Norfolk.

188

Enters a train of bullock-wagons, each covered with a tilt, and dragged by many yoke of oxen driven by a Kaffir boy, owned by a race of pious Dutchmen, who thought, as Scotchmen think today, that God himself professed a special interest in their welfare. Big-boned the Dutchmen, and loose-jointed, bearded with Newgate frills,[301] after the Dopper[302] manner; married to vrows of a not very appetising type, whose sole idea of women's rights was to produce a man child every year.

These pious folks were marksmen before the Lord, and horsemen up to a certain point., but never excelling in the art like the Texans or Australians, and without the personal pride which sits so well on Mexicans, Arabs, and Gauchos when in the saddle. Preachers and strong in prayer they were, serving a God who seemed a devil, as set forth by themselves. In their relations with the natives harsh and cruel, as those who feel their faith is the sole true one, and owns good rifles, are apt to be.

Withal not moneygrubbers, and liking even better to hear the singing of the lark than the mouse cheeping in church or Stock Exchange. Haters of modern progress in the form we know it, as they had all been artists or anarchists. This homespun, six-foot, semi-Huguenot, semi-Batavian race soon overspread the land, setting up kraals and houses and a Bethel here and there, and started in to kill the game and to enslave the natives, after the manner of the Spaniards in America and of the English in Australia.

The lives they led resembled (with differences) the lives passed by the Israelites of old in Canaan, their flocks and herds covering the land. Had they set down their fights with the native tribes, and chronicled their and their neighbours' villainy, they might have made a bible almost as curious, though not so *accidentle*, as the old one. But whilst they drank their coffee, smoking their pipes, under their low verandahs, gazing at nothing over the veldt, or rode to town to take the sacrament three times a year, another race was drawing nearer them day by day.

The semi-Portuguese, half-Dutch, half-English Cape Colony, and the territories which the Boers had trekked from to escape the joys of modern life, had little by little all been occupied by God's Englishmen.

Their advance had been of a different nature to the Batavian Hegira.[303] Little by little

---

[301] Whiskers under the chin and jaw.
[302] Pertaining to the Dutch Reformed Church in South Africa.
[303] A migration or journey. From Hejira, the journey of the prophet Mohammad.

(as our custom is) we had - by fighting here and buying there, peddling our gin, extending our influence, opening our markets and broadening our phylacteries - found that to the north the land of Ophir[304] lay. Nothing excites our wrath more fully than to see rich mineral lands in the hands if others. It seems to strike us a sort of coming between the Lord and His anointed.

Agriculture, of course, is necessary, for we must eat; but it should be the work of the fellaheen, of low-riced peasants of the Latin races, or of bankrupt Jew-swept farmers in Dacotah. We should be free to exploit the world and the above referred to Helots.[305]

We have a mission to perform, and to be free to follow it we must have gold and diamond mines in order to obtain a market for our sized cottons and our trash from Birmingham. What matters it to us that, like the Israelites of old or modern Mormons, the Dopper Boers had braved the hunger and the perils of the wilderness to listen without fear of interruption to a Dutch sermon?

Superior morality is not bound by treaties, so no matter that in 1875 and at other times we had agreed to leave the Transvaal to the Boers. Britons were never slaves to treaties when gold was found in an adjoining country. Especially when in the case of pinchbeck[306] Cortes had been growing up not without points of resemblance in his character to him who died in Castilleja de la Cuesta.[307] Cortes, 'tis true, with all his faults, was a brave captain, exposing himself on all occasions like the meanest of his soldiers. History does not relate that Rhodes has been in battle or exposed himself to any peril, except perhaps of bankruptcy.

In love of money and of power he seems at least to equal the conqueror of Montezuma. There the resemblance ends, but some men like to resemble others in their faults. The man of fate was slightly corpulent, in face Napoleonic, with the dull fishy eyes of those who love to dominate; he passed his life just like Trimalchio,[308] amongst his sycophants, thinking (like Louis XI.) that all men, himself included, had their price, taking his Olivier le Daim[309] from Scotland, but hitherto without a Commines- to

---

[304] An Old Testament 'El Dorado.' Genesis 10.
[305] Slaves ruled by Sparta. A subjugated population.
[306] A brass alloy, a cheap imitation. A reference to Cecil Rhodes.
[307] The death-place of Cortes in Seville.
[308] A character in the 1st century AD Satyricon by Petronius. One who through hard work and perseverance attains power and wealth.
[309] A favourite of Louis XI of France. (c.1428-1484) A snide reference to Dr. Jameson.

chronicle his exploits. What was more natural than that after the cycle of bad trade the British aristocracy should turn almost as one peer to any one who showed them chances of wealth unsoiled by work, freed from all responsibility, and almost without risk, except of reputation?

So the Rhodesian wand was waved, and Kimberley arose, like Venus, from the mud, decked out in diamonds, extra Callipyge[310] as benefits a Hottentot. A sordid, dusty in summer, muddy in winter, wilderness of shafts of mines, a hell for mules and oxen, for Kaffirs and for honest men, black, white, or yellow, and a most perfect paradise for Houndsditch Jews and money-grubbing Christians and a sure haven for the demi-mondaine who, in London or in Paris, has outlived her market. Dukes, peers, and even princes, with spavined officers of cavalry, company-mongers, and all the crew of those who bow the knee to all "Amphytrions ou l'on dine,"[311] rushed to share the spoil. When Kimberley itself became too small, and all the territories which may be lumped together as Fraudesia Magna were colonised, then came the usual little wars, the smashing of poor Langalibele,[312] and the various exploits which made the names of Rhodes and Jameson.[313]

'Tis pity when a good Scotch doctor - valiant, moreover, and a good administrator - must leave his guinea-pigs and conscientious vivisection to run a-soldiering. Even the scientific head will turn at times with the flattery of fools.

More pity still when honest unsuspecting men are put forth by designers to take the chestnuts from the fire. When it was found that Salisburia, Randolphia, and Wild Cattia, with British Bankruptana Land, were rich in nothing but the tetze, men's eyes began to turn to the Dutch Naboth's[314] vineyard beyond the Vaal.

~

---

[310] Beautiful buttocks.
[311] A paraphrase from Moliere's 'Amphitryon': "Le véritable Amphitryon est l'Amphitryon où l'on dîne." The person who provides the feast (whether master of the house or not) is the real host.
[312] Langalibelele (c1814 - 1889). King of the Hlubi, a Bantu tribe.
[313] Sir Leander Starr Jameson (1853-1917) A Scottish doctor and close associate of Cecil Rhodes, who led the failed raid by Rhode's private army into part of the Bechuanaland Protectorate, bordering the Transvaal in November 1895, in an attempt to overthrow the Boer government. According to Rudyard Kipling, his famous poem 'If—' was written in celebration of Jameson's personal qualities at overcoming the difficulties of the Raid. It has been suggested that Jameson's relationship with Rhodes was also sexual, but this has never been substantiated. However, neither man married, and, in 1920, Jameson's body was disinterred in England, and buried next to Rhodes in what became Zimbabwe.
[314] Kings 1: 21. The owner of a vineyard coveted by King Ahab.

# FRAUDESIA MAGNA II

*The Saturday Review*, 4th of April 1896.

Beyond the Vaal for almost fifty years the Boers had had free play for self-development. They passed their lives as it seemed to them with profit. They ruled and licked their "niggers," shot their game, rode round their herds, were born, married, died, and left no epitaphs. What if they used no pocket handkerchiefs, and went to bed, fully dressed, and in their boots? Many a good man wishes to die with his boots on rather than in a bed. What matter if they showed but little aptitude for business, and generally refused to enter into the sweet joys of modern life?

If ledgers, telegrams, with shoes, trains, telephones, and vaccination normal schools and School Boards, rights of women, homes for lost dogs, and social purity left them unmoved, they showed an aptitude for other things perhaps as unimportant. With rifle in their hand, on a half-broken horse, they loped across the veldt, on a dark night going as surely where they wanted as a dog returning home. At almost any distance in reason, the Roineck soldier whom they aimed at was as good as dead. If they were, perhaps, a little brutal in their ways, it is the wont of those who live as they did. A healthy, barbarous race of folks, speaking no language but their own, and loving field-sports; given to hospitality and elementary vices.

It is the glory of the British Government never to profit from experience. Sometimes I think the Anarchists are right in saying that government itself is what is wrong; for men who in their private lives, as grocers, lawyers, auctioneers, or soap-boilers, seem quite intelligent, no sooner enter Governments than they run stark mad.

After the example of the East India Company and the various Chartered Companies of times gone by, it seemed a little risky to try another. No Bourbon ever profited so little by facts as British statesmen. So once again we peddled off Imperial responsibility to a job lot of peers, princes, company-promoters, magistrates, and others of those for whom the Prayer Book bids us pray when Parliament is sitting. What happened might have been foreseen even by a member of a County Council.

With much profession of "Imperial interests," "the duties of a conquering race," of "extension of the beneficent influence of British progress," the Chartered Company set out to run its course. First, it annexed a lot of territory which seems not worth a penny; then almost quarreled with the Portuguese; smashed up the Matabele, without a reason, except that it was said that their territory was rich with gold. But all the same their chiefest aim and object seems to have been to pick a quarrel with the Boers.

The "stickit"[315] captains with the herd of those who could not pass examination, the officers on leave [sic] from the British army,[316] the company-promoters and the rest seem to have thought that on them lay the onus of revenge for our defeats at Bronkerspruit and Majuba[317] - at least they said so in the bar-rooms. So that the feeling of antagonism which nearly a generation of peace had almost stilled daily became more keen betwixt the Britishers and the Boers.

Two of one family scarcely can agree in business and it may be that the Boers and ourselves were too akin to pull together. What wonder that the ignorant and semi-barbarous Dutch farmers thought they had met and smashed the power of Britain after their victories! What wonder that the English farmers and settlers chafed under the rough taunts of men as brutal maybe as themselves!

The Anglos-Saxon race, great as it is, wants above every other race the restraining influences of civilisation to make it pleasant to deal with. Therefore doubly was Imperial control of paramount necessity on the Dutch frontier. Unfortunately, some twenty years ago, gold had been found in the Transvaal. When we consider that the Premier of the Cape was emperor at Bulawayo, and possibly largely concerned in mining enterprises at Johannesburg, the reason of the constant bickerings of Englishmen and Boers becomes quite plain.

The Government of the Transvaal seems to have been quite aware of what was sure to happen when the mines were opened in Johannesburg. On the one hand a pastoral population living in the country, and on the other a mass of all the heterogeneous scum which always floats to gold mines. Still, gold mines in South Africa seem to collect a somewhat different population from that which congregated in California and Australia. In neither of the latter countries was there a native population to be found ready to work; therefore the fortune-hunter had to do his digging for himself, and thus became capable of facing hardships, and not a swaggering capitalistic boaster ready to talk and careful of his carcass like the Outlander of Johannesburg.

---

[315] Stuck. Usually referring to someone who cannot get promotion. It may also be a literary allusion to S. R. Crockett's short story: 'The Stickit Minister' (1893), written in the 'Kailyard' style, which Graham despised.
[316] The implication here is that there was British Government and army complicity.
[317] British defeats during the First Boer War 1880-1881.

Gold-mining is pleasant sport enough when, seated in your office, you fleece the public in a Christian manner and let the niggers do the digging. Pleasant moreover in a sort of Bedford Park or Turnham Green with a good climate; for at Johannesburg the "artistic" terra cotta and red brick Victorian Queen Anne aesthetic style of architecture has had full sway, and alternates with blocks of buildings in the Palladian Ebenezeresque; with all the horrors of plate-glass, and free advertisements, fashionable suburbs, native quarters of the town, residences of our prominent citizens, and everything a Houndsditch Jew, or New Cut Christian suddenly made rich, might sigh for.

Add to these beauties of art a situation in a dreary plain; spice well with loafers, Kaffirs, Jews, and a few Malays, some Dutchmen come to town to sell their wool, dozens of tramps, plenty of Englishmen upon the make, with others on the burst, and more or less you see the place. There is of course the aristocracy - that is, of money - and the controlling spirit of that well-known revolutionary party which lured poor Dr. Jameson to Krugersdorp[318] and then made terms with Kruger[319] whilst he was fighting.

In a place composed as is Johannesburg, one does not look for Christian virtues, as the people are all there in order to make money, and not to preach the Gospel. Still, a little courage does not come amiss even to money grubbers. Then, too, we English are a generous race, and virtue in distress, even in theatres, is always a trump card. Yet here were Englishmen fighting, as they perhaps believed, for the lives of Englishmen, and still the Reform Committee of Johannesburg, instead of mounting more or less barbed steeds, was capering nimbly in Paul Kruger's chamber to the lascivious pleasing of a dudlesack.[320]

We are told that the chief spirits were athletes to a man, one of them being the champion runner of South Africa; and no doubt their strength, just like their hearts, was in their heels. As yet not one of the capitalist revolutionaries has denied the soft impeachment of the letter to Dr. Jameson. Till that is done, the leaders of the Outlanders must be set down as cowards. Indeed, it seems but little valour was in the place; for in the ignoble panic which ensued we hear of burly Cornish miners trampling

---

[318] The site where Jameson's force was repelled by the Boers.
[319] Paul Kruger (1825-1904). An Afrikaner political and military leader who served as President of the South African Republic (or Transvaal) from 1883 to 1900.
[320] A European bagpipe.

194

on children and throwing women out of railway carriages in their extremity of terror. That "Cowards' Van" was written on the cattle-trucks which carried them, unless the writers of the legend were Boers, seems to have been a little hypercritical on the part of the men of valour like the reforming runaways, who planned the scheme and failed to face the music.

Let us examine for a moment what was the position of the foreigners within the town. No doubt they bore the greatest burden of the taxes, and no votes; but then their object in Johannesburg was to make money, and not to pose as social emancipators. The Boers, no doubt, regarded all of them, even the richest, as a set of money-grubbers whose souls were in their pockets, and to whom votes were quite unnecessary. I do not say that the Boers were right; but men who, like the Boers, fight better than they talk are apt to take this view of men of business.

Then comes another question. In the reforming schemes so well thought out by the Reform Committee it does not seem a place was found for the "niggers" who worked the mines. Suppose the *coup d'état* had not miscarried, how had the position of the Kaffir workers been benefited? 'Tis strange the Cornish miners never thought of joining in the demand for votes. Might it have been that they looked to the Boers to protect them from the greed of Christian and Jew capitalists?

And the historic raid itself, the foray of the well-born moss-troopers,[321] commanded by the younger sons of peers and officers of Household Cavalry on leave, all honourable and very pushful men.

No one denies that a Transpontine[322] *Pax Britannica* hung over the land. All was at peace. The Matabele smashed, the native tribes in general almost cowed, no quarrel between the Courts of Windsor and Pretoria.

True there had been a fall in Chartered shares, and generally a feeling that the gold in British South Africa, outside the Transvaal, might all be carried in a hat-box. Nothing, as far as we know, had transpired to ruffle the relations between the rival claimants for the future throne or Presidential chair of the South African Republic or Empire. Hofmeyr[323] and Rhodes, although no doubt hating each other like true friends, still

---

[321] Soldiers of fortune, mercenaries, who roamed Scotland in the mid 17th century.
[322] Latin: Across the bridge. In this case, 'overseas.'
[323] Jan Hendrik Hofmeyr, 'Onze Jan,' (1845-1909). An Afrikaner politician and journalist.

outwardly were one.

Paul Kruger had not signified that he intended to attack the capital of Cape Colony. We are gravely asked to believe that peaceable Dutch farmers, as stolid as if they had come from Aberdeenshire, were about to butcher citizens whose only crime was to have asked for votes, and put the honour of their wives in peril. Had they been Arabs, Indians, Turks, Armenians, or Cossacks, the thing might have been true; but Dutchmen and Dutchmen of the Dopper type, it passes credibility.

Our mission (if we had one) in South Africa was to show the benighted people how Englishmen behave in matters national and international. Therefore, for months before the event we allow our Chartered Company to mass police on the frontier of the Transvaal. We allow our fellow-countrymen in Johannesburg to boast of the rifles and Maxims which it turned out they had not got, and to insult the National Anthem of the country in which they lived, in open theatre. Then came the raid led by the Scottish Doctor, luckily not clothed in the habit of old Gaul.[324]

Being a doctor, and therefore used to blood, he seems to have kept what little head the flattery he had received for his exploits against the Matabele had left him. At any rate, he faced the dangers of his silly expedition like a brave man, and still has time, if fools will let him, to take a quiet Scottish practice in Aberdeen or Peebles, and beat his sabre back again into a bistoury.[325] When it was known in England that the brave five hundred had not run away, but stood some hours of fire, how the pæans of British pluck burst forth! When in the past have Britons ever quailed, even against far greater odds than those of Krugersdorp?

But, then, 'tis said how splendid was their conduct. Look at the distance they covered in the saddle. It now appears the distance from the frontier to Krugersdorp is about one hundred and twenty miles, thus giving two days' ride of sixty miles a day.

Now, though I am myself a man by nature quite as unwarlike as any other Outlander, and look on a horse as only a trifle less terrific than a tiger, I am told by those who know, that our Indian cavalry frequently accomplish sixty miles a day, and in a climate far severer than the climate of South Africa. And then the hardships that they underwent, the men and horses being represented as having passed two days without

---

[324] Kilted.
[325] A scalpel.

provisions, which seems strange when, in the evidence at Bow Street, it is sworn that every twenty miles there was a sort of barroom for the men and stables for the beasts.

It may be that the valour, or at least the skill, of both the Boers and Jamesonians has been overestimated. To the civilian mind it seems a little curious that the Boers should have fired for thirty hours upon a handful of mounted men halted on an open plain, and only killed some twenty of them. But if the shooting and the tactics of both sides were poor, their power of imagination seems to have been immense. The Boer loss is put down at anything from three hundred to six thousand, their dead from four to about three hundred.

In fact, imagination seems to have been about what there was most of in the field of Krugersdorp. One thing, 'tis true might have been done, but was omitted. In times gone by your Englishman died game. If in a sea fight he got the underhand, he nailed his colours to the mast and went down cheering. No matter what the odds by sea or land, he seldom capitulated. Cervantes who himself had fought in the great battle of Lepanto, observes that the soldier makes a better show dead on the battlefield, than safe in flight. He might have said the same about capitulation, if at the time the word had been in the Spanish dictionary.

It does not fall to the lot of every one who comes under capitulation almost without conditions to meet a conqueror like old "Oom Paul."[326] If he had ranged the whole five (or four) hundred in a row and shot them in the market-place of Johannesburg, we might have pitied, but could not have avenged them. I who write these lines have seen five hundred men full of life and hope - that is, the hope that most men have of not too unpleasant life and easy death - stuck up against a wall and "executed," and can well remember at the last fire all who remained erect were one old man smoking a cigarette, and quite composed, and a young soldier clasping a crucifix. However, in South America men "play and pay," and are not returned as "empties" to the mother-country, to become the heroes of the nation they have disgraced.

It may be, if good Father Charleroix[327] were to write the story of our doings in South Africa, that he might give a different answer to his own three questions. Laying aside the blessing of the true faith, which I suppose some of us must have introduced

---

[326] 'Uncle Paul.' Paul Kruger.
[327] A French Jesuit priest (1682-1761). The first historian of French-colonised North America.

into South Africa, where are the other blessings (apart from gin and powder) which we have given to the natives?

No one can say the Chartered Company has been a blessing, even in disguise. If to work hard and be a sort of helot is a blessing, the Dutch and English rulers have done much good; for now, I understand that Kaffirs have to show at the year's end a tale of days worked for their conquerors. Labour twice sanctifies the Kaffir (and the Briton); it blesses him who toils, for in itself it carries sanctity; it also blesses him who profits by the labour, and surely that is much. If want of faith, and love of gold and greed for power, with lack of common courage (which a bulldog has) to stand by friends in peril, are an example, why the natives are greatly in our debt.

England, perhaps, is justified, if not by works, by her humiliation; for, once again, the whole world thinks us liars.

No one will credit that the personally conducted picnic from Mafeking was kept a secret from all in London and the Cape. We still are brave and true, honest and generous, as Britons always have been; but a censorious world, perhaps, will call the qualities in doubt.

In the whole sordid and tinpot affair none have emerged with credit. Rhodes is a sort of unofficial exile, his Charter almost doomed. Hofmeyr has rounded on his friend, and Thatcher[328] cannot draw. The fifteen pushful warriors of Bow Street are becoming a joke for Gods and men, and the curtain seems about to fall on a dismal farce.

From the rank wash of scum and duckweed rises out "Oom Paul," like a Batavian Neptune, and so triumphant that he is reported to have sent to Manchester for pocket handkerchiefs (for the first time in his life), to be made of good stout bunting, striped like the Union Jack.


## THE IMPERIAL KAILYARD: BEING a BITTER SATIRE on ENGLISH COLONISATION

*Justice: The Organ of Social Democracy*, 5th of September 1896.[329]

In order to prevent misapprehension, I may say at once that I am for Liberty,

---

[328] "Captain" Frank Thatcher who had been part of the Jameson Raid, and who had tried to paint the debacle as an heroic failure in the *Illustrated London News*.
[329] Also a pamphlet published by The Twentieth Century Press.

Property, and Old England; that I believe in virtue, magnanimity, righteousness, British fair play, the rights of man, and other things of that nature.

Believing as I do in the above national articles, and holding as I do that if such things exist they were invented and patented in England, and that it is impossible without infringement of copyright for any foreign nation, or any individual member of a foreign nation, either to use, aspire to, or in any way to become possessed of any of the aforesaid qualities, or virtues, I own that some recent events have caused me to doubt a little as to the hereditary continuity of moral qualities. I do not think that these doubts render me of necessity either a bad citizen or a disloyal subject. Let me say, therefore, in extenuation of my views, that I am neither an Anarchist nor a member of the Church of England. In my childhood I remember being stirred almost to enthusiasm when I was informed that wherever the British flag floated, all were free and equal before the law, irrespective of race, position, or colour.

All free and independent - the poor elector independently blacking boots, and the rich elector as independently running his course as the bridegroom of the scriptures - it pleased my elders to thus instruct me, and though, with the natural scepticism of youth, I received the information with the distrust that all coming from my elders merited, yet, with the diplomacy of the weak, I forebore to question statements, which I might have been compelled to believe by superior force. The sanctity of British soil, the superior virtue and chivalry of my countrymen, their justice, toleration, and fair dealing with all stronger than themselves, and their generous commercial attitude to weaker nations than themselves, grew to be my more serviceable creed.

With this, and a firm belief in the immutability of female virtue, I felt myself fairly equipped to face the world. The many sacrifices of principle and common-sense, that most men have to endure in order to adjust themselves to the exigencies of their belief, I went on making cheerfully and for years, in order to adapt myself to the creed I had been nurtured in, and only the evidence of my senses and the testimony of an occasional newspaper have caused me to reconsider my position upon the two cardinal items of my ethical programme.

Slowly but surely I have been compelled to abandon the second article of my belief, so that to-day, except from a purely legal standpoint, even seduction seems less founded on probability.

In relation to the first, it may be my mental vision has become distorted, for who am I to set myself against the universal self-approbation of a mighty empire? Nothing of all this need discourage a philosopher. The world was made for us, that is for Englishmen, and if in certain portions of it Norman French law conflicts with Roman Dutch, both are agreed that Hollander, Royneck [sic],[330] and Africander, must rule in Africa. There were, I think, some natives, as Kaffirs, Zulus, Hottentots, Basutos, and still there are some Matabeles, but what of that? None of them ever wore a *hault de chausse*[331] or rode a bicycle. Therefore it is clear that Britons are not bound by the same moral standard in their dealings with them, as if they were Europeans.

Principles, Maupassant has justly said, are by their very nature false and sterile. Are they not ideas reputed fixed and immutable? Fixed and immutable ideas in a world where all is changing, where light is an illusion, where sound is an illusion of our senses. I do not mean to say that Maupassant is, as a philosopher, likely to replace Tupper in England, but still even from a Frenchman you may sometimes gather wisdom.

Principles, of course, are acted on by isothermal lines. That which is right in London, is inexpedient at Buluwayo [sic]. Commerce is founded, as are politics, upon expediency, and Britain is the home of commerce.

It may be now and then in opening up a new found territory that some slight injustice may be done. But what of that? No change can be accomplished without some class, some race, or individual suffering some loss. Surely, then, the death or wounds, captivity, or even the extermination of some few thousand savages, cannot be weighed against the blessings of the telegraphic service, postal communications, free trade in drink, or the retailing of the same after the plan of Gothenburg.

Let us then keep on and spread the light, make ever broader the phylacteries of our empire, open up markets, and make ourselves hating and hateful to all mankind. To ensure a self-supporting and prompt millennium, all that is wanted is more markets. Therefore, we must grab all we can, and where we can, even if now and then a grabber is forced to herd with criminals, as a first-class misdemeanant. The phrase to "open up the country" stirs one's soul. Visions of Drake, of Hawkins, and of Captain Kidd, of Aaron Burr, of Claude du Val, Jack Shepherd, Xenophon, Sir Walter Raleigh, and

---

[330] Afrikaans: 'Redneck.' A British person, or English-speaking South African.
[331] Breeches.

other noble spirits, who launched their barques into an unknown sea in hopes to find the Indies, rise and excite our minds. The explorer, hunter, trapper, lumberman, and "mustanger" with their rifles, cap of skins, lean horse, long knife, and their flint and steel; with their large faith, endurance, spirit of adventure, and occasional brutality, rise from the fiction of Mayne Reid,[332] and trouble our imagination.

Hakluyt and Pemberton and Mungo Park, with Burton, Burkhardt and the rest, as Captain Cook and the Valhalla of the Spanish navigators, who first filled the maps with names, have drilled us to think well of all adventurers. As boys we followed their adventures, wept at their troubles, fought with them in imagination, sailed with them, and were knighted alongside them by good Queen Bess, or Ferdinand the Catholic on their return. Thus it is in part our minds are moulded to judge favourably of conquerors from youth. Then the odds seem so great. Cortes in Mexico, alone upon the causeway battling for his life, Rhodes or Pizarro charging amongst the thickest of the foe, seem so heroic. Still, if we pause to think, the odds are all the other way. War club, assegai and boomerang, bolas, parang and krise, even if wielded by thousands avail but little against quick-firing guns. In stern reality the "native" is the hero, and the European "conquistador," as Beit, Barney Barnato, Selous,[333] -Rhodes and Co., nothing but cowardly interlopers, presuming on superior weapons.

To open up a territory, then, is something glorious in itself, and also adds to the area of the British Empire. Paterfamilias, when he finally gets off his useless son, imagines him in Africa, extending British influence somewhat as follows:

A fine young fellow in his knickerbocker breeches and tan gaiters, with large straw hat and moral tone, riding about the country, giving orders to obsequious natives. A splendid shot and horseman, though a duffer of the duffers ere leaving home. Distance is sure to make a man a marksman and a rider, though in point of fact most colonists seldom discharge a gun, and as for riding, only those born in the country, or who have gone there very young, ever venture upon a horse except it be as quiet as a cow.

In young hopeful's district his father sees him manfully fighting the wilderness

---

[332] Thomas Mayne Reid (1818-1883). A Scots-Irish writer of popular boys adventure novels, mostly set in the Wild West.
[333] Frederick Courteney Selous DSO (1851-1917). An English explorer, soldier, and big-game hunter, famous for his exploits in Southeast Africa. A close friend of Cecil Rhodes and Theodore Roosevelt. Reputedly his real-life adventures inspired H. Rider Haggard to create the fictional Allan Quatermain.

and making money, though he does no work; for work degrades a man who does not profit by it. Throughout the districts all the farms are owned by gentlemen. In the bush stores no sale of alcohol or gunpowder is permitted to the natives. Trifling with the native women is prohibited by law. On Sunday, in the log-built church shaded by palm trees, the preacher (a graduate of St. Bees) holds forth on home, on British pluck, and inculcates the elementary virtues. All is quite homelike, except the offertory, which sometimes dwindles owing to the lack of circulating medium.

After some five or even seven years are passed, Hopeful returns with liver and fortune, quite unstained by toil, a little boastful about our Empire, perhaps a little inclined to drink, sunburned, but still refined and quite a gentleman.

Reality beholds him in a palm tree hat, red shirt, high boots, and redolent of gin and strong tobacco, crammed in a hut with three more graduates of Oxford, a dead, decaying horse before the door; his cook a native woman, who washes for the camp, and serves by turn at night as concubine to all four. If he elects a country life, he soon becomes a brute, an honest, whisky-drinking brute, treating the natives not unkindly, but in the British way that now and then brings on a mutiny in India or a revolt in Matabeleland.

If he stays in the country he makes no money, sometimes works hard, at intervals lies back for weeks, cursing his folly for leaving England. Needless to say, he gathers nothing worth gathering about the land he lives in. Its botany, geology, its flora never appeal to him. Its fauna may be good for sport, but the damned Dutch, the infernal natives, or the cursed prairie fires, for everything has its condemnatory adjective in his vocabulary, render game scarcer day by day.

If on the other hand, he casts his lot amongst the dwellers in the towns, his fate is often different. At first, of course, he tries some business which a gentleman can enter without contamination. Sets up as a horse-dealer, or in the wine trade, and comes to grief. After a while he goes upon the local stock exchange, buys, sells, cheats, wins, and takes the steamer home - a millionaire - to build his palace in Tyburnia.[334]

Take him for all in all, the Briton colonises well, and would do better if he could ever look at anything from any other standard than that of Tooting. Neither in Canada,

---

[334] The area between Paddington Station and Hyde Park, in London's West End.

Australia, Tasmania, nor any portion of the earth, where hitherto we have carried ourselves, our flag, our beer, and our institutions, have we developed characteristics like those which Africa calls forth. In our dealings with the natives in older colonies, our intolerance has been tempered by lack of ammunition, and a sort of furtive kindness, which lurks in our natures, if the object on which we exercise it is submissive. One sees a carter crack a whip, with a report like thunder, at the horse he cleans and feeds, and loves far better than his wife, and which he never touches with his thundering whip. He likes to crack it, merely to show his power and to remind the horse what is in store for it, if it should rebel. Such was the Briton's attitude in days gone past. He did not generally ill-treat the "nigger" - only despised him in a sort of amicable manner. In Africa the scene has changed, and the "nigger" has no rights at all, except, of course, to clear out to the inferior lands and work for master at the rate that master chooses. We know, of course, that birds of Paradise, with the small heron, the humming bird, the giraffe, zebra, and all living things, which can be made in any way to minister to fashion, must disappear.

In the same way the "nigger" is also bound to go. What business has a man in his own country to hunt and shoot, refuse to till the soil, or till it only by the labour of his wives, buying no ploughs from us? What right has anyone to anything, if he can make no rifles to defend it? It may be we have gone a little fast in Africa. At least, the howl of hatred raised by all Europe and America against us, during the past six months, would seem to prove it. Not that I think the French, the Germans, or the Scandinavians, would have behaved an atom better than ourselves. The fault lies in our mode of life and the facilities for quick communication, even more than in ourselves. In former days, the colonist planted there for life, he had to learn the native ways by contact with them, and in the end he got to understand and to treat them more on an equality. To-day a steamer in a fortnight or three weeks takes a man home to England, and so he never rubs his English angles off, and still remains a stranger in the land he lives in. Throughout South Africa, we have had full scope to civilise the natives. We have dressed them in our clothes, and tried to fashion them as much as possible in our own image. We taught them commerce, established schools in which they learned geography, history, and as much arithmetic as was expedient for them. When possible, we took away their wives, and forced them to rely on prostitution in our own way, to satisfy their natural

203

polygamic tendencies which all men have. We found their native beer too weak, and gave them whisky. Even their diseases seemed too childish for our conversing and we brought the small-pox and syphilis under their observation. Lastly, their "gri-gris" and "fetishes" did not seem apt to us, and so we sent our missionaries to spread the true faith, each missionary belonging to a different, and differing sect, and setting forth the tenets of the faith according to his individual ignorance of its true nature. And we have prospered greatly.

Commerce has prospered, fortunes have been made, and towns have risen, where ten years ago, the springbok and the hartebeest roamed o'er the veldt. The natives are in full revolt against our power and all goes well.

How though does all this spreading of the empire, waving of the flag, thundering of cannons and of speeches in our own praise react upon us? Much the same way as slavery reacted on the planters in South Carolina, who were themselves as much degraded by their "institution" as their "niggers." Never before has such a tone of boasting spread over all the nation. Never before have officers and gentlemen entered into such low and base intrigues as the one the world has talked so much about. Seldom before have Englishmen not fought, when fighting came in their way, to the bitter end. Certainly never in the history of our race have there been such determined efforts to defeat justice, or such an outcry when that justice tardily did justice on some electro-plated filibusters.

But more than all, a tone of callousness is spreading over our dealings with the natives of South Africa. Young gentlemen write letters to the *Westminster Gazette* dwelling with pleasure on an execution in Bulawayo. The twitching of his face, the kicking of his legs, "the nigger's cheek," the weather at the time; all is dished up as if it were a matter his mother would be glad to hear of. Reporters, as in duty bound, report or else invent the casualties upon the "native" side; chronicling with much fidelity "the killing of some sixty 'natives' by our 'brave fellows.' "

If, on the other hand, a friendly native happens to get killed, he is returned as "slaughtered." On rare occasions when an imperial Englishman is slain, he has a special paragraph all to himself, generally headed in leaded type, "Massacre of Another Englishman." Lord Grey, who was, I remember, not at all a swaggerer or even very fond of blood at Harrow, is almost always nearly under fire; if not he, then Mr.

Cecil Rhodes has heard the firing quite distinctly from his tent. That way "Buncombe"[335] [bunkum] lies. "Buncombe" itself is harmless, even amusing, but when, after the description of a fight, a sentence closes the article [which] deplores that owing to the natives falling flat among the bush the machine guns could not play properly upon them, the case is different. Readers will see at once what cowardly brutes the Matabele are. At great expense the Chartered Company had introduced quick-firing guns to enable them to cope with the assegais and old trade guns of the Matabele. But not content with that we had endeavoured by our own example to make them understand how white men think and fight, and to enable them to comprehend fair play and patriotism and our other qualities.

All was as nothing. At the first attack the savage instinct was too strong, and shame of shames, instead of standing in the usual way to be mowed down, these barbarous wretches threw themselves upon the ground, rendering other tactics useless, putting us to vast expense in ammunition, and showing the world it is impossible to civilise such a degraded people. Our missionaries, I take it, are to blame for not instructing the chief and headmen of the "niggers" that the first duty that a Matabele owes to Queen Victoria is to stand upright like a man and let our gunners have a chance to play their Maxims in a proper way upon them.

Again, we have the episode of the alleged "shooting" of the native god M'Limo. On this occasion two "heroes," an American and a Briton, set out to capture this official in his own house. In an open and heroic fashion they approached him with gifts, and what the writer describes as "offertories," but leaves us in the dark as to what these "offertories" were. "Accosting him, they said they came to beg his blessing." How like a Briton their conduct was. No artifice after the foreign fashion; merely his blessing, which they must have been in need of. "Being decoyed by M'Limo into his cave, and seeing the treachery of the natives rendered capture imminent, and finding, in the circumstances, it was impossible to capture the prophet alive, Burnham, without further hesitation, shot him in the cave." A most heroic deed, heroically conceived, well carried out, and quite successful but in one respect, and that is that it was a lie, for recent telegrams declare the M'Limo is alive. Such an adventure, if it had occurred, might

---

have been justified by the result. As it appears, it is apocryphal. It seems to show the kind of faith that Europeans keep with the natives of South Africa, even in their moments of imagination. No one doubts that eventually that the Matabele will be conquered, and that our flag will wave triumphantly over the remnant of them, in the same way as it waves triumphantly over the workhouse pauper and the sailor's poor whore in the east end of London. Let it wave on over an empire reaching from north to south, from east to west; wave over every island, hitherto ungrabbed, on every sterile desert and fever-haunted swamp as yet unclaimed; over the sealer amid the icebergs, stripping the fur from the live seal, on purpose to oblige a lady; over the abandoned transport camel, perishing of thirst on the Soudan; and still keep waving over Leicester Square, where music halls at night belch out their crowds of stout imperialists.

~

## BLOODY NIGGERS

*The Social Democrat,* April, 1897.

That the all-wise and omnipresent God, to whom good people address their prayers, and for whose benefit, as set forth in the sustentation of his clergy, they hoard their threepenny bits all through the week, is really but a poor, anthropomorphous animal, is day by day becoming plainer and more manifest. He (Jahvé) created all things, especially the world in which we live, and which is really the centre of the universe, in the same way that England is the centre of the planet, and the Stock Exchange is the real centre of all England, despite the dreams of the astronomers and the economists. He set the heavens in their place, bridled the sea, disposed the tides, the phases of the moon, made summer, winter, and the seasons in their due rotation, showed us the constant resurrection of the day after the death of night, sent showers, hail, frost, snow, thunder and lightning, and the other outward manifestations of his power to serve, to scourge, or to affright us, according to his will.

Under the surface of our world he set the minerals, metals, the coal, and quicksilver, the platinum, gold, and copper, and let his diamonds and rubies, with sapphires, emeralds, and the rest, as topazes, jacinths, peridots, sardonyx, tourmalines, or chrysoberyls, take shape and colour, and slowly carbonise during the ages.

Upon the upper crust of the great planet he caused his plants to grow, the trees, bushes of every kind, from the hard, cruciform-leaved caramel to the pink-flowering Siberian willow. Palm trees and oaks, ash, plane, and sycamore, with churchyard yew, and rowan, holly, jacaranda, greenheart and pines, larch, willow, and all kinds of trees that flourish, rot, and die unknown in tropic forests, unplagued by botanists, with their pestilent Pinus Smithii or Cupressus Higginbottomiana, rustled their leaves, swayed up and down their branches, and were content, fearing no axe. Canebrakes and mangrove swamps; the immeasurable extension of the Steppes, Pampas, and Prairies, and the frozen Tundras of the north; stretches of ling and heather, with bees buzzing from flower to flower, larks soaring into heaven above them; acres of red verbena in the Pampa; lilies and irises in Africa, and the tacuaras, the istlé and maguey, flax, hemp, esparto, and the infinite variety of the compositæ,[336] all praised by name.

Again, in the Sahara, in the Kalahari desert, in the Libyan sands, and Iceland, he denied almost all vegetation, and yet his work seemed good to those his creatures - Arabs, Bosjemen, reindeer, and Arctic foxes, with camels, ostriches and eider ducks who peopled the waste spaces. He breathed his breath into the nostrils of the animals, giving them understanding, feeling, power of love and hatred, speech after their fashion, love of offspring (if logic and anatomy hold good), souls and intelligence, whether he made their bodies biped or quadruped, after his phantasy. Giraffes and tigers, with jerboas, grey soft chinchillas, elephants, armadillos and sloths, ant eaters, marmots, antelopes, and the fast-disappearing bison of America, gnus, springboks and hartbeest, ocelot and kangaroo, bears (grisly and cinnamon), tapirs and wapiti, he made for man to sheet, to torture, to abuse, to profit by, and to demonstrate by his conduct how inferior in his conception of how to use his life, he is to them.

All this he did and rested, being glad that he had done so much, and called a world into existence that seemed likely to be happy. But even he, having begun his

---

336 A large family of dicotyledonous plants.

work, was seized with a sort of "cacoethes operandi," and casting about to make more perfect what, in fact, needed no finishing touch, he took his dust, and, breathing on it, called up man. This done he needed rest again, and having set the sun and moon just in the right position to give light by day and night to England, he recollected that a week had passed. That is to say, he thought of time, and thinking, made and measured it, not knowing, or perhaps not caring, that it was greater than himself; for, had he chanced to think about the matter, perchance, he had never chosen to create it, and then our lives had been immeasurable, and our capacity for suffering even more infinite that at present, that is, if "infinite" admits comparison. However, time being once again created and man imagined (but yet perfected), and, therefore, life the heavy burden being opposed [sic] on him, the Lord, out of his great compassion, gave us death, the compensating boon which makes life tolerable.

But to return to man. How, when, why, wherefore, whether in derision of himself, through misconception, inadvertence, or sheer malignity, he created man, is still unknown. With the true instinct of a tyrant (or creator, for both are one), he gave us reason to a certain power, disclosed his acts up to a certain point, but left the motives wrapped in mystery. Philosophers and theologians, theosophists, positivists, clairvoyants, necromancers, cabalists, and Rosicrucians and alchemists, and all the rabble rout of wise and reverend reasoners from Thales of Miletus down to Nietzsche, have reasoned, raved, equivocated, and contradicted one another, framed their cosmologies, arcana, written their Gospels and Korans; printed their Tarot packs, been martyred, martyred others (fire the greatest syllogist on earth), and we no wiser.

Still man exists, black, white, red, yellow, and the Pintos of the State of Vera Cruz. A rare invention, wise conception, and the quintessence of creative power rendered complete, for we must think that even an all-wise, all powerful God (like ours) improves by practice.

An animal erect upon its feet, its eyes well placed, its teeth constructed to masticate all kinds of food, its brain seemingly capable of some development, its hearing quick, endowed with soul, and with its gastric juices so contained as to digest fish, flesh, grain, fruit, and stand the inroads of all schools of cookery, was a creative masterpiece. So all was ready and the playground delivered over beautiful to man, for men to make it hideous and miserable.

Alps, Himalayas, Andes, La Plata, and Vistula, Amazon, with Mississippi, Yangtsekiang and Ganges, Volga, Rhine, Elbe and Don; Hecla and Stromboli, Pichincha, and Cotopaxi, with the Istacihuatl and Lantern of Maracaibo; seas, White and Yellow, with Oceans, Pacific and Atlantic; great inland lakes like Titicaca, Ladoga, all the creeks, inlets, gulfs and bays, the plains, and deserts, the geysers, hot springs on the Yellowstone, Pitch Lake of Trinidad, and, to be brief, the myriad wonders of the world were all awaiting newly-created man, waiting his coming forth from out of the bridal chamber between the Tigris and Euphrates, like a mad bridegroom to run his frenzied course. Then came the (apparent) lapses in the creator's scheme. That the first man in the fair garden by the Euphrates was white, I think, we take for granted. True that we have no information on the subject, but in this matter of creation we have entered, so to speak, into a tacit compact with the creator, and it behoves us to concur with him and help him when a difficulty looms. Briefly I leave the time when man contended with the mastodon, hunted the mammoth, or was hunted in his turn by plesiosaurus or by pterodactyl. Scanty indeed are the records which survive of the Stone Age, the Bronze, or of the dwellers in the wattled wigwams on the lakes. Suffice it, that the strong preyed on the weak as they still do to-day in Happy England, and that early dwellers upon earth seem to have thought as much as we do, how to invent appliances with which to kill their fellows.

The Hebrew Scriptures and the record of crimes, of violence, and bad faith committed by the Jews on other races, need not detain us, as they resemble so entirely our own exploits amongst the "niggers" of to-day. I take it that Jahvé was little taken up with any of his creatures, except the people who inhabited the countries from which the Aryans came. Assyrians, Babylonians, Egyptians, Persians and the rest were no doubt useful and built pyramids, invented hanging gardens, erected towers, observed the stars, spoke truth (if their historians lie not), drew a good bow, and rode like centaurs or Gauchos. What did it matter when all is said and done! They were all "niggers," and whilst they fought and conquered, or were conquered, bit by bit the race which God had thought of from the first slowly developed.

Again a doubt creeps in. Was the creator omniscient in this case or did our race compel him, force his hand, containing in itself those elements of empire which he may have overlooked? 'Twere hard to say, but sometimes philosophers have whispered that the Great Power was careless, working, as he did, without the healthy stimulus of competition. I leave this speculation as more fit for thimbleriggers, for casuists, [337] for statisticians, metaphysicians, or the idealistic merchant, than for serious men.

Somehow or other the Aryans spread through Europe, multiplied, prospered, and possessed the land. Europe was theirs, for Finns and Basques are not worth counting, being, as it were, a sort of European "niggers," destined to disappear. Little by little out of the mist of barbarianism Greece emerged. Homer and Socrates with Xenophon, Euripides, Pindar and Heraclitus, Bion, Anaximander, Praxiteles, with Plato, Pericles, and all the rest of the poets and thinkers, statesmen and philosophers, who in that little state carried the triumphs of the human intellect, at least as far as any who came after them, flourished and died. Material and bourgeois Rome, wolf-suckled, on its seven hills waxed and became the greatest power, conquering the world by phrases as its paltry "Civis Romanus," and by its "Pax Romana," and with the spade, and by the sheer dead weight of commonplace, filling the office in the old world that now is occupied so worthily by God's own Englishmen. Then came the waning of the Imperial City, its decay illumined by the genius of Apuleius and Petronius Arbiter. Whether the new religion which the pipe-clayed soldier Constantine adopted out of policy, first gave the blow, or whether, as said Pliny, that the Latifundia[338] were the ruin of Italy, or if the effeminacy which luxury brings with it made the Roman youths resemble the undersized hermaphroditic beings who swarm in Paris and in London, no one knows.

Popes and Republics, Lombards, French and Burgundians, with Visigoths and Huns, and the phantasmagoria of hardly to be comprehended beings who struggled in the dark ages like microbes in a piece of flesh, or like the Christian paupers in the English manufacturing town, all paved the way for the development of the race,

---

[337] A person who uses clever but unsound reasoning on moral issues. A sophist.
[338] Roman estates employing large numbers of peasants and slaves. Pliny the Elder objected to the profit-orientated nature of these large enterprises.

perhaps, intended, from the beginning, to rule mankind. From when King Alfred toasted his cakes and made his candles marked in rings (like those weird bottles full of sand from Alum Bay) to measure time, down to the period when our present Sovereign wrote her "Diary of the Highlands" is but a moment in history of mankind. Still, in the interval, our race has had full leisure to mature. Saxon stolidity and Celtic guile, Teutonic dullness, Norman pride, all tempered with east wind, baptised with mist, narrowed by insularity, swollen with good fortune, and rendered overbearing with much wealth, have worked together to produce the type. A bold, beef-eating, generous, narrow-minded type, kindly yet arrogant; the men fine specimens of well-fed animals, red in blood and face; the women cleanly, "upstanding" creatures, most divinely tall; both sexes slow of comprehension, but not wanting sense; great feeders, lovers of strong drinks, and given to brutal sports as were their prototypes the men of ancient Rome; dogged as bull-dogs, quick to compassion for the sufferers from the injustice of their neighbours; thinking that they themselves can do no wrong, athletic yet luxurious, impatient of all hardships yet enduring them when business shows a profit or when honour calls; moralists, if such exist and yet, like cats, not quite averse to fish when the turn serves; clear-headed in affairs, but yet idealists and, in the main, wrong-headed in their view of life; priding themselves most chiefly on their faults, and resolute to carry all those virtues which they lack at home to other lands.

Thus, through the mist of time, the Celto-Saxon race emerged from heathendom and woad and, in the fullness of the creator's pleasure, became the tweed-clad Englishman. Much of the earth was his, and in the skies he had his mansion ready, well aired, with every appliance known to modern sanitary science waiting for him with a large bible on the chest of drawers in every room. Australia, New Zealand, Canada, India, and countless islands, useful as coaling stations and depots where to stack his bibles for diffusion amongst the heathen, all owned his sway. Races, as different from his own as is a rabbit from an elephant, were ruled by tweed-clad satraps expedited from the public schools, the universities, or were administered by the dried fruits culled from the Imperial Bar. But whilst God's favoured nation thus had run its course, the French, the Germans, Austrians, Spaniards, Dutch, Greeks, Italians, and all the futile remnant of mankind outside "our flag" had struggled to equal them. True that in in most particulars they were inferior. Their beer was weak, their shoddy not artfully diffused right through their cloth, their cottons less well "sized," the Constitution of their realm less nebulous, or the Orders of their Churches better authenticated, than were our own. No individual of their various nationalities by a whole life of grace was ever half so moral, as the worst of us is born. And so I leave them, weltering in their attempts to copy us, and turn to those of whom I wished to write when I sat down, but the exordium, which of course I had to write, has stood so long between us that I fear my readers, if I happen to attain to such distinction, are wondering where the applicability of the title may be described.

I wished to show, as Moses told us, that God made the earth and made it round, planted his trees, his men and beasts upon it, and let it simmer slowly till his Englishman stood forth. It seemed to me that his state became anthropomorphous, and I doubted, if, after all, he was so wise as some folks say. In other portions of the earth as Africa, America, Australia, and in the myriad islands of the South Seas people called "niggers" live.

What is a "nigger?" Now this needs some words in order to explain his just position. Hindus, as Brahmins, Bengalis, dwellers in Bombay, the Cingalese, Sikhs and Pathans, Rajpoots, Parsis, Afghans, Kashmiris, Baluchis, Burmese, with the dwellers from the Caspian Sea to Timur Laut, are thus described. Arabs are "niggers."
So are Malays, the Malagasy, Japanese, Chinese, Red Indians, as Sioux, Comanches, Navajos, Apaches with Zapatecas, Esquimaux, and in the south Ranqueles, Lengwas, Pampas, Pehuelches, Tobias, and Araucanos, all these are "niggers" though their hair be straight. Turks, Persians, Levantines, Egyptians, Moors, and generally all those of almost any race whose skins are darker than our own, and whose ideas of faith, of matrimony, banking, and therapeutics differ from those held by the dwellers of the meridian of Primrose Hill, cannot escape. Men of the Latin races, though not born free, can purchase freedom with a price, that is, if they conform to our ideas, are rich and wash, ride bicycles, and gamble on the Stock Exchange.[339] If they are poor, then woe betide them, let them paint their faces white with all the ceruse[340] -which ever Venice furnished, to the black favour shall they come. A plague of

---

[339] It may be that Graham is ironically reflecting on his own quarter-Spanish ancestry.
[340] A poisonous skin-whitening cosmetic.

pigments, blackness is in the heart, not in the face, and poverty, no matter how it washes, still is black.

In the consideration of the "nigger" races which God sent into the world for whites (and chiefly Englishmen) to rule, "niggers' of Africa take first place. I take it Africa was brought about in sheer ill-humour. No one can think it possible that an all-wise God (had he been in his sober senses) would create a land and fill it full of people destined to be replaced by other races from across the seas. Better, by far, to have made the "niggers" white and let them by degrees all become Englishmen, than put us to the trouble of exterminating whole tribes of them, to carry out his plan. At times a thinking man knows scarcely what to think, and sometimes doubts whether he is the God we took him for and if he is a fitting Deity for us to worship, and if we had not better, once for all, get us a God of our own race and fitted for our ways. "Niggers" who have no cannons, and cannot construct a reasonable torpedo have no rights. "Niggers" whose lot is placed outside our flag, whose lives are given over to a band of money-grubbing miscreants (chartered or not) have neither rights nor wrongs. Their land is ours, their cattle, fields, their houses, their poor utensils, arms, all that they have; their women, too, are ours to infect with syphilis, leave with child, outrage, torment, and make by consort with the vilest of our vile, more vile than beasts. Cretans, Armenians, Cubans, Macedonians, we commiserate, subscribe, and feel for. Our tender hearts are wrung when "Outlanders" cannot get votes. Bishops and Cardinals and statesmen, with philanthropists and pious ladies, all go wild about the Turks. Meetings are held and resolutions passed, articles written, lectures delivered, and the great heart of Britain stirred as if stocks were down. But "niggers," "bloody niggers," have no friends. Witness "Fraudesia," where Selous cants, Colenbrander hangs, whilst Rhodes plays "bonnett," and Lord Grey[341] and Co. add empires to our sway, duly baptised in blood.

So many rapes and robberies, hangings and murders, blowings up in caves, pounding to jelly with our Maxim guns, such sympathy for Crete, such coyness to express opinion on our doings in Matabeleland; our clergy all dumb dogs our politicians dazed about Armenia; "land better liked than niggers," "stern justice meted

---

[341] Sir Edward Grey (1862-1933). British Liberal statesman. Best remembered for saying: "The lamps are going out all over Europe, we shall not see them lit again in our life-time," at the start of WWI.

213

out" - can England be a vast and seething mushroom bed of base hypocrisy, and our own God, Jahvé Sabbaoth, an anthropomorphous fool?

~

Graham's final major anti-imperialist diatribe of this period was published in the Manchester-based *Sunday Chronicle*, just eight days before the celebrations for Queen Victoria's Diamond Jubilee.

## EXPANSION of EMPIRE
*The Sunday Chronicle*, 13th of June, 1897.

We have indeed made broad the phylacteries of our empire during the past quarter century. In every corner of the world some epoch-making little man[342] has been extending our national power on an insecure footing and building his own fortunes on the solid rock of five per cent. Truly an age of expansion, national expansion, and international expansion; an age of panning pro-consuls, successful financiers, of hybrid "conquerors" of the gin, blood, and iron species, a "flag-waving" century, a patriotic, albeit Jingoesque and Chauvinistic, century which has seen forty millions of people

---

[342] Probably a reference to Dr. Jameson.

incorporated in a quarter of a century into our empire, to the somewhat periwig-pated and pseudo-rumbustious national antheming of Mr. Rudyard Kipling.[343]

Well, it is done, and hardly a corner of the known world remains in which the name of Britain is not mentioned with a curse. That this should be so only goes to prove the jealousy, bad faith, and envy of all foreigners. In our heart of hearts we know that we are right in all we do. What more can man desire than the approval of his conscience? That we all enjoy. Conscience, I take it, is a British product, and once across the Channel it withers, dies, or as some folks think, was never known.

\* \* \*

Alone of Christians, Catholic or Protestant, we hallow Sunday, making it an image of our future state, drawn from the Nonconformist point of view. We speak the truth, cleave to a single standard for our money, marry one wife, though practising polygamy on the sly. Our cannons, ships, torpedoes, gin, gunpowder, cheap guns, sized cotton, hardware, hats, boots, dog-carts, fox-terriers, our East End of London, Cradley Heath, our loyalty, self-righteousness, the ease with which we swallow every kind of drink, prove us a chosen race. We made the "gentleman" and took a patent out in order to defend ourselves from the infringement of our copyright by foreign counterfeits. A sense of duty governs all we do, we recognise that we are pioneers, our mission is to civilise mankind, to teach them commerce, introduce our faith, keep others out, extend our trade, and pose as patterns of the virtues about which we talk, but seldom practice, upon economic grounds. Still forty millions in a quarter of a century, is going rather fast. Xerxes and Hannibal, Cæsar and Alexander, with Genghis Khan and Tammerlane, Cortes, Pizarro, Hastings and Clive, with Othman, Ali, and the other scourges of mankind who in past times pursued the path we follow now, ne'er went so fast, but spent their lives in doing that which we now accomplish in the lifetime of a horse. That proves without doubt the march of progress and shows our weapons are superior to theirs, and the superiority of weapons marks high-water line in the advancement of our race. Good guns, superior ships, the best torpedoes, quick-firing rifles, and a well-

---

[343] Graham hated Kipling's political views - what Cedric Watts describes as: 'the semi-Darwinian mystique of Kipling's imperialism.' The writer and critic, Edward Garnett, had written to Graham: 'Kipling is *the* enemy [. . .] He is a creator; and he is *the genius of all we detest.*' Letter, 26th of January 1899, The Manuscript Collection of Admiral Sir Angus Cunninghame Graham, NLS.

trained army, taken from useless toil to serve abroad, are what a nation most may pride itself upon.

* * *

The comfort of the average man, the advance of art [,] of literature (even of science), the rate of wages, standard of national life, all of these are nothing, so that the limits of our empire are pushed further on. Now that a few short years will see the whole of Africa partitioned out between ourselves, the French, the Dutch, the Belgians, and the rest, comes in the doubt of who is gainer by all we have achieved. Markets, I know, are wanted for the advancement of trade. That is to say, that the rich men who profit by our trade want to find out new fields to which to send their goods.

But as at home our population is not stationary, and as abroad the world is not illimitable, where does the gain come in? The manufacturers of other nations send their goods to every corner of the earth, profits grow less and less, and so it may be that we have conquered Africa in vain. One thing is certain, that hitherto our rule has brought no blessings to the natives of the place. Once call a man a savage, and it is straightway assumed he has no rights. No "nigger" loves his country, cares for his wife, his children, values his property, clings to his customs, or can feel the sentiments which are alleged to animate the whites; all that he longs for is to have a master to order him about. Shall trade and commerce, empire, morality, religion, cottons, hardware, and "our flag" all languish from the persistence of the "niggers" in the place where they were born?

It cannot be that the waste places of the earth were not designed for us, designed for those, in fact, who by their industry can turn them to account. If we desist, the French, the Germans, Belgians, and the rest will all rush in, ravish our markets from us and unfurl their spurious "flags" (made of cheap bunting), to our national disgrace. So once committed we must perforce advance till from the Niger to the Cape our rule prevails, with Pax Britannica, one gentleman in every parish of all Africa, a sanitary inspector, County Council, division between classes, snobs, cads, prigs, and all the joys which make our life at home so gay, so fascinating, and so entirely past the comprehension of all there men.

* * *

If, therefore none have gained, either in Africa or yet at home, by all that we have done, what will the inexorable judge posterity pronounce upon our deeds? Men,

216

children, women all blown up in caves, baskets of hands sent in to Belgian chiefs in the damned Congo hell; raids, hangings, shootings in Rhodesia; Selous "a gunning," with the Bible in his hand, shooting his blacks, returning to his tent to praise his God, and out again to slay. Rhodes setting forth his dictum that he likes "land before niggers;" the Portuguese in Delagoa Hay behaving as they did in times gone by; these are the blessings which the sordid European race for L.S.D.[344] has brought on Africa.

Granted the "niggers" have shot down our men, murdered the children of our settlers, fired their farms and driven off their cattle, were they not after all, true patriots like to the Scots at Bannockburn, Spartans at Thermopylæ, better than Cretans, as good as Cubans; or is all changed, and virtue, vice, patriotism mere names, and liberty a thing unknown where men are black? Those who have lived on frontiers know that in all cases white men are to blame, and that their presence, not their actions, if only men could clear their minds of cant, justifies every Indian, nigger, or member of an "inferior race" to exercise his rights to turn them out.

*  *  *

Las Casas,[345] writing to the King of Spain, tells him that he should not permit the atrocities which go on in the Indies every day, "but which atrocities the tyrants who perform them style 'conquests' thinking thereby to blind your Majesty to their atrocity." This was a Spaniard writing to a Spanish King three hundred years ago, a bishop such as have been few, apostle to the Indians as Colenso[346] was apostle to the Zulus, a man who in those days crossed the Atlantic thirteen times, in perils oft, in journeyings away, suffering without complaint the stripes laid on him by the tongues of fools, and every line he wrote might be applied to Africa to day.

Our national disgrace is Africa. Even an Indian famine caused by our rule, which throughout India renders our Queen the "Queen of famine and the Empress of black death." does not cry out so strongly to the few Englishmen in whom a sentiment of elementary justice lingers, as does Africa.

What signifies a protest here and there to the self-approbation of a nation such as

---

[344] Pounds, shillings, and pence.
[345] Bartolomé de las Casas (c.1484-1566) A 16th-century Dominican friar, Spanish historian, and social reformer.
[346] John William Colenso (1814-1883). An English mathematician, missionary, and social activist, who was the first Church of England Bishop of Natal Province, South Africa.

217

ours? Put down the "slave trade," abolish human sacrifices, stamp out polygamy, is still the cry. These may be worth objects, but when once achieved see that forced labour does not replace the trade, that prostitution does not occupy the place polygamy once filled, and as to human sacrifice, what sacrifice exceeds the daily sacrifice of factory or mine.

Let us expand, push out our limits, let our standard stream unfurled in atmospheres where once the date palm was the only flag; let us get markets, honestly if possible, but still get markets; let us boast, brag, hang, shoot, massacre, introduce our spirits, syphilis, and rule where they have been unknown; let us oust the French and Dutch, with Belgians, all nations but our own; and having done so, let us count cost at home and ask ourselves what it has all been worth, and if our "conquests," performed by tyrants who seek to blind "Our Majesty" to their real deeds with sounding phrases, have brought relief to any single struggling poor man in all those hells called Wigan, Preston, Leeds, Bradford - in Manchester, or Cradley Heath.'

~

Graham's most controversial utterance on the subject of Empire took place at a conference entitled 'Nationalities and Subject Races,' held in Caxton Hall, Westminster, between the 28th - 30th of June 1910, which attracted a large and enthusiastic international audience. Graham chaired a session on Poland and Ireland, and the resurgence of the Irish language, but had his opportunity to share his views during the fifth and final session, entitled 'Proposed Remedies':

## CONFERENCE SPEECH: 'NATIONALITIES and SUBJECT RACES'
30th of June, 1910.[347]

I will be brief. We have heard speeches from people competent to deal with various sectional parts of the subject. I will now, with your leave, go back to the main basis of the Conference, which really is, Imperialism: its Cause and Cure. The microbe of Imperialism is one of the most insidious in its approach in the whole history of pathology. In the same way that a man takes diseases, scarcely knowing how, or when, or from whom, so does Imperialism attack a nation and sap its vitality almost unknown

---

[347] Report of Conference, held in Caxton Hall, Westminster (June 28-30, 1910), pp.142-146.

to the nation itself.

We have seen in the past the decadence of the Roman Empire, mainly through the spread of Imperialism. We have seen the decay of the great Spanish Empire in the New World through its inordinate expansion and through its inordinate Imperialism. It sapped the vitality of both of these Empires by allowing them to spend force in the uttermost portions of the earth – force which they should have kept for the consideration of their own questions in their own countries for the solution of those great social problems to which we Socialists her in England and throughout Europe are addressing ourselves.

Much has been said this evening about India. It would ill become me to speak about Imperialism in India after men so much better qualified than I am to speak on the subject have addressed you. But Imperialism in India is almost a typical case. It has run the same course in India, in the archetype that it is running to-day in South Africa, in Egypt, in the Congo, in the regions of Peru and Columbia, and wherever they are exploiting nations and peoples throughout the world. First in India we had the humble company of traders. Who would have thought from such very small beginnings so mighty a Upas tree[348] as this British rule in India would have extended its baleful influence?

After the traders we had the natural disputes with the natives of the country. We sent our soldiers, some of them in those days giants, prepared to sacrifice all their blood, their lives, their treasure for what they considered was the benefit of humanity, the extension of civilisation, and the propagation of their faith and their empire throughout the world. Those men, those circumstances, produced a Lawrance,[349] they produced a Mountstuart Elphinstone,[350] the produce in a lesser degree Lord Canning, and many another man who laboured according to his lights to administer justice and really to introduce civilisation to those countries.

But little by little, and all unknown to the governing classes, the insidious bacillus

---

[348] *Antiaris toxicaria*, a tree in the mulberry and fig family, containing a deadly poison. 'Upas' from the Javanese word for poison.
[349] John Laird Mair Lawrence, 1st Baron Lawrence (1811-1879), a prominent British Imperial statesman who served as Viceroy of India from 1864 to 1869.
[350] The Hon Mountstuart Elphinstone (1779-1859). Scottish statesman and historian, associated with the government of British India. He later became the Governor of Bombay. Graham's mother, the Hon. Anne Elizabeth Elphinstone-Fleeming (1828-1925) was his niece.

of Imperialism was step by step undermining the humanity and the noble ideals of these people. It has been well said by several on the platform that the danger of Imperialism is greater to the Imperialist than it is to the people who are governed. Take the case of India to-day, seething with discontent from the Punjab to the Cormandel Coast; take the influence of Government and Imperialism upon the quondam Radical, Lord Morley.[351] Little by little we have seen him false to that principle which he has defended through a long life of usefulness. Who to-day is suppressing free meetings in India, who to-day is imprisoning citizens without trial, who to-day has called forth the indignant protests that electrified us from the lips of citizens of India; who but Lord Morley? Oh, the pity – the man who has denounced the aristocracy and the hereditary principle more strongly than any other statesman in our modern life.

It was the same with administrators under the old Spanish rule, with many of the men of whom civilisation could be proud, but their ideals, their pride, their nobility, were inevitably sapped by the same forces, by having to act as governors, as the nobility and the fine ideals of Lord Morley have been sapped by his having to apply the coercive *régime* to such a country as India.

We have also heard this evening much of Egypt. The last speaker has dwelt upon the necessity of conforming to the Egyptian ideals. It seems to me that if we do not conform to the Egyptian and the Indian ideals we run the risk in both of these countries of Sicilian Vespers[352] of enormous magnitude. I am not one of those people whom the word assassination terrifies. Some deeds are written in letters of gold, deeds which we Westerners reverence and hold in honour, and it may be that the most timid constitutionalist of us all, if placed in the same circumstances as El Wardani[353] was placed in Egypt, might have acted – I say *might* have acted – in a similar way. Of one thing I am certain, that no sophistry, no wheedling or cajoling of the governing power, no distortion of the facts by the reptile Press (always ready to throw over the whole world and to back up tyranny and to say a word in favour of injustice) will ever make

Egyptian Nationalists hold the name of El Wardani other than in such honour as

---

[351] John Morley, 1st Viscount Morley of Blackburn (1838-1923) was a Liberal statesman, writer and newspaper editor. He was Secretary of State for India between 1905 and 1910.
[352] Bloody rebellion.
[353] Ibrahim el Wardani (1887-1910), executed for the assassination of the Egyptian Prime Minister, Boutres Ghali Pasha (grandfather of the UN General Secretary, 1992-1996) on the 20th of February, 1910. Ghali had been accused of favouring the British in the 'Denshawai Incident.' See passim, p.80.

that attaching to the name of the slayer of General Brobrikoff. [sic][354]

This Imperialism is making snobs and cowards of us all. It is sapping the vitality of all of us; we are all guilty of it; all those who do not raise a protest on platform or pulpit, or by pen, in some ways, are guilty of the stain of it. Think what a mean thing it is – think what a little thing it is, the modern Imperialist as embodied in its prototype, Ex-President Roosevelt.[355] Think of the advice that he tendered a few weeks ago in Cairo to the Nationalist party, and think of the meanness, of the bacillus infecting without the knowledge of its infection; think of the meanness of a Secretary of Foreign Affairs[356] in this country who was content and is content to shelter himself behind the extravagant impertinence of a perambulating Yank.

Imperialism means the degradation of all our ideals; Imperialism means a vast concourse of small men under the shadow of a great waving flag; it means the sending out of our soldiers to stamp out the liberties of other countries It is from little nationalities that your great men come, and I put it to every sane man and every sane woman in this assembly, whether after all, as Bruce said at Bannockburn, freedom is [ ][357] a noble thing, and whether if an angel from heaven were to descend to-night and to propose to govern us for our benefit, whether in a short time the mildest of us would not become revolutionaries and the angel have turned into a devil.

I have been asked to propose my remedy. I have no remedy but that of common sense and to endeavour as far as lies in us to fit all these nations for self-government, and to help them to that particular form which they chose to select. And finally, as I hate the idea of empire, if it were necessary to break up the British and every other empire in the same way as it is proposed to break up the Poor Law system, I should do it, because empires and poor laws are the due complement of each other, and both of them are disgraces to humanity."

---

[354] Nikolay Ivanovich Bobrikov (1839-1904) Russian Governor General of Finland. He was assassinated by the nationalist nobleman, Eugen Schauman (1875-1904). in Helsinki, who shot and killed himself directly afterwards, becoming a Finnish national hero.

[355] Theodore 'Teddy' Roosevelt (1858-1919). On the 3rd of March 1910, at the University of Cairo, Roosevelt praised British rule in Egypt, and vilified El-Wardani, adding: "The training of a nation to fit itself successfully to fulfil the duties of self-government is a matter, not of a decade or two, but of generations."

[356] See passim.

[357] The transcriber of Graham's speech had incorrectly copied down 'freedom is not a noble thing.'

Graham's friend, Edward Garnett, witnessed this speech with his son David, then aged 18, but already well acquainted with his parents' circle of émigré Russian anarchists. Many years later, David recalled the event in his memoirs:

The only speech I heard, which was not completely boring, was delivered by Cunninghame Graham. Looking like Charles I, with his aristocratic features and Vandyke beard, and exquisitely dressed, he held up a thin, carefully manicured hand and began his speech with the words: "I am not one of those who tremble [sic] at the word – ASSASSINATION!" There was a storm of applause, which prevented his proceeding for some minutes, and it was obvious that all the delegates, whatever the colour of their skin, were consumed with the passionate longing to commit murder. Although I was very uncritical at that age, it did strike me that Cunninghame Graham's remark was one of the silliest I had ever heard. He was in no danger of assassinating or being assassinated. He had no reason to tremble.[358]

~

Graham had publicly declared himself to be a republican,[359] and it is hard to imagine that he regarded the British monarchy, the source of all political patronage, class, and imperial values, with anything less than abhorrence. His true feelings had been expressed some years earlier in this extract:

How can the veriest Tory get up any enthusiasm about a set of beings who have nothing Royal about them either in appearance, habits, or in reality. The fact is, they are not real kings or queens, but merely official puppets, and created by Parliament. Who but a fool could excite himself at the spectacle of that stout, bald-headed German gentleman, the Prince of Wales?[360] Excellent, if you like, performing all the offices an unconscious automaton would perform as well, but oh, how uninteresting.

Can anyone contemplate the hideous Hanoverian tribe of foreign princes without being moved to disgust at the creatures themselves, and to pity for the nation that tamely submitted to be ruled by them?[361]

However, openly attacking the monarchy, during a period when the large bulk of the population was both jingoistic, and paranoid with the fear of foreign agents and anarchists, was quite another matter.[362] In *Might Majesty and Dominion* (above), he had attacked it tangentially, by contrasting the pomp and circumstance of Victoria's funeral

---

[358] David Garnett, *The Golden Echo* (Chatto & Windus, 1953), p.119.
[359] 'Mr Cunninghame Graham M.P. and the Liberal Party,' *The Glasgow Herald* (7 November 1889), p.10.
[360] The future King Edward VII.
[361] Cunninghame Graham, 'The Royal Grants,' *The Labour Elector* (10 August 1889), p.92.
[362] The Siege of Sidney Street, involving two Latvian revolutionaries, had occurred only a few months earlier.

with the grubby poverty of everyday life. In the following piece, on the coronation of her grandson, the dreary George V, he questions monarchy's relevance, as other than an outdated show of upper-class arrogance and complacency.

## BOVRIL

*Justice: The Organ of Social Democracy*, 22nd of July, 1911.

By a strange mistake at the Coronation ceremony it seems that Bovril must have been substituted for consecrated oil. That is the only explanation I can give for the extreme materialism of the whole show.

Streets barricaded, and the stern bull-dog face of Lord Kitchener of Khartoum repelling everybody, and soldiers, soldiers, and still more soldiers, everywhere.

The crowds that did not come; the air, as of a Scottish Sabbath, on the town.

The decent uncovering of heads without a cheer.

The harassed looking king, the unsympathetic queen, virtuous and good no doubt, but not forthcoming. The display of abject wealth, for wealth, too, has an abject air at times.

The foreign kings and princelets reminding one of their historical progenitors who used to swell the Roman triumphs.

The Indian troops, martial, but monkyfied.

All these, and the great gulf between the thin black lines of people in the street, looking like flies stuck on the glazing of a stale Bath bun, and the rich, seated like guilty creatures at the Follies on their red baize seats, all made the Coronation only a modified success, fit for a moderate, decent, home-keeping and perplexed crowned head.

Still, it would be unkind to charge the failure of this great whip-up for Imperialism upon King George.

He did his best no doubt, submitting to it all like a crowned lamb.

The fault lies on the press, with its absurd vaticinations,[363] and most of all upon the organisers of the show.

They, rich and sceptical, materialistic to the core, caring for nothing but the Ritz and Carlton, for Hurlingham and Ranelegh, for Melton and for Monte Carlo, were convinced that all the people were of the same mind. To them the sixty-thousand

---

[363] Prophesies.

soldiers were a sign (set in the mud) of their eternal power, their might and majesty, and their dominion of the poor. The foreign princes were proof positive that Englishmen – that is, themselves and theirs – were chosen by the Lord to dominate the world.

The orb, the sceptre and the red-flannel-covered seats were but so many proofs of their superiority to those who stood about the streets.

Kingship to them meant money, motor-cars, luxury, and, above all, security in their possessions. They thought, apparently, that the great bulk of those who never in their lives rode in a motor, except a penny bus or Black Maria (now, I believe brought up to date), were influenced by the same appeal.

Hence came their error, and hence the failure of the whole thing to stir the imagination if the crowd.

What might the organisers of the Coronation have achieved had they but had the sense!

I write, of course, taking things as they are, not as a Socialist; for, as St Paul says, he who fights, fights to prevail, and I suppose the organisers wanted their show to draw.

In the first place, the experience of the world through ages past has shown that it is quite impossible to move the mass of humankind merely by bread alone.

Even if you gild the loaf the people will not rise to take it with a shout. Ideas, and they alone, have ever really swayed mankind. Take Christianity and Buddhism, the great reform that the inspired driver of the camels in the Hedjaz initiated; lastly, take Socialism.

Does anyone suppose that men will come to Socialism solely upon account of the material advantage it holds out? If so they have not grasped what Socialism means,

Had but the Court officials recollected that underneath the sceptre and the crown, the orb, and all the rest of the old properties[364] brought from the Tower, that there was something deeper, they could not have failed. We know that the whole ceremony is but a tinkering cymbal,[365] the ghost, as it were, of something that went out long years ago.

Still, in its time it had real significance. Theoretically the king humiliates himself before his God. He bows the knee. He is then stripped to the shirt.

Only when he has sworn to shield the widow and the fatherless, to protect the weak,

---

[364] Props.
[365] Corinthians 13:1.

to curb the strong, and to administer true, equal justice betwixt man and man, he is invested with the mantle and the crown.

This in itself, in days gone by, was a solemn covenant that the king made with God and with his people.

To-day it has become a spectacle for peers, for peeresses, for sweaters and their wives to gape at, whilst the real people stand afar off in the street.

Had it been so contrived that all this interested them, as it had interested their forbears once upon a time, they might have come in millions to line the streets, just as they did to see King Edward's funeral only a year ago.

Dullards, with Bovril in their head instead of brains, folk slow and unimaginative themselves, who thought that all the world was just as dull and unimaginative as they were themselves, ordained it otherwise.

The people love a show, they said, because a show was all they, sunk in their stupid luxury, could understand.

They had their show.

Their soldiers lined the streets. The subject princes of their Empire ambled along, decked in their golden chains and looking ill at ease. Sweaters and peers, with peers and sweaters, Liberals and Tories were in their thousands.

What wonder, then, that publicans and sinners held aloof and made the thing a frost?[366] It all came, I am sure, from the unlucky substitution of either of Bovril or of Lemco[367] for Chrism[368] oil.

[366] Slang: Snubbed or ignored.
[367] Like Bovril, a processed meat powder.
[368] Anointing.

# THE INTERNATIONALIST

Only a fine contextual line divides Graham's anti-imperialist writings and his many articles and letters which deal with foreign adventuring and international intrigues. Both indeed deal in the end with large powers exerting their wishes by force of arms, or economic pressure, on smaller nations or indigenous populations. As a friend of the downtrodden, and someone who took a very jaundiced view of so-called 'progress,' these causes exercised his pen in later life, and within these, we must include Ireland and Scotland.

However, Graham was no armchair critic. He was a renowned world traveller; he had been swept up in a revolution in Argentina, had known Buffalo Bill and Sitting Bull, had been burnt out by Mescalero Apaches in Texas, had taught fencing in Mexico, had prospected for gold in Spain, and, dressed as a Turkish doctor had tried to reach a forbidden city in south-west Morocco, among many other adventures and first-hand experiences.

1889 had been a year of disappointment and frustration; he and his new Labour party "which had no policies and no funds" had been castigated by the Liberals, and sneered at by the TUC,[369] who saw Keir Hardie and Graham as dangerous revolutionaries. Graham was also under huge financial pressure; his trial defence had cost £2,000, and his constant travelling to speaking engagements around the country was exhausting and expensive, during a time when his income from his Gartmore estate had dropped during an agricultural depression, adding to the considerable debts he had inherited from his father.[370] The pressure of work was taking its toll on his health and on his marriage, and in mid-November he joined his wife Gabrielle in Spain. From Valencia, they travelled to Lisbon, where he interviewed Portuguese socialists for *The Labour Elector.*

## LISBON REVISITED

*The Labour Elector,* 21st of December, 1889.

The *Alagoas* [371] has just arrived bringing the ex-Emperor of Brazil, Dom Pedro de Alacantara. When a nation turns its ruler adrift in a hurry it should select a better steamer than *Alagoas*, or should at least communicate to Mr. Plimsoll first.[372] Such an

---

[369] *The Scotsman* (5 September1889), p.4.
[370] Over £100,000.
[371] An 1,800 ton steamer, built on the Clyde.
[372] Samuel Plimsoll (1824-1898). A Liberal MP and social reformer. He devised 'The Plimsoll Line,' which indicated the maximum safe draft of a ship. Graham's inference is that the ship was unseaworthy, or at least overloaded.

abominable old tub I never saw. I used to think Ulysses (not Grant, but King of Ithaca) made a pretty long passage of it from Troy, but after poor Dom Pedro's recent experience have come to the conclusion that his passage was an ordinary one after all. But all the same "Long Live the Republic. Long Live Liberty and all the rest of it." But why? That is what I am not sure of. Take Chamberlain, Mr. Mundella, Messrs. Bryant & May, [373] Phethean, Sir Charles Dilke, Archibald Forbes, Augustus Harris, Captain O'Shea, Sir Charles Russell, and Charley Beresford, shake well together, add of Boulanger one slice, Paul Deroulede[374] an ounce. Flavour with a few Portuguese slave merchants from Mozambique and a French journalist or two, and you have the ingredients of a new Brazilian ministry; the whole added to a stew of Generals and Colonels out of an *Opéra Comique*.

Nevertheless, "Long live Liberty, etc." But why?

I do think sometimes that Athenians must have felt like lynching Socrates with his "Why?" However, I am a long way from your readers and feel safe on that score.

A good emperor put out, and a lot of needy rogues put in. But then the Republic. The soil of America abhors an empire, as naturally as the stomach of a schoolboy a vacuum. At least many wealthy but dull men say so. How much better we should all wag without these wealthy dullards. Did the electors of a country have but the faintest perception of their own interests, how many supple-bodied gentlemen now nightly dislocating themselves as clowns and harlequins would be peacefully slumbering (how shall sleeping offend?) and an *entrechat*, a *pirouette* (well executed, of course) would be so much more useful to them than the hogs-wash we are so plentifully dieted upon. But d__n these digressions.

What I want to know is, what have the negroes of Goyaz, the herdsmen of Rio Grande du Sul, the mulattos of the mines of Geraes, the lumberers of Bahia, gained by the affair?

Long live the Republic (Federal, I think) of the United States of Brazil.

Here, you brute buck-nigger, black my boots, and quickly too. A Republican should go clean-footed (and clean-handed if possible). Get out early into the coffee-fields, my

---

[373] A British match manufacturer. In July 1888, Graham was involved in a campaign led by Annie Besant to improve the wages and conditions during the London Match Girls Strike.
[374] Paul Déroulède (1846-1914). French author, politician, and patriot.

coloured brethren - the Empire is gone and you are free - as free as I am. Work from six till night, for you are a citizen of Brazil. It is a pleasure to toil in the service of a Republican.

"Can you, then, deny," said to me an oleaginous Portuguese merchant, "that this Republic is a step in the right direction?" And in the language of Camões[375] did I try to explain to him, by way of allegory, as I shall to you: In the town of Puita, near Guayaquil, on the Pacific Coast, no vegetation grows. Therefore, the inhabitants (an imaginary race) did on the high white cemetery walls of their town depict certain green palm trees, to their infinite content. But Providence, ever jealous (as it would appear) of the efforts of mankind to supply its omissions, Providence, I say. No mule or donkey would ever pass those trees without staying to contemplate or essay to nibble, curse the driver never so wisely. What remained, therefore, for the County Council (let John Burns[376] take heed) but to repaint the trees blue - yes, bright blue - removing temptation from the browsing pachyderms. At the same time did they preserve a semblance of a forest to the blameless Puitans. I have spoken; let him who has the ears of understanding upon him, refrain from the Republican bray till he is sure of the Republican provender.

To resume the thread of my discourse at the other end of the skein. Yesterday, the Editor of the *Protesto Operario*[377] and other friends took me to see the ancient Jewry, now the poorest quarter of the city, the former inhabitants having generally sought out more golden Jerusalems for themselves in London or Paris. Honest Portuguese labourers herd and swelter in the forsaken dens. There, in the steep irregular lanes, do the wives and families of the descendants of the men who sailed with Vasco Da Gama, who crossed the ocean with Columbus, live and move and have their being. Portuguese civilisation, as like our own as one humbug to another, deported 210,000 of them this year alone. From all sides comes the cry of taxes and syndicate, of oppression, of long hours, of short wages, of starvation, of misery, of riches, of hypocrisy, of Republicanism, and all the various ingredients that make the hell-broth of

---

[375] Luís Vaz de Camões (1524-1580). Considered Portugal's greatest poet.
[376] A firebrand Socialist. He and Graham were arrested during 'Bloody Sunday' in Trafalgar Square in 1887, and imprisoned. In 1889 he became a Progressive member of the first London County Council, and in 1892 the MP for Battersea. He was generally regarded as a betrayer of the socialist cause.
[377] *Worker Protest* (1882-1893). The organ of the Portuguese Socialist Party.

our nineteenth century civilisation.

So, sitting in the sun and watching the misdirected efforts of some underfed men and starving oxen to drag some logs of campeche-wood up a steep hill - smoking a little, and thinking not much - did I begin to indite this to you, intending to have written of the ships, of the crowd, of the sun, of the broad-flowing Tagus, and of many other things which I have happily omitted; and even at this moment, in a cloud of dust, passes Dom Pedro, silent and contemplative as I remember him of old, strolling in the market-place of Rio, and smiling on the little naked black children; and in my mind's eye do I see the newly-fledged Brazilian Deputy bawling at his "coloured brethren": "Here Cæsar, are my boots blackened yet, you hound? I must rush off to the Senate, and, in the interests of human liberty, record my vote against the Eight Hours Bill." And so, no more at present from your special correspondent in Lisbon.

According to Anne Taylor, this article lacked his customary verve, and that Graham had remarked to a friend: "I could write plenty more if I was not right over a stable in which two mules were fighting, and if I had not, for the want of blotting paper, to get up at the end of each sheet and take a little sand out of the wall with a knife to dry what I had written." But, significantly, Taylor adds: 'Here, suddenly, after years of arid polemic, was a brief glimpse of a new kind of writing that was beginning to come more often and more easily to him: to say what he saw; to describe what he, and others, did, he discovered was intensely satisfying'[378] and which, when it matured, turned him into one of the finest sketch writers of the period.

~

In late 1890, and early 1891, three pieces on the plight of the Sioux Nation appeared in *The Daily Graphic*, described by John Walker as: 'an anguished cry from the heart against the cruel treatment of the American Indian.'[379]

---

[378] Taylor, p.218.
[379] John Walker Ed., *The North American Sketches of R. B. Cunninghame Graham* (Edinburgh: The Scottish Academic Press, 1986), p.25.

# THE AMERICAN INDIANS: GHOST DANCING
*The Daily Graphic*, 29th of November 1890.

The special correspondent of the *Sun* at Pine Ridge, Dakota, keeps us informed of the movement of the Indians now massing their forces at Cherry Creek.

Glancing over the evening papers we see that the Sioux are dancing the Ghost Dance, and learn that in the opinion of the perspicacious correspondent the settlers expect to be robbed and murdered. Some of us may say, "Confound these Indians, they ought to be shot down." Yes, smokeless powder is your true civiliser after all. There is no good Indian but a dead Indian, which we know is true, for have not the American humorists declared it, and has not a tender-hearted public in two continents affirmed their declaration with a laugh. Artists wish they could be present to see the ceremony. Those who, in pursuit of money have been in the "Territory," the whisky sellers, the Bible peddlers, the land speculators (having caught the phrase from some frontier man), tell us the "Indians is pizin," and, like Peter, seal the lie with an oath.[380] The general public glances over the telegrams from Omaha and hopes there will be no bloodshed, then returns to discuss the recent political scandals and the prurient details connected with the private life of party leaders,[381] which, of course, we all know are of vastly more importance than the extermination of legions of heathen Indians. Still, there are few who really know what is going on in the snow at Cherry Creek, what the Messiah really is that the Indians are looking for, and who the ghosts are who are dancing. A Ghost Dance to the Sioux is what the Holy War is to the Mohammedan, what the last prayer (faith present or faith absent) is to the Christian. The Sioux can stand it no more; therefore they are dancing to the ghosts of their forefathers to arise and help them against their enemies. Only an Indian superstition. Looking for a Messiah. Waiting for the Las Casas[382] who will never come.

I wonder if the British public realizes that it is the Sioux themselves who are the ghosts dancing. Ghosts of a primeval race. Ghosts of ghosts who for three hundred years, through no crimes committed by themselves (except that of being born), if it be

---

[380] Actually, Saint Paul. Romans 1:9.
[381] A reference to the ongoing scandal surrounding Charles Stewart Parnell, and the divorce proceedings against his lover Katharine 'Kitty' O'Shea, on the 15th of November.
[382] Bartolomé de las Casas (c1484 - 1566). A Dominican friar, was granted the official title of 'Protector of the Indians' by King Ferdinand II of Spain.

not a crime to love better the rustle of the grass than the shrieking of the engine, have suffered their long purgatory. Ghosts who were men. The Messiah these poor people are waiting for, our poor people here in London also look for. But both will look in vain. Justice will not come either to Cherry Creek, no, nor yet to Whitechapel. The buffalo have gone first, their bones whitening in long lines upon the prairies, the elk have retired into the extreme deserts of Oregon, the beaver is exterminated to make jackets for the sweater's wife, the Indian must go next, and why not, pray? Is he not of less value than the other three? Let him make place for better things – for the drinking shop, for the speculator, for the tin church. Let him realize that in the future, where he changed his peltries for beads and powder, two gills of whisky shall be sold for a quarter. Men say the change is good (but good is merely relative), perhaps good enough for him, but death, indeed, for all the ghost dancers.

Civilization, perhaps, one day will remember them when the civilized Indians commercialism is creating, are dancing around the flames of European capitals.

But Rocky Bear and the Little Wound, Short Bull and Sleeping Water have had enough, they have taken horse, mounting lightly as drops of water (from the offside) silently, in single file, never stopping to squat and pass the pipe round; each man knowing his pony by the mecate,[383] they are marching on Cherry Creek. But the Kiowas, the Cheyennes, the Arapahoes, the Comanches have braided their horses' manes. They (who before civilisation loved one another as the dwellers in Liddesdale and Bewcastledale[384] did of old) are friends.

They have mounted their best horses, they are coming through the day, they are coming through the night, across the frozen prairie (the dry grass hardly crackling beneath the bronchos' feet), they are passing the whispering red woods, coming through the lonely canyons, marching silently as ghosts on Cherry Creek, across the lands that once were theirs to take counsel with the ghosts of those their former owners.

Better that they should come and smoke and dance, "dance for ten days without food or water," better far that they should die fighting, than by disease and whisky. Outrages they will commit, of that there is certainty, but all they do can scarce atone for all they and theirs have suffered. Tricked by all, outwitted, plundered by the

---

[383] A bridal rope, traditionally of horsehair.
[384] Warring areas on either side of the Scotland-England Border.

Christian speculator, better far that they should die fighting, and join the ghosts who went before them. This I want the world to recognise, that even Indians do not contemplate their own extermination without centuries of suffering. We might have taught them something, they might have taught us much, soon they will be all forgotten and the lying telegrams will speak of "glorious victories by our troops." Once more sin will be committed in the name of law and progress. It is a hard case to decide on, no matter from what side you approach it; these men have lived too long, better, therefore, they die fighting. No one will regret them (but myself) - except, perhaps, their ponies, who may feel their new owners' hands heavy on the horsehair bridle. The majesty of civilisation will be vindicated, one more step towards universal hideousness attained, and the Darwinian theory of the weakest to the wall will have received another confirmation to strengthen those who want to use it against the weakest here in Europe.

~

SALVATION by STARVATION: THE AMERICAN INDIAN PROBLEM
*The Daily Graphic*, 22nd of December 1890.

The first act in the concluding drama of the existence of the Sioux Indians is played out. Apparently in direct violation of the President's express orders, the Indian police arrested Sitting Bull, with the natural consequence that a rescue was attempted and a fight took place. In the fight, Sitting Bull, who was heard giving his orders in a loud voice, fell pierced by a bullet. This is an old trick, well known in Spain and in Mexico, and throughout the frontiers of the United States.

The escort appears at the frontier town without the prisoner. Officer reports prisoner endeavoured to escape, and, in the struggle that ensued, was accidentally shot. Quite so; that is to say one of two things happened - either the prisoner was offered a suppositious occasion to escape, and shot in the attempt, or else he was deliberately murdered in order to save time, legal expenses and the problematical Spanish-American or Uncle Sam's justice (sic).

This would seem to have been the end of Sitting Bull - deliberately murdered to stop him from asking for food for his tribe. "Minds" in Boston's "first families," in the south, and that noxious product of civilisation, the Anglified American, the man who secretly laments that there is no peerage in America, will talk of Lutz and Pijano. The editors of Western papers will talk of the safety of the settlers being at last secured by the removal of Sitting Bull, and worst of all, the American public as a whole will believe them and think a piece of poetic justice has been performed.

Poetical, no doubt, but as for justice - as far removed from anything connected with it as was the other specimen of American "justice" executed three years ago in Chicago, and for the self-same reason, namely, that the culprits asked for bread. American justice! American justice to Indians, above all, is a minus quantity. American justice to anyone who dissents from the gospel of cent per cent means the bullet or the gallows; to the Indians it has meant starvation or the bullet. What wonder that they should have chosen the bullet.

Still, it is a cheering thought that most of them (I hope not Sitting Bull) have been baptised, and that their souls will be saved, though their bodies have been starved by the Christian American Government. Sitting Bull was right in his lifelong policy that the whites are the mortal enemies of the Indian race.

Whether in Patagonia, on the pampas, or on the prairies of the North West, the treatment that the whole Indian race has received, whether at the hands of Spanish or English Americans, is a disgrace and a scandal even to the disgrace and scandal facetiously called civilisation, - in which the doctrine of whether the iron pot strike the earthenware pot, or the earthenware pot float against the iron pot, fuel for the earthenware pot has become a gospel.

Everyone who knows the Indians seems united on one point - that the recent disturbances are due to starvation and to the deliberate withholding of the covenanted rations from the wretched Indians. As Mr. Moreton Frewen[385] says in the *Pall Mall*: "Theirs (the Indians') was the cattle (the buffalo) on a thousand hills. Theirs was the whole country, the prairie, the woods, the rivers, and they were free." It would seem - and I speak not as a sentimentalist who takes his Indian (coloured) from the pages of Fenimore Cooper, but one who has passed many a night staring into the darkness watching his horses when Indians were about; it would seem that food were a little enough thing to grant them in their own country. True, I am one of those who think

---

[385] A writer on monetary reform, who served briefly as Member of Parliament for North East Cork.

that the colour of the skin makes little difference to right and wrong in the abstract, and who fail to see so much difference between an Indian sitting over a fire gnawing a piece of venison, and a tailor in the East-end of London working in a gas-lit den sixteen hours a day for a few shillings a week. It does not much matter, though the bulk of mankind declare that a prairie with corn growing on it, and a log house or two with a corrugated iron roof, is a more pleasing sight than the same prairie with a herd of wild horses on it, and the beaver swimming in every creek.

That is their opinion, and they will not, I am sure, deny me the right to express mine, that, as the Spaniards say, "*Hay gustos que merecen palos.*"[386]

But the gain of civilisation. You would not surely allow these rich lands to remain for ever in the hands of a few wandering savages? Again, I say that to me the mere accident of a little colouring matter in a skin does not alter right or wrong and that the land was theirs, no matter to what uses they put it, centuries before the first white man sneaked timidly across the Atlantic.

Those who are loudest now (the settlers in Dakota) for the final extermination of the Sioux fail to grasp that, when Dakota is all settled, they themselves will in the main become as dependent on the capitalists as the Indians now are on the United States Government, and that the precedent of rigorous measures with the starving Indians will be used against themselves.

I would, even at the eleventh hour, secure the Indians in a fertile territory, and prohibit any white man from settling among them, except he were a man of proved good character.

I would in that territory make it a criminal offence to supply drink to any Indians.

I would exclude all missionaries except those of the Roman Catholic faith, for in my experience of missionaries the Roman Catholics alone have seemed to me to understand them.

Lastly, I would endeavour to set up cattle ranches among them, for in my experience of Indians this is the occupation to which at present they are best suited.

My frontier friends may smile at my idea of Indians as ranchers, and exclaim, with expressions which I spare your readers, that the Indians would eat all the cattle in a

---

[386] Spanish: 'There are tastes that deserve sticks.'

week. All I can say is, I have seen the Indians in the Gran Chaco, and on the frontiers of Chile, no whit less savage than the Sioux, make first-rate ranchers when drink was away. At least we owe the men from whom we have taken their all, replacing doubtfully the beaver and the buffalo with whisky and smallpox, some reparation beside a small-bore bullet.

Even in America, where public opinion is, perhaps, more brutal than in any other country of the world, surely a flush of shame must rise to the faces of honest men when they receive the telegrams from Dakota. It puzzles me to think, except the horse, what benefit the Indian race has gained from civilisation.

Perhaps, though, it is better that the evil should come quickly, for it will come at last. In the next generation or so they will be gone, and then the Americans will organise picnics on a grand scale to visit the historic places in Dakota and Montana, where the curious and picturesque peoples (*vide* advertisement to cheap circular trips from New York to Dakota) "who once inhabited our continent, lived and smoked their red calumets."[387]

This article was published one week before the infamous Battle of Wounded Knee (also known as The Wounded Knee Massacre), on the Lakota Pine Ridge Indian Reservation in South Dakota. By the end of the attack, 150 men women and children had been killed, with 51 wounded. Some estimates put the death toll much higher.

**THE REDSKIN PROBLEM**: "BUT 'TWAS A FAMOUS VICTORY"
*The Daily Graphic*, 5th of January 1891.

"Our special correspondent" at Pine Ridge, Dakota, whose dispatches I have read with such heartfelt pleasure for the last month, has had the opportunity lately of assisting in one of the most healthy manifestations of the spirit of civilisation that it has been the lot of any special correspondent (out of Africa or Egypt) to chronicle for many years. I freely admit I am dense, and density is as the sin of witchcraft, but be that as it may, I never yet was able to discover why it is, when a body of white troops, well armed with all the newest murderous appliances of scientific warfare, shoot down men whose ignorance of proper calling clearly proves them to be savages, the act is invariably

---

[387] Peace-pipes.

spoken of as a glorious victory. There are some things which be too hard for me, and the way of the serpent on the rock is as easy of comprehension in comparison to it, as is the fact that the particular political party to which I choose to belong is composed of upright and righteous living, whole-souled patriots, and that the other fellows are all either rogues or fools, or an amalgam of the two.

If, though, the previous fact is difficult of comprehension to me, how much more so is the converse fact that, if the aforesaid braceless, breechless knaves, in precisely the same manner, shoot our "glorious troops," their proceeding becomes a "bloody massacre," a "treacherous ambuscade," or something of a low-priced nature of that sort.

I should have thought that sauce for the Indian savage was also sauce for the white rowdy who swarms in all the frontier corps, even if the latter worthy was acquainted with the priceless boons of boiled shirts and plug hats, and worshipped his fetish in a stifling meeting house instead of on the open prairie. Still that in no wise alters the case that there has been a glorious victory of the American troops at Pine Ridge. Very pleasing to read that after three centuries the good old racial feud between Indians and whites is being fought out in the good old way.

Let it be once granted that there is no good Indian but a dead Indian. Does that apply, though, to Indian women and children? I see that our "brave troops" remorselessly slaughtered all the women and children, and our special correspondent, in estimating the "bag," remarks that by this time probably not more than six children remain alive out of the whole Indian camp.

Can anything more miserable be conceived than the forlorn position of the wretched Indians, when at the break of day they found their camp surrounded by troops, when, at the same time, we remember they were probably half-starving, and that the recent severe weather is as summer compared to the winter of Dakota.

I cannot imagine anyone reading (always from our special correspondent) and not feeling the profoundest pity for the wretched Indians. The spectacle of them sitting silently in a semi-circle. One would have thought, would have appealed to anyone but an American frontier soldier. We are told that the Indians planned an ambuscade, but it would seem a curious kind of ambuscade that 120 men should allow themselves to be surrounded by 500, backed by artillery. That many of the Indians – now so fortunately dead – had murdered settlers and fired ranches I have little doubt. That the whole

236

Indian question (like the question of the unemployed in London) is a most difficult and piteous one no one will deny. Still, though, hardly anyone who knows Indians can refrain from thinking that in this instance there seems to have been a deliberate attempt to goad them to fury in order to shoot them down. Any old Indian fighter will agree with me that to attempt to deprive Indians of their arms by surrounding them at daybreak with troops was certain to produce a conflict. The Indian resents nothing in the world like an attempt to deprive him of his weapons.

He is almost born with them. His little bow as a child grows with him, becomes strong and tough with him, and is buried with him. It is no more his fault that generations on generations have been accustomed to go armed than it is the fault of a mustang, born a pacer, to refuse to trot.

It is as ridiculous to expect an Indian to love work as it would have been to expect a Highlander of the '45 to take to typewriting rather than cattle-lifting as a means of subsistence.

Indians will (and experience both on the pampa and the prairie have taught me this) only deliver up their arms at a time of solemn treaty or in the presence of overwhelming force. Five hundred men were enough to destroy, but not enough to overawe, one hundred Indians.

No one should have known this better than the officer in command of the troops. Therefore, I believe the whole affair was arranged beforehand by men who knew perfectly well what would happen. One's very soul revolts in disgust from the account of the cruel butchery, the shooting down of fleeing savages with Gatling guns, the useless and cruel slaughter of the women and children.

The only consolatory feature of the whole affair is that the Indians seem to have fought like demons and inflicted severe loss on the troops before they were exterminated.

I had hoped that the matchless pen of Bret Harte[388] would have raised a protest against the doings in Dakota; if the protest had been made it would have run through the American press like wildfire, and surely must have produced some good. Soon, I suppose, we shall hear of some more glorious victories of the same kind, and then the ghost dancers can all dance together in some other world, where we may hope there

---

[388] A writer of popular Wild-West fiction, who for a short time was the United States Consul in Glasgow.

may be neither Gatlings nor any other of the pillars of civilisation to annoy them.

It seems a pity, too, to waste so many good Indians who might have been so advantageously used to turn honest pennies for enterprising showmen, if no other method of utilising them occurred to the great American Republic. However, I may be permitted to make my moan over the women and children at least, for I doubt much if they had committed any weightier crimes than the unpardonable one of living.

Now that they are dead they will furnish an excellent repast for the coyotes; and, for the Indians, they would have died hereafter; and, after all, what does it matter? For, as Montaigne says, *"Quoi, ils ne portaient pas des haults de chausses."*[389] [sic]

In 1921, *Scribner's Magazine* (New York) published Graham's article *Long Wolf*, which brought to public attention the forgotten grave of the chief of the Ogallala Sioux, in West Brompton Cemetery, London. Long Wolf had fought at the Battle of the Little Big Horn, and had died of pneumonia, aged 59 while touring with Buffalo Bill's 'Wild West.' In 1991, after reading Graham's article in a second-hand book, the gravesite was rediscovered by a Worcestershire housewife named Elizabeth Knight. In 1997, after a long campaign with his descendants, Long Wolf's remains were reinterred near the site of the Wounded Knee massacre.

~

The 10-week Spanish–American War in 1898 was a conflict stoked up by the American yellow press to wrest control of Cuba, and take possession of Puerto Rico, Guam and the Philippines. Future President Theodore Roosevelt (who had written to Graham suggesting subjects for a book)[390] had led his "rough riders" during the campaign on Cuban soil, and declared it "a splendid little war," and it ushered the USA onto the geopolitical stage.

While Britain (particularly) and the United States still talk about "the special relationship," Graham had no doubt back then what this relationship was, and to whose advantage it worked.

---

[389] French: "What, they do not wear breeches?" Montaigne, *Essays XXX* 'Of Cannibals.'
[390] President Roosevelt's son, Kermit (1889-1943), wrote: 'My father had been for many years and eager reader of all that Cunninghame Graham wrote [. . .] I thought at the time that here was a writer that could make Buffalo Bill and his era live and speak and act for our children, and our children's children.' 'Introduction' to *Rodeo* (1936).

238

## WAS IT WORTH IT?

To the Editor of *The Saturday Review*, 3<sup>rd</sup> of February 1900.

Sir, - During the Spanish-American war, I was one of the few who maintained that it was both base and impolitic to throw over our old ally Spain and humiliate ourselves before the United States in the vain hope of alliance with that Power.

My views were held to be sentimental. Events have proved them practical and have shown that the "Pan-Anglian" rhapsodists were the true sentimentalists. That our conduct was base, is I think amply proved, by the fact that we sided with the stronger side against the weaker.

True we did so, with many platitudes about "progress," "civilisation," and "Pan-Anglianism."

Progress and civilisation are not mere matters of flags (barred, or striped, with due garnishings of stars and caps of liberty), but include such things, as shorter hours of labour, lessening of division between classes and kindly treatment of coloured races. Are the working hours in Cuba shorter today than they were under the Spaniards? Those who know the American capitalists can answer this question.

As to division of classes, anyone who knows New York can speak as to the unfathomable gulf between the rich and poor in that city.

Lastly when did anyone hear of intermarriage between an American and a coloured woman? Yet such intermarriages often took place in all the Spanish colonies. It may be that ere long, Lynch Law will be introduced into Cuba, and that possibly will be the sum of the Cuban gain.

To speak of the Philippines is an offence, the last state of those unhappy islands being at present a disgrace to humanity and civilisation. I now come to the impolicy of our actions. We threw over and insulted Spain in her necessity, thus securing one more enemy in Europe, when we had already not a single friend but herself. Moreover we deliberately sacrificed the help of a nation, which though fallen upon evil times must always be taken into account in all settlements of naval and military questions on the Mediterranean coasts; a nation also which in the event of a war between France and England could materially help either power.

What have we gained by all our squirmings and grovelings before the United States?

239

An Open Door. Yes, and a booted foot to kick us through it. It was ever the sneak's reward to be thus treated.

But have we even gained the Open Door?

That remains to be proved.

It may stand ajar whilst President McKinley is in office; but there are not wanting indications that should the Democrats enter into power it would immediately be slammed in our faces.

It should not be forgotten that the United States is a strongly Protectionist Power.

Let us now come to the present time. Our affairs in South Africa are not in a brilliant condition. We have had our reverses, and all Europe has laughed in chorus.

According to the "Pan-Anglian" theory help and commiseration should have come from "our own flesh and blood," from "our cousins beyond the sea," from "that great and growing people derived from the same stock as ourselves and akin to us in thought in language and in sympathy (sic)."

Have they come?

On the contrary from one end of the United States to the other enthusiastic meetings in favour of the Boers have been held against us.

At those meetings we have been denounced as "oppressors" as "pirates" as "robbers" and as bullies.

It may be that these epithets are our due; but surely those who uttered them ("our own flesh and blood") must have forgotten the meaning of the word "Kewby."[391]

Money has been collected at these meetings and forwarded, to the "patriots of the South African republics rightly struggling for liberty."

More than that, on Monday last it was stated in the United States Senate, that 95 per cent of American opinion was opposed to us in the present contest.

All alliance with us has been repeatedly and contemptuously repudiated, not only at public meetings, but by American statesmen.

It is hard to teach an old dog to do new tricks, and harder to remove by a few after-dinner speeches the rooted antipathy of a hundred years. We have failed in receiving, not only the sympathy, but almost the neutrality of the United States, as it is stated that

---

[391] Unknown.

240

a loan is to be negotiated in that country for the Transvaal Government.

It is certain that from no country have such emphatic protests come about "food stuffs" being declared "contraband of war," as from the United States.

It now remains to be seen if that country will be the first to receive an envoy from the South African Republics. It is possible that the first offer of intervention may come from America, that is if 95 per cent of the population hate and despise us, and sympathise with the Boers.

Truth and Justice (for all I know) may be somewhere or other; but if they are, they were "there" when, with insulting language, we threw over Spain our ancient ally, and came magnanimously to the assistance of America, squirming and sniffling on our bellies, to receive the smallest measure of favour.

Was it worth while, so to foreswear ourselves for such a despicable cause, and have not events proved that we acted impolitically [sic] and in a base and miserable fashion?

Was it worth while?

In some doubt,

I remain, Sir, yours faithfully, R. B. Cunninghame Graham.

~

## COALS OF FIRE.
To the Editor of *The Saturday Review*, 17th of February 1900.

Sir,

As yours was the one journal (as far as I know) in all England, to advocate prudence and reflection before professing sympathy, holus bolus, with the United States in their war with Spain, without receiving from them any reciprocity, I venture to address you again upon that subject.

That one nation is free to offer its sympathy to another is incontestable; but that a nation, who already has few friends (I forgot our faithful friend Italy in my last letter), is prudent in rushing in, without making conditions, requires proof. We are (I think) a commercial nation; it is our pride and our boast; we pat our stomachs when we say it, at times, we seem to value ourselves more upon our commercialism than upon our truth or honour.

241

But I submit that it is not acting on sound business principles to give up goods without some guarantee of the purchase money being paid.

Now what we gave to the United States was in reality goods (we are a commercial nation), and those goods, i.e. our sympathy and our help against the intervention of the Powers, have never been paid for.

Therefore, as a member of a commercial nation I protest against such a flagrant departure from sound business principles and against the frittering away of the national assets (sympathy and help), without fitting return.

But though the United States has proved, in this matter, a fraudulent debtor; Spain on the other hand has behaved as befits an ancient ally.

Though in the States the insults of the Yellow Press fall thick and fast on England, her people and her Queen, and meetings are daily being held in which we are reviled, in Spain only a fortnight ago a pro-Boer meeting advertised to be held in Barcelona was proclaimed by the Government as an infringement of neutrality towards a Power with which Spain was at peace.

Certainly Spain owes us little. We sat still and saw her stripped of her colonies, under lying and specious protests, which deceived no one, least of all ourselves.

But it appears that fair dealing and honourable treatment are to come from the ally whom we betrayed and meanly sacrificed, and insult, abuse, and dishonourable treatment from our own Anglo-Saxon (sic) kinsfolk, to whom we groveled so much and from whom we are now receiving a deserved cold-shouldering.

The above view is I submit a common-sense and a practical view of international alliance. Alliances (unlike Anglo-Saxon marriages) are not made in heaven.

They are made on earth, and conducted (or should be conducted), purely on business principles.

No alliance (except for brief periods of filibustering) is possible between commercial competitors. It is a commonplace of the Political Economists, not of Marx and the Socialists but of Marshall and the Plutocrats, that "the wars of the future will be for markets."

But this is so, and I do not doubt it. As we are a commercial people, clearly we run most danger from our keenest competitor, the United States. If this is not so, then the axiom re "wars and markets," falls to the ground. But if sentiment is to rule and not ordinary commercial principles, where is the sympathetic attitudes which our statesmen assured us would be superinduced if we threw over Spain and bravely came to the assistance of the big battalions?

I am, Sir, yours faithfully, R. B. Cunninghame Graham.

~

Graham's debts, and his failure to win Camlachie in 1892, seems to have precipitated a crisis, during which he apparently contemplated suicide.[392] Caroline Benn writes that (along with Hardie), Graham and his wife Gabrielle were 'unrecognized manic depressives,'[393] but Tschiffely only describes an occasional tendency toward the morose.[394] Gabrielle's mental state might be gauged by the fact that at this time, and up to her premature death in 1906, she was smoking between one and two hundred cigarettes a day.[395] Their financial crisis deepened, and in 1900 they were obliged to sell Gartmore House and estate, which broke Graham's heart, and left him with feelings of ancestral betrayal.[396] However, it was probably the saving of him, and he was now free to spend more time abroad, pursue his literary career, and re-engage with politics.

Since 1891, while still an M.P., Graham had been a regular visitor to Morocco, travelling to remote areas, the climax of which was his famous journey in late 1897, aged 46, towards the forbidden city of Tarudant on the edge of the Sahara Desert, disguised as a Turkish doctor. This journey ended in failure when he was captured and imprisoned by the local Kaid, but it resulted in his most celebrated book - *Mogreb-El-Acksa* (The Far West), hailed by many as the finest travel book ever written. In 1904, France and Spain carved out zones of influence in Morocco (so-called 'protectorates'), which drew in Germany (with Britain and the United States standing in the wings), precipitating *The Moroccan Crisis*, and the country would remain destabilised until the mid 1920s. During this period, Graham travelled there many times, reporting on conditions, and was at one point the 'Special Correspondent' for *The Glasgow Herald*, (the newspaper that had consistently criticised him during his parliamentary career). His many articles, on the complexities of the ever-changing political situation, as the European powers jockeyed for influence, exclude any attempt at a comprehensive engagement, but the following letter demonstrates the depth of his knowledge and involvement.

---

[392] John Lavery, *The Life of a Painter* (London, Cassell & Co), 1940), p.89.
[393] Benn, p.46.
[394] Tschiffely, p.24.
[395] Ibid., p.269.
[396] A moving description of their last day at Gartmore can be found in Graham's sketch: 'A Braw Day,' *The English Review* (November 1911), pp.609-14.

Graham travelling incognito as Sheik Mohammed El Fasi.

## THE POSITION IN MOROCCO:
Letter to *The Glasgow Herald*, 15th of August 1912.

"Sir - I was much struck with your leading article on the situation in Morocco this morning. May I, without offence, call it Liberal!

Mulai Hafid[397] has indeed been a victim of circumstances. Without doubt he is a cruel and bloodthirsty man, as his conduct on several occasions has proved, but at the same time he was a patriot, and did all he could to preserve the independence of his country, in the same spirit that Wallace showed of old Scotland. Your readers must not be too ready to assume that a little more colouring ("pigmentum") in the skin of necessity takes from a man the love of country. Neither can a little more or less tincture of civilisation be held as a disqualification. We have no documentary evidence that Wallace took more than an occasional bath, or "kist his sark"[398] as often as does a modern paladin. For all that, only a Southron [399]would deny that he was patriot.

To return to Mulai Hafid, who by the injunctions of his creed is a great bath-taker, and by the immemorial custom of Sultans of Morocco certainly never wore any of his

---

[397] The Sultan of Morocco from 1908 to 1912.
[398] Scots: Doffed his shirt.
[399] An Englishman.

clothes more than once, his position was doomed to failure from the first. The French had (in the interest of the bondholders) deprived him of all revenue, except what he could extort directly from the tribes. All the Custom Houses were held by France to secure the pound of flesh of the Christian Shylocks who had advanced money. After a certain amount of squeezing the tribes rebelled, and this was the opportunity for the French. Then followed a sham relief of Fez. The truth was that it was never in danger. How a strongly-walled city, well supplied with quick-firing guns, could be in danger from a rabble of tribesmen with gas-pipe, flint-lock guns passes my powers of imagination. Our compatriot, Mr M'Ivor M'Leod the British consul, remained quietly in Fez during this hypothetic siege. I think his wife and family were with him. The French and German consuls, also friends of mine, never thought of moving, though at any time they could have come down to the coast.

You say that Mulai-Abd-al-Assiz[400] was . . . "a shallow trifler and as profligate in his instincts as Ismail of Egypt."[401] I passed three weeks at his Court, seeing him every day riding out, and talking with him repeatedly, and may fairly say that I knew him pretty well. I know him still, and dined with him in Tangier in the month of April. Certainly he was a "shallow trifler" during the time he was Sultan. He was very young, and many Europeans, who ought to have advised him against extravagance and folly, were only too ready (in order to make money) to push him on rather than to restrain him. I do not think he had "profligate instincts" or was the least like Ismail of Egypt. Ismail was a far abler man, and knew perfectly well what he was about. I never heard Mulai-Abd-el-Assiz accused of profligacy other than buying a mail coach in a country where there are no roads, or ordering an enormous steam launch to go on a little river about as big as the Luggie.[402]

The whole episode of the French intervention in Morocco has been a sordid affair, and stained with great and unnecessary bloodshed. It has resulted in placing both shores of the Mediterranean in the hands of Powers that could close it to us in the event of the entente cordiale coming to an end. I say Powers advisedly. France has never allowed Spain to fortify the northern frontier Puycerda and Figueras, thus leaving a space of

[400] The Sultan of Morocco from 1894 at the age of sixteen, until he was deposed in 1908.
[401] Isma'il Pasha, known as 'Ismail the Magnificent,' the Khedive of Egypt and Sudan from 1863 to 1879.
[402] A rivulet, which flows from the border of Graham's old constituency in Lanarkshire, and enters the River Kelvin at Kirkintilloch. An extraordinary, but not untypical comparison.

some 80 miles free, through which she can march an army. This, though it is unknown to many Spaniards, is the reason that has made France the controller of the destinies of Spain for at least a century.

It is also the reason that made many of us who know Morocco welcome the presence of the Germans in Agadir as a counterpoise to the power of France. Too many people forget that from Tangier to the island of Perejil the distance is but nine miles. With Spain controlled by France the entrance to the straits could be closed with ease and Gibraltar rendered useless, or obliged to surrender through want of provisions, which could not possibly arrive from land.

In any case France will have a long and costly business on her hands, and one which possibly may stir the taxpayers into revolt. Moreover, if the present movement in the south succeeds under the leadership of Mohamed-el-Hibu, the son of the great desert Marabout Ma-el-Anin,[403] France may find herself faced by a new empire in the Sus.[404]

You say that France can bear the financial strain of a long filibustering expedition better than Italy or Spain. That is so, but you go on to say that Spain has reaped no glory and even less in material results by her piratical incursion to the Riff. Once more I say that is so; but why omit all reference to Italy, who surely has neither laid up glory nor mere cash in Tripoli? Lastly, I think you may as well also include France. Glory is surely not added to the laurels of a nation by the bombardment of defenceless towns, such as was Casa Blanca, and money, what possibly can be gained by the acquisition of a poor country such as Morocco, stuck, moreover, as thick as is a wasps' nest with wasps, with turbulent, fierce tribes.

I am, etc., R. B. Cunninghame Graham.

PS - Your readers may be surprised that I refer to Morocco as a poor country. There are a few choice bits in it, but they are small; and as to minerals, in spite of all that we have heard - where are the mines?

---

[403] Leader of the resistance against the French and Spanish in 1884-1885.
[404] The name given to the southwestern part of Morocco before the establishment of the French and Spanish 'protectorates.'

~

In November 1912, a Parliamentary Committee examined the alleged killing of an estimated 30,000 Amazonian Indians[405] (which became known as 'The Putumayo Affair'), through starvation and mistreatment, under the control of The Anglo-Peruvian Rubber Company that was registered in London, and had three British directors. The man believed to be responsible was the 'rubber baron' Julio César Arana, who appeared at the hearing, and whose power and intimidation had prevented any proceedings against him in Peru.

## UP THE RIVER
*The Nation*, 31st of May 1913.

Father Gumilla, Jesuit and missionary, has left us many and curious descriptions of the Indian tribes, both of the Orinoco and the Amazon. In those days, Tarayacu and Uyacali were well known mission stations. Manaus was but a port for canoes trading in a small way. Iquitos, only a name at most, had a mission and a few trading huts.

---

[405] This estimate was given in a report by the British diplomat Roger Casement who had visited the Amazon in 1910, and who was subsequently knighted for his work there, and in the Congo. 'Sir' Roger Casement was executed for treason in 1916, in Pentonville Prison, (where Graham had been incarcerated), for attempting to enlist German support for an Irish uprising during the First World War. Graham would write to his friend W. H. Nevinson on the 27th of November 1927 about Casement: 'His father was deputy grand master of the Orange Lodges of Armagh. Sir Roger was a bitter, black Ulster Protestant, who, when [Joseph] Conrad and I knew him first, had no words but of contempt for Irish Catholics . . .'

The Putumayo was known but to a few Brazilian and Peruvian half-breeds, and the Indians lived their natural lives - lives interspersed with fighting and ritual cannibalism, just as Gumilla has described. Walking once through some zoological prison where the animals were caged either behind bars or walked about upon the edge of ditches too wide for them to cross, all looking dull and languid, fat and overfed, and all as bored as is the average member of the legislature, a friend remarked: "I often think these beasts are happier here than they could be if they were all at large." I looked at him, pained and amazed, for he seemed quite a reasonable man, and a few minutes only had elapsed since he was talking, with a glistening eye, about the freedom of Albania.

He saw my look, and said, "I think so, for in the deserts and the woods they suffer hunger, mange, and wounds. They fight with one another, and in old age they die of hunger miserably."

Seeing I had a crank to deal with, I rejoined: "All that you say is true; but they have liberty. If they fight it is with one another, and no one ever heard of tigers setting out to exterminate another race of beasts; they only eat when they require food. True, in this horrid place of torture they have a sufficiency to eat; moreover, there always is a plentiful supply of fools to gaze at them. When they have mange, ointment is rubbed into their skins, and so on. Therefore, to make them happier still and take away even the desire for anything but life-sustaining food, to make all perfect, why not castrate every one of them, and, having drawn their teeth, feed them through horns with gruel made of meat?"

That is the problem with the Indians. Julio Arana knows it well, for in examination he stated: "These Indians are freer than ourselves. They have no business, no commerce, worries, or troubles such as we have here, and they know all the forest tracts and streams, just as we know the streets here in our cities and our towns." He added: "The Indians are happier than we are"; and again, "for full three hundred years these Indians have resisted civilisation."

All this he said in the flat, toneless Spanish that men speak away up the rivers in the Tropics, with the slow drawl that seems inborn in those with an admixture of Indian blood. As he spoke, slowly, cautiously, without a trace of hesitation, without the least annoyance at the questions that were showered at him, plausible, deft in confusing issues, with an air of knowing what he talked about, the committee room, the nervous chairman with his spectacles, the lawyers in their wigs, the pressmen jotting down their copy, the ladies in their furs, the audience of the strange heterogeneous people that law courts, committees, and other places where there is no entry money to be paid always assemble, seemed to melt away into the mist which filtered in through the open leaden-paned windows, from the Thames.

I saw another river, yellow and turbid, running between the banks of alluvial soil, with hard-wood trees growing down to the edge. Here and there it left bare banks of sand, on which basked alligators. Here and there were clearings, with a trader's house, a little landing-place, and two or three canoes. Occasionally islands broke the stream, and on them waved bamboos and palms, feathery and light, and from them to the river's bank flew parrots and toucans. Heron's fished in the iguapés and cormorants sat on dead branches of the trees. Canoes shot out from underneath the dark, metallic-looking vegetation, and in the stream an Indian stood drawing his bow to shoot fish in the shallows. Along the narrow sandy trails now and then Indian women marched in line, naked except for a white cloth, and monkeys chattered in the trees. Sometimes I thought I saw a tribal battle, with loud ear-piercing yells and arrows whistling through the trees. Terrible as it seems after the Balkan War and the invasions of both Tripoli and of Morocco, several men were slain. Prisoners were taken and sometimes tortured; but all of them died game. A cruel sight it was, ten times more horrible than the thought of the half-eviscerated men who lay, a month or so ago, in Thrace and frost-bitten, crushed by passing wagons, gnawed by wolves, and their eyes picked out by crows, because the Indians were not Christians, and fought to please themselves.

Yet Julio Arana, who alone of all the people in the Committee Room except one or two of his underlings, who stood about, olive-skinned, undersized, and looking pinched with cold, myself, and Hardenburg,[406] had seen these kind of Indians in their native state, and he deliberately said: "These Indians are happier than ourselves." Here my mind worked back to the Committee Room, and Julio Arana, tall and broad-

---

[406] Along with Roger Casement, the American journalist Walter Hardenburg (1886-1942) had exposed the atrocities carried out by Anglo-Peruvian Rubber in what has been described as: "perhaps the most terrible page in the whole history of commercialism."

shouldered, with a skin the colour of the stomach of an alligator, small and dull Indian eyes, boots made (possibly in Iquitos) by a trunk-maker, and dressed win "store clothes," was sitting down, having more than held his own with his examiners.

One could not but admire his vast audacity. His strong and prognathous skull showed him a man of power, perhaps not intellectual; but cunning and resourceful, pitiless and bold. His under jaw, powerful as a gorilla's, looked as if it could have closed, like a steel trap, upon your hand. His head gave the impression that you might strike it with a hatchet till your arm ached, and make as little show upon it as on a stump of greenheart in his own native woods.

Brazilians, Columbians, Peruvians, one and all smile when you talk of him and say

"Of course, we know Arana . . . he is the rubber man."

"Cruel?" you ask; and they reply, "Not personally, as far as we know. He is a rubber man, and to get rubber you cannot go about in gloves."

So Julio Arana in the flesh, bound in his hat and hosen,[407] the bold, soft-spoken, keen-witted Peruvian, with his keen wit set in his athletic body, left my mind on which he had so strongly stamped his picture, left the Committee Room without a stain on . . . his ability, having admitted this most important fact, that there "had been atrocities, although exaggerated in the account." No doubt that most atrocities are coloured by those who tell them. Still, the natural indication of the witness does not palliate the crime.

What matters it if the victims of the Inquisition are to be numbered by the thousands or in tens? Calvin is damned for all eternity for having burned one man. Damned in the minds of those who think that all the souls of all mankind since the Creation would have been saved too dearly if but one man was forced to pass through fire to any kind of god.

Arana got up from his chair, bowed, and withdrew, and in the corridor stood talking through an interpreter to a confiding Irish priest. The worthy man thanked him in a rich brogue for all his kindness done through is agents to some young Franciscan friars just landed in Iquitos. Arana smiled, showing a row of strong, white teeth that would have graced a shark, and with a gesture seemed to put the friars away

---

[407] The Book of Daniel 3:21

from him in the same spirit that Cromwell waved away the crown. Then, without looking to the right or left, he walked down the pseudo-Gothic corridor, followed by his clan.

Then came the turn of Hardenburg, the man to whom Europe and America is indebted for the knowledge of the facts. "Make yourself a Redeemer, and you will be crucified," so runs the Spanish saying; and this is just as true to-day as it was nineteen hundred years ago in Galilee. Poor and unknown, accused of forgery, and of blackmail - all revelations of the treatment of the Indians, Arana and his kind stigmatised as blackmail - when he had taken his position, just in the middle of the semi-circle, all craned to see the kind of man he was.

Just as Arana speaks a nerveless and slow Spanish, so does Hardenburg speak slow Western English. Perhaps the climate makes all men of European race born in America, speak slowly and drawlingly. English and Portuguese and Spaniards, Brazilians, Argentines, Mexicans or what not, all speak but little, and speak that little slow. Pale with the pallor of the man of Northern European stock who has had fevers in the Tropics, brown haired, brown eyed, and rather bald, clean-shaven, and self possessed, the witness sat as impassive as a Sphinx.

His rather worn blue serge suit fitted him closely, and gave an air of neatness to disfigure, not quite American and still not English, which conveyed somehow the feeling that he had lived long in hot countries, and was accustomed to thin boots and clothes. Little enough about him to arrest the eye, except a square piece of "aventurine,"[408] known on the Pacific coast as "gold-stone," that dangled from his chain.

Briefly and quite conclusively he disposed of both the charges of blackmail and forger; touched on the outrages on in passing, referring no and then to passages which he had written in his book. Nothing compelled him to appear; he came, just as Arana came "on a lone hand," in the same way that he, three or four years ago, unknown and friendless, sought the offices of "Truth."[409]

All questions put to him were answered briefly, and to the point, in the strong accent of his native land, but in a pleasant voice. Nothing sensational occurred in his

---

[408] A green quartz.
[409] The British publication that first broke the story in 1909.

examination, and those who had listened to him, hoping to hear a tale of horrors or violent attacks on Arana, were disappointed in their hopes. The interest in the man was in himself, not in what he brought out before the Committee of the House.

As he spoke on, one saw him an engineer upon the Cauca Railway in Columbia. In one's mind's eye one watched him hire his horses at Buenaventura, on the Pacific coast, followed him on the road to Pasto and to Popayán. "All the world after is but Popayán," the proverb goes. What curious and old-world haciendas he stopped at on the road to those two historic and most clerical cities one can conjecture easily.

No doubt, as evening came on, bringing with it the pain between the shoulders that long days on horseback at the "Trotccito" brings, he saw the vast old building in the distance, rode to the gate, passed through Zaguan, and found himself in a great courtyard like an Eastern caravanserai.

A long, low range of sheds, roofed with red tiles, ran round the walls, and under it he got off and tied up his beasts. When they were cool, he, or his peon, led them to the great well right in the middle of the yard and watered them, and set out to buy them fodder and provisions for himself. Perhaps he had a little stuccoed room with a bench made of white cement at one end on which to lay the bed. Perhaps he slung a hammock between two pillars of the shed; or, perhaps, lighting a fire, lay down beside it, after his supper and a smoke. Some days he plodded on through forest paths in semi-darkness, under gigantic trees, all interspersed with strong bejucos as thick as boat ropes. At other times his way led up rough mountain paths, on which he stumbled, drenched in perspiration, dragging along his horse. Again, he would have days on open plains, on which the sun played like a furnace, and the heat ascending from the earth rose up to meet the glare of the fierce sky. Sometimes he passed a group of huts buried amongst banana trees, round which fed scraggy goats. In the old towns he rested probably a day or two, wandered about the streets, and saw the Indian market, with its silent crowd, seated before their wares, or, entering the dark, cool churches, sat down exhausted with the heat.

His coming would excite a mild sensation, and priests would ask him if he was a Christian, telling him, perchance, with pride, of how before the battle fought at

Boyacá, Bolivar,[410] finding no one to serve Mass, mounted his horse, and called out: "Are there amongst the ranks some men from Popayán?" and when three or four stepped out at his call, said, "That is right. You, Pepe, serve the Mass." The long trail over, and arrived at the head waters of Putumayo, there would be the hire or buying of a canoe and the search for paddlers. All this time he had travelled through a country quiet as Devonshire; but now the scene was changed. As he dropped down the river, paddling with the current, resting between the hours of ten and three to dodge the heat, and in the evening dragging the canoe up into some open spot for fear of tigers, he would pass Indian tribes.

At first, quite savage and unused to see white faces, they treated him with confidence; but by degrees the sight of his canoe made them escape into the woods.

As he was quite in ignorance of what was going on in the rubber districts, this would astonish him, but still he paddled on. Finally, one hot afternoon, the "Iquitos," a steam launch, passed them down the stream, her crew all shouting, and a man firing a shot across his bows. She passed, and Hardenburg having paddled his canoe ashore, was wondering if it were not the safest thing to do to run unto the bush.

Then, steaming down the river, fresh from the taking of La Union, drunk with new rum and blood, came the launch "El Liberal."

The rest is history, and the tale of his being taken prisoner, learning about the horrors, and his book,[411] is known to the whole world.

What is not so well known is that there, far away "aguas arriba" (up the river), is a vast system of great forests cut by and into rivers, and often inundated, so that an enormous lake extends for leagues.

There the remainder of the Amazonian Indians are delivered over to the scum of the whole world, for such a scum as is the half-breed population in the great No-man's-land between the three republics cannot be matched on earth.

Un 1670, good Padre Figueroa - he was martyred by the Cocumas just at the junction of the Huellagas and Apuré (affluents of the Amazon) - in his "Revelation of the Missions of the Conception of Jesus in the country of the Maynas," has the following:

---

[410] Graham wrote that his grandfather on his mother's side, Admiral Charles Elphinstone Fleeming of Cumbernauld (1774-1840), had befriended Simón Bolivar, 'El Libertador.' (1783-1830). Cunninghame Graham: 'The Admiral,' *The Saturday Review* (3 November, 1900), pp.546-548.
[411] *Putumayo: The Devil's Paradise* (1912).

"Two-thirds of all the Indians die from diseases contracted from the Spaniards. Only God knows the occult design of Divine Providence that when the Evangel enters their houses the result is so many illnesses and such mortality."

The ways of Providence are indeed hard to fathom. Only a child, and those who are born with faith, as Padre Figueroa was, are children to the end, would ever try to sound them, or to do aught but marvel at the great unfathomable plan.

Forests and forests and still more forests; rivers and swamps, and still more rivers and more swamps; Morichi palms, Tacamajaca, Urundei, and Greenheart, millions of hardwood trees and feathery bamboos; a wilderness of slime and mud; a chessboard cut into gigantic squares by rivers, and a sun that shines out wearily through the mist; a world of humming birds, of parrots, pink flamingoes, and macaws sailing like through the still, heavy air; a world where monkeys chatter, and where the tapir bursts through the underwoods, and the great manati floats awash upon the streams, and where insects hum like the faint drumming of a tom-tom on a tropic night; such is the Putumayo.

In it man has a little place - a place as humble as mankind has in the whole world; but a place that he filled happily according to his lights.

His destiny lies in the tweed-clad laps of those assembled in Committee, having the knowledge both of good and evil, just as if they were gods.

The fate of these poor Indians lies in their hands; these tribes to whom good Padre Figueroa brought, as he thought, glad tidings of great joy, and to whom Julio Arana brought the lash.


The Committee's deliberations were brought to an end by the Great War. Arana died penniless in 1952, aged 88.

# □□□□□□
# SCOTLAND

From 1896, until his death forty years later, Graham wrote over thirty Scottish sketches. Solemn, often tragic, vivid descriptions of old-world gentry, local worthies, and eccentric relatives, all of whom were disappearing – 'being born unfit for progress.'[412] The overall pace and effect is languid, his Scotland is benighted, its people are stolid and stoic, but have lost the vital spark of spirituality and joy, resulting in the loss of the older, heroic type. As John Walker points out: '[. . .] nationalists of the 1930s [. . .] have tended to forget that in the early stages of his career [. . .] Graham had treated with a vitriolic realism the defects of the Scottish character and the abuses and vices of the national way of life.'[413] However, this might also have been his reaction against the 'Kailyard' school of writing, which depicted a cosy continuity, camouflaging the destruction of communities and social cohesion, which it purported to exalt, disguising life's harsh realities, and ameliorating the need for radical action. Imperialism is not something that only happened abroad, and this is where Graham's political campaigns, his anti-imperialism, his histories, his sketches, and his portraits, find reconciliation – in his gauchos, his Jesuits, his Apaches, Sioux, and his old-world Scots.

In Ireland and Scotland, land ownership and the plight of subsistence farmers, or crofters, was a burning issue throughout the 19th century, with pressure exerted by landlords to 'clear' them from the land, resulting in mass migration (often forced) of hundreds of thousands of people. Henry George's books and speaking tours which proposed that the land belonged to the people by right, that private ownership should be abolished without compensation, and that the occupants should become tenants of the State, provided a lightning rod for growing discontent. As a direct result of George's Scottish tour in 1884, the Scottish Land Restoration League was formed, followed by the Highland Land League, and its Parliamentary arm, The Crofters' Party, which succeeded in getting four M.P.s elected. [414]

Graham saw the issue of land ownership in Scotland as of enormous importance, at a time when the plight of the crofters in the Highlands had spilled into open rebellion. His radical views on the subject, which, unlike Henry, proposed the nationalisation of the land, are all the more remarkable coming from the lips and pen of a landlord whose properties bordered the Highlands:

---

412 Cunninghame Graham, *Thirteen Stories* (Heinmann 1900), p.x.
413 John Walker, 'Cunninghame Graham and the Critics' (*Studies in Scottish Literature* Vol.19, 1984), p.113.
414 Graham had demurred from standing against their candidate, James Shaw Maxwell in Glasgow at the 1885 general election, in return for which they supported his campaign in North-West Lanark.

Military again for the West Highlands. The old Tory dodge. The unfortunate people starve, and the Tory Government, to their cry for meal, answer with bullets. Points for our readers: Are deer game? Have the crofters broken any law? Have they injured any man? Have they destroyed the work of any man's hands? Scotland is a free country – quite – it appears; for a crofter to starve in, or a deer to eat his crops in. I wish – and surely there is no harm in wishing – that there were not a deer, a grouse, or a salmon in all the Highlands. If there were not, we might see more sheep, more agriculture, more men, and fewer Cockneys and German princelets.[415]

**THE DESTITUTE CROFTERS**: MEETING OF GLASGOW SYMPATHISERS
*The Coatbridge Express*, 28th of December 1887.

It is not often that a public man has addressed a Glasgow audience under heavy bail.[416] I stand in that position tonight, and when a man is on bail it is very easy for him to give vent to seditious language. Now, I am aware that if all those assembled at this meeting were to go into the witness-box and swear that I had not used seditious language, if a

---

[415] Letter to *The Coatbridge Express* (30 November 1887), p.2.

[416] Graham was still awaiting trial for his part in the riot in Trafalgar Square.

policeman had sworn that I had, your testimony would be to no avail. (*Laughter.*) Therefore I do not intend to put you to the proof by speaking anything that might be considered seditious this evening.

I suppose, after all they must look upon political [words illegible] told them to do so. But I think it is a science that has been pushed as far as they would like it to go. Let them take up old General Stewart's book on the Highlands[417] a genuine representative of old crusted cobwebbed Toryism, but nevertheless a humane man, a man of feeling, a Scotchman, and a Highlander who knew the sufferings of the people among whom he lived. They would find that in those days of which General Stewart wrote, although there was not much wealth in the Highlands, there was no starvation. Mark the irony of the civilisation process. The driving out of the human beings had been a complete failure. (*Cheers.*) What I will say is - Burn political economy and buy a Bible; they are cheap now, because, I suppose, fewer people read them as formerly. (*Laughter.*) You will find in the Bible, not perhaps, better political economy, but more humanity than they are accustomed to experience in the administration of present day government.

The crofter question is not a new one; it is a grievance of long-standing, and one which now, at all events, no serious politician can afford to burke. It is one of these questions we must set ourselves seriously to solve, like the question of the unemployed in London, like the Irish question, like the poor we always have with us, we must have the Highland question, unless the crofters take it into their hands to work our their own salvation by taking a leaf out of the Irish book and making the country unendurable to the ruling classes. Now, that is not sedition; at least it is not sedition in England and Scotland, for there is no coercion here, but in Ireland it would be sedition, and only yesterday we have seen a Roman Catholic priest dragged into prison for using language not one whit stronger, and for all we know by this time he has been waited upon in his cell by five warders, knocked down, and stripped of his clothes. (*Shame.*) This has already been done in the case of other political offenders in Ireland, but then it was done in the name of law and order. (*Shame.*)

The crofter question has rapidly developed itself. It is a question that obtrudes itself

---

[417] Major General David Stewart of Garth, *Sketches of the Character, Manners, and Present State of the Highlanders of Scotland'* (1822).

257

on men's minds, and it is a question above all others that interests us, and that directs the attention of men to first principles. (*Cheers.*) When people begin to look into first principles - the people who are called the mob and the swinish multitude, as the Tories call them - when they begin to look into first principles it becomes rather dangerous for the ruling classes. (*Cheers.*) It was so in '93 in France, and in '48 all over Europe, and now it is going to be dangerous, too, when the scales of Toryism have fallen from their eyes, and when like a giant rising from sleep the working class realises the power they have got, and band themselves together and cry, "Hold, enough!" We must have justice in Ireland; we must have justice for Scotland and Wales; we must have a municipality for London; we must have justice done to the suffering crofters in the Highlands. (*Cheers.*)

I have often said lately, in speaking to the unemployed in London, that they have their rights and wrongs, but they also have their duties. Now I want to say that the crofters also have their duties. If self-preservation is the first law of nature it is the duty of the crofter, not only to himself, but his wife and family, to ring the chapel bells, to set the heather ablaze, to form land leagues, to adopt plans of campaign, and generally to make the situation for the landlord untenable until the democracy in Glasgow and other great cities throughout the Empire have first settled the Irish question and then come to their assistance. (*Cheers.*) I condemn weak and self-seeking Liberal leaders for standing by in masterly inactivity whilst the most cherished interests, and even the lives of the people, are imperiled, and I ridicule the Government proposal for depopulating the Highlands by means of emigration. Depopulation should begin in another direction. First, the landlords should be made to emigrate, and when they had gone, the deer should give place to men. (*Cheers.*) I blush to think that in a civilised age any government should make such an infamous proposal. (*Cheers.*) A hundred years ago, before the deer forests were established, the Highlands supported then what was a growing population in comfort, and surely there is no reason why the land could not do the same now, when the population had been thinned by the brutal system that has prevailed so long. (*Cheers.*) Instead of the Government giving money for emigration, let them give it to enable the crofters to acquire and cultivate land that has been robbed from their forefathers. (*Cheers.*) If they do not do that, they have deliberately shut their eyes to signs of the times, and made up their minds to face bloodshed and revolution in the future.

(*Cheers.*)

I know it is not the custom in this country for a woman to speak on a public platform, particularly in Scotland, but the times are so critical, and the disposition of the ruling classes is so tyrannical, that I hope I may be pardoned if I venture - as it has always been woman's mission to speak for the friendless, and to alleviate as much as possible the wrongs and miseries of humanity. I know that there are some who say that in Great Britain that there are practically no wrongs to liberty, and that the law is equal to all, and that all we have to do is obey it (*Hear, hear, and laughter.*) If this is so, surely there is something wrong in the present condition of the laws in the Highlands - in the Highlands! the Highlands, the pleasure grounds of the rich - that beautiful and romantic country where so much of the old-world feeling and patriotism lingers that we find so late as 1745 the whole population take up arms to do battle for an idea. (*Loud cheers.*) Who is not stirred to the innermost recess of his heart when he reads of the seven men of Moidart? [418](*Cheers.*) Who is there that would deny the heroism of these men? In these days the Highlands few men, and what men! Now civilisation marks as its aim the popularity of the deer while the best of the pastures are given over to sheep, and the Highlander is thrust from his post to be the backbone of other nations, and to carry out opposition to the home country so far from Lochaber and civilisation - condemned the remainder to more civilisation.

But laws are equally just in Great Britain. (*Laughter.*) The law, for instance, which gives one man the power to turn another man's family out into the snow; that gives one man the power to make his brother his slave, to work for him for starvation wages - (*Loud cheers.*) - that made the deer live more securely than men. Civilisation, religion, morality, law - what things have not been called upon in your name! And what do we find at this moment? That at Christmas-tide the message of peace and good-will was delivered amongst men. Should it not turn the Christmas dinners to ashes in our mouths? (*Loud cheers.*) Shall we not ask ourselves if it is a venial offence to kill the deer for food - deer fattened most probably upon their own miserable crofts? (*Cheers.*) But no - the deer is more valuable than men. "Hands off," says property; "Bring the soldiers and police" cries morality; "Let us read a sharp lesson to those who refuse to starve in

---

[418] Companions of Prince Charles Edward Stuart at his landing in Scotland in 1745.

the richest country in the world," shouts civilisation.

But this civilisation of ours, with its fearful failures, its heart-breaking inequalities, contains within itself that which will inevitably cure or destroy it. (*Hear, hear.*) The very crowding of men together in great cities has given them the opportunity by their alms, and the power of their votes to undo much of the evil which has crept into our midst as silently and as unlooked for as the star of Bethlehem, the constellation Cassiopeia. And, above all, the crofter question is essentially one for women. Do not women bear to the full every hardship of the crofter's lot? Do they not suffer - aye, and in silence, not in action, which makes suffering so much keener - (*Cheers.*) - so infinitely more heart-breaking? Do they not suffer when their fathers and their husbands are driven out by the pangs of hunger to the bare hillside to hunt for deer? And may it not be that the knowledge that one woman has had the courage to face an audience to express, or endeavour to express the interest she feels in their lot, and the deep sympathy she feels for them, may stir the heart of some poor crofter's wife when the meal is running low - when in the long winter nights she sits crouching by the embers listening to the howling of the wild wind down the glen, her heart burning with the bitter sense of injustice and wrong, and her children crying to her for bread which she cannot give them. (*Great cheering.*)

~

Graham's life long commitment to Scottish home rule is not in doubt. Anne Taylor describes him as 'the principal begetter' of The Scottish Home Rule Association, along with Keir Hardie, in May 1886,[419] and he became its first Vice-President. However, his active participation in the early Association is difficult to unearth, and it is likely that his focus remained on Irish Home Rule as a necessary precursor to Home Rule for Scotland (not yet full independence), in what became known as 'Home Rule All Round.'[420] A non-party organisation, the SHRA was inspired by the establishment of The Scottish Office in 1885, and Gladstone's conversion to the idea of Home Rule for Ireland. During its checkered and bifurcated history, it attracted many political activists from the Left, including future Prime Minister Ramsay MacDonald; the militant socialist

---

[419] Taylor, p.317. This may be partly true, Graham and Hardie were founder members, but, according to Roland Muirhead, it was established by the Edinburgh printer and author, Charles Waddie (1836-1912). (Letter from Muirhead to Graham, 2 May 1927, NLS Acc: 3721:7). Waddie was certainly the driving force (along with the renowned classicist, Professor John Stuart Blackie), and the unflagging propagandist behind the original SHRA, but, it had dissolved well before his death in 1912.

[420] Waddie apparently first coined this popular expression. See *The Glasgow Herald* Obituary (6 February 1912), p.7.

M.P., James Maxton; future Secretary of State for Scotland, Tom Johnston. The Red-Clydesider, William 'Willie' Gallacher, trade unionist, and Communist M.P., would serve as its President. Between 1889 and 1914 Scottish home rule was debated fifteen times in Parliament, including the introduction of four Bills. In 1913 such a Bill passed its second reading, but World War I intervened. In 1918, the SHRA was reconstituted and funded by Roland Eugene Muirhead,[421] a pacifist, and socialist businessman, who had previously been a member of the Independent Labour Party. It was Muirhead who gently badgered the now peripatetic Graham, who spent his time between his house at Cardross[422] in Argyleshire, and his Mayfair flat, with frequent trips abroad during the Winter months, to become re-engaged in Scottish politics. Graham was elected President of the SHRA in 1927, and continued as President of The National Party of Scotland, and Honorary-President of The Scottish National Party, when the various home rule groups finally merged in 1934.

Graham's approach to Scottish home rule was entirely pragmatic,[423] a means by which social change could be more speedily implemented. He may also have considered Scottish and Irish home rule as a means of undermining the ossified power structures he had hopelessly attacked as an M.P., and a means by which the Empire could be eroded from within, as in this letter to *The Saturday Review*:

> Bulgaria, Roumania, Servia, Norway, have all seceded from Greater powers within the memory of man. Finland and Hungary, Poland and Ireland, with Bohemia and Macedonia, all mortally detest their union with great oppressive States. Nothing but force keeps any one of them a portion of the great empires to which respectively they all belong [. . .] the whole trend of modern thought and economics is towards the evolution of small states, and every great unwieldy Power, our own included, is on the verge of a break-up and a return to its component parts.[424]

It was only a Britain united that could have forged and sustained such an Empire, perhaps it would take a Britain divided to demolish it. As it transpired, in the case of Scotland, the opposite was nearer the truth.

---

421 Muirhead had also spent part of his youth in Argentina. Muirhead, letter to Graham (15 June 1929). NLS.
422 'Ardoch,' Graham's home between Dumbarton and Helensburgh.
423 "They did not want a Parliament to sit and quote Burns or sing the praises of whisky or kilts." *The Glasgow Evening News* (1 July 1892), p.7.
424 Cunninghame Graham: 'Spain and Catalonia,' letter to *The Saturday Review* (30 June 1906), p.819.

~

On the 9th of April 1889 Graham spoke in support of a Scottish Home Rule Bill put before Parliament by Dr. Gavin Clark M.P. (Caithness), seconded by William Hunter M.P. (Aberdeen North), and this can be seen in the first substantive attempt to introduce legislation on this subject in Parliament. Renouncing the idea of 'separation,' Clark and Hunter based their argument primarily on the fact that Scottish 'nationality' was increasingly ignored, and that changes to legislation were painfully slow due to general parliamentary neglect, where time was taken up with Irish and colonial matters (the kind of Irish filibustering as described in his 'A MEMORY of PARNELL,' above). Speaking in support of the motion, Graham took a more hardheaded approach:

## SPEECH ON HOME RULE
The House of Commons.
9th of April 1889.

I wish in a very few words to support the Motion of the hon. Member for Caithness, but I wish to do it on vastly different grounds and reasons from any of those which have been urged by hon. Members who have spoken to-night. I do not wish to support this proposal specially on national grounds. I thoroughly agree with an observation that fell from the hon. Member for Caithness when he said that, though there is a great and growing feeling in favour of Home Rule in Scotland, it runs on other lines than those of the Radical programme. I do not wonder at that, because, personally, I never could find out what were the lines of the Radical programme. I believe, Sir, that there is a great and growing demand for Home Rule in Scotland, but it comes, in my opinion, from no sentimental grounds whatever, but from the extreme misery of a certain section of the Scottish population, and they wish to have their own Members under their own hands, in order to extort legislation from them suitable to relieve that misery. That may seem an extreme proposition to state in this House. Hon. Members from Scotland are often fond of representing Scotland as a sort of Arcadia, but I think that, in face of the misery existing in the Highlands and Islands, that we have women in Aberdeen to-day toiling for 6s. or 7s. a week; that we have 30,000 people in Glasgow who herd together in one room; and in face of the fact that we have a Socialistic agitation on foot in the East and West of Scotland, I must say I do not think the condition of the poor in that country is one very much to be envied. I think it will be found that the same reasons which impel a certain section of

262

the Scottish people to be dissatisfied with the legislation served out to them from this Parliament are not the reasons which have been alleged by other hon. Members. On many public questions public opinion is far riper for legislation than in this country. Not one Member who has spoken, although it must be patent to all hon. Members, has referred to the rising opinion in favour of land legislation in Scotland. I should like to ask the hon. Member for Roxburghshire whether he could go down to his constituency and speak to the free and independent electors there, and say much against the theories of Henry George,[425] for example? And I would like, furthermore, to point out to the House that on the question of labour legislation in Scotland we are much farther advanced as a country than in England, especially on the eight hours' question. In the matter of free education and many other questions, the people of Scotland are greatly in advance of those of England, and it is for these reasons, and not for sentimental or national ones, that I think this House will soon be called on to face the demand for a Legislature for Scotland. We have an absolute detestation in Scotland of all propositions dealing with the solution of the land question by means of emigration. It would not, I fancy, tend to enhance the popularity of any hon. Member in Scotland to go down to his constituency and propose to emigrate the crofters *en masse*. He would soon be met by the suggestion that some of the landlords and capitalists of the country could be emigrated with much greater benefit to the country. It has been said that in the event of the institution of a Scottish Legislature we should largely be represented by the merchants of the country. To that statement I say, God forbid! I believe I speak the feelings of a large section of the Scotch people when I emphatically state that, were such a Legislature ever created, we should find the working classes much more represented than is the case here. Thus, I think that, taking into account the large expression of opinion that has undoubtedly been given to-day by the Scottish Members, and taking into consideration the great pressure that will soon be brought to bear from social causes upon this House from the electorate of Scotland, we have not come here with an absolutely futile or fatuous proposition when we have, for the first time, endeavoured to press the cause of Scottish Home Rule upon the House of Commons.

---

[425] See passim.

The House divided: Ayes 79: Noes 200.

Keir Hardie commented:

> Dr. Clark deserves credit for pushing on his Scottish Home Rule resolution to a division in Parliament. True, the only member who showed any true appreciation of what Home Rule would ultimately lead to was Cunninghame Graham. Dr. Hunter's nice picture of a Scottish Parliament composed of smug, bald, pot-bellied shopkeepers is too laughable to be taken seriously. With Mr. Graham we say in all seriousness. 'God Forbid.' Of course the G.O.M. [The Grand Old Man] was cautious, and threw the onus on the people of Scotland. In this he is perfectly right. I believe the people of Scotland desire a Parliament of their own, and it will be for them to send to the next House of Commons a body of men pledged to obtain it.[426]

~

Except for lip service in his early election campaigns, Graham made no secret that he despised the Liberal leader, Gladstone 'with all his heart and soul.'[427] The following flight of sometimes surreal rhetorical acrobatics, describing Gladstone's speech in Edinburgh on the 27th of October 1890, is Graham in playfully reckless mood, and includes a long humorous passage on Italian and African fetishism,[428] juxtaposed with passages of faux diffidence:

## MIDLOTHIANISM[429]

*The People's Press*, 1st of November 1890.

Alarms, excursions, processions, the myriads of the old form joined to the thousands of the new, all Edinburgh afoot for the third time, to see the arrival of Mr. Gladstone.

Will he go for Scotch Home Rule? Is he going to climb down on Disestablishment?[430] What will he say about the eight hours? How bad all this is for the people. Take notice, no one seemed to think that their wishes on any of the

---

[426] *The Labour Leader* (April 1889).

[427] A. F. Tschiffely, *Don Roberto: R. B. Cunninghame Graham 1852 - 1936* (Heinemann, 1937), p.195.

[428] The subject of fetishism was probably inspired by current anthropological debates on the origins of religion. See contemporary works by Grant Allen, Herbert Spencer, and Andrew Lang. J. G. Frazer's 'The Golden Bough,' also began publication in that year.

[429] Midlothian, which included Edinburgh, was Gladstone's constituency. Although born in Liverpool, Gladstone was of mixed Scottish parentage, half Highland and half Lowland, giving him, as some thought, a contradictory, dual personality. His biographer John Morley described him as: 'a highlander in the custody of a lowlander,' and an adversary as: 'an ardent Italian in the custody of a Scotsman.' (If we substituted 'Spaniard' for 'Italian', we might have arrived at an accurate description of Graham himself.)

[430] Disestablishment of the national churches of Scotland and England was a contentious issue of the period.

above-mentioned subjects were worth a moment's consideration. No one asked whether the measures were right and just and equitable in themselves, but merely if a certain distinguished old gentleman of eighty thought them advisable to adopt in the exigencies of party welfare.

What went they forth for to see?[431] A reed shaken by the wind, or a wind shaken by a reed of eighty years growth. Pitiful commentary on universal counting of noses, lamentable and impotent conclusion of a generation of education. Popular government reduced to a Punch and Judy show, and this not amongst the Neapolitans, the Andalusians, the inhabitants of Tarrascon [. . .] but amongst my own pious, whisky-drinking, east-wind wrinkled compatriots, the Scotch. The best educated (as we delight to call ourselves) nation in Europe, the people amongst whom politics is the subject of daily, almost hourly conversation, were out to a man to learn what the state of their own opinions were. I want no one to think I am against fetish worship in the abstract - fetish, from the Portuguese *feitiço*. Oh, dear no; it has always seemed to me one of the highest forms of human intellect, that is as beneficial in Naples as Dahomey.[432]

At small cost you buy your fetish, and call it respectively in the two localities "Gri-Gri," or San Gennaro,[433] as it has done nearly every year for the last seventeen hundred years.

At Naples you, with hideous aniline pigments, daub him an acrid blue or agonising green. In the Cameroons you attain the same aesthetic result with cinnabar and yellow ochre. In either case, you have your fetish at a capital outlay of, say 4½ d.

Think, though (properly understand), how useful he is to you when made. Is there a foul insect (at Naples)? Have sardines left the coast temporarily? Does the English traveller object to pay more than ten times the price for conveyance from the P. and O. steamer to the mails. Do any of those contingencies arise that even ruffle the smooth current of the lives of "*brava genti*,"[434] out with San Gennaro and pray to him, pray till the wind changes, the fish return, or till a richer and foolisher, or, maybe, not "personally conducted" lot of tourists appear.

---

[431] Luke 7:25. "But what went you out to see? A man clothed in soft raiment?"
[432] An old West-African kingdom. It became a French colony in 1894, and is now modern-day Benin.
[433] St Januarius, the Patron Saint of Naples. A fourth century martyr, whose relic of dried blood is said to miraculously liquefy every year.
[434] Italian: Fine folk.

Similarly in Dahomey a leopard goes off with three or four of your best assegais sticking in him. A crocodile eats a portion of your family, or devours a goat or pig, in fact, let any contingencies arise, from ravages by lions to the introduction of small-pox by the Christian teacher, and "Gri-Gri," is your trump card.

Now comes the practical nature of this truly practical (and really estimable) form of worship.

San Gennaro will not give a fair wind. What, then, shall the true believer pray in vain? Is faith so common an article that we can waste it even in Naples?

By no means.

Pluck him (San Gennaro) from his position of honour in the bows of the felucca,[435] lash him well on the gunwale, tie a string round the neck of him, and tow him astern till he arrives at a better (and more miraculous) frame of mind.

So with Gri-Gri. Stick him full of assegais, like a porcupine on a writing-table, subject him to some resolute government till he too will do righteously. As a last resort, take both the fetishes and burn them up to ashes, remembering that the initial outlay on them was but fourpence halfpenny. Fairly comprehend, fetish worship is a delightful belief for a thinking man - that is, of course, in Naples or Dahomey, where people rule their fetish, and do not let the fetish rule them.

In Midlothian, though, all is different, and I confess to me the worship is not conducted on the same commercial principles or with as just an understanding of the laws of supply and command.

What can be fairer? You keep a sort of debtor and creditor account - fair winds, good long prayer.

Good fishing - new coat of paint.

Success in hunting - offering of Indian corn.

Immunity from crocodile or missionary - a lump of sugar cane.

All this is very reasonable.

No self-respecting Neapolitan, or dweller in Dahomey would allow his fetish to get above himself, or to be Jeshuran[436] kicked. How different in Midlothian. Fetish may be dumb for months, say what we do not want, refuse to tell us what our opinions

---

[435] A traditional wooden boat used in the Eastern Mediterranean, particularly, Egypt.
[436] Jesurun: (Isaiah 44:2) A symbolic name for Israel probably derived from a root signifying 'to be blessed.'

266

really are, in fact, may so disport itself that in Dahomey or Naples it would inevitably be subjected to deposition, and we are quite content.

We want a Scottish Home Rule breeze, for instance.

Fetish won't blow to the value of a tinker's curse; we are contented.

We see our miners toiling for long hours, our signalmen and pointmen almost taking root at their respective places, we want an Eight Hours' Bill; fetish is silent. We are delighted.

We are tired of worshipping in and paying for a national kirk, and want to see, *per contra*, a rabble rout of sanctimonious Muggletonians[437] and other preachers rise and waddle through the land (that is the way they are made). *Feitiço* is quite silent, or perchance to our importunate prayers responds, the Greeks were colour blind. Enormous versatility. As Mo says, "O, *toute puissance de l'orviétan.*"[438] Still, though, I can't help thinking (where's the harm in thinking even though no one does it nowadays in Scotland, and to be singular is to be wicked) that it might be better for a leader to have a policy.

When Scotland has her mind made up.

How if Scotland has no mind, and therefore cannot make it up.

Five years of absolute surrender of individuality on the part of the worshipper, five years of waiting on the part of the fetish, for worshippers of money have, it appears, reduced them both to jelly-fish condition. Still a great old fetish, after all, a man of monstrous vitality, vast erudition, and one who, if throughout the course of his life he had ever really chosen to place himself at the head of the democracy of England, might have led them, at least, a day's march out of the wilderness of poverty.

Perhaps, though, he has placed within their reach the power of their sons to do so.

*Ah! si la jeunesse savait, si vieillesse pouvait.*[439] But so it is, and will be whilst the world is world, and it is matter of the commonest notoriety that every midshipman can sail the ship far better than the captain.

Not any captain, though, sir, as I once heard old Chatterton exclaim at a crowded meeting of Christian socialists, when Fleming Williams spoke of our Master, Christ.

---

[437] A small 17th Century Protestant sect that opposed philosophical reasoning.
[438] French: "O, by the power of orviétan": a 17th century quack panacea.
[439] French: "Ah! If youth knew, if old age could."

Now, to the gains of this same *tournle* in Midlothian. Why was it that in the teeth of the east winds, the people mustered thick in Princes Street?

For words of light and leading on three matters - Eight Hours' day, Scottish Home Rule, Church Disestablishment. The two latter not of much importance after all, and mercifully so, as it happened, for de'il a crumb of comfort got the worshippers on either of them.

Union of England with Scotland, not a pleasant thing. Still, though, perhaps, or if, or *per ambages*,[440] as we might say - if in the future, or perchance the dim future - for it is unwise to pin oneself to anything in particular - if, then, in the far-off period, which I hope may ne'er arrive, the Scottish people might, would, or should discover they have a mind, and prefer being swindled by their own lawyers in Edinburgh instead of undergoing the operation at the hands of the London ones, I will, if I am alive, take the matter into my best consideration and resolve it for them. Meanwhile, let the clansmen wait.

Scotland must wait, and pass the interval with whisky and prayer. So with Disestablishment, about which no sensible man cares very greatly, at least till the labour question is settled. With the eight hours, the Fetish spoke in quite a different style.

He has seen the signs of the times, and, according to his wont, in the self-same way that in the case of the Irish Church, and other matters, he gave all the best arguments for not doing so when about to yield, so too he has done in this instance. We take it that the G. O. M. intends to vote for the Eight Hours Bill for Miners, that is, if the miners make noise enough about it in the interim.

If for instance, they sharply reprove Roby[441] for his meanness in trucking for their votes (against his manifest conviction), and then saying, as he did after the election, that Home Rule was all his joy and that the Eight was a mere secondary affair.

Meanwhile, this is Midlothianism. Let no one doubt, or if they do, communicate with Naples, or with Cormandel,[442] where a similar state of belief exists.

Never to think, always to wait, and wait, and wait. Wait, whilst the poor in the

---

[440] French: To put in a roundabout way.
[441] Henry George Roby (1830-1915). A Liberal M.P., and classical scholar
[442] Coromandel. A peninsula on the North Island of New Zealand.

Cowgate swelter in lodgings suitable for swine. Wait, whilst the "hinds"[443] of Haddington are worked to death and paid less than a London docker.

Give up all individuality and be content with open mouth and fast shut eyes, to remain content and give up all reform till over every workhouse in Milesia[444] waves a green flag.

~

Graham not only wrote his articles, histories and sketches, he was much sought after as a writer of Introductions and Prefaces[445] to the works of others, particularly for travel books, writing almost 50 during his long career. Although not strictly a 'political' piece, the example below is a wonderful oddity, introducing a book by J. Morrison Davidson,[446] a socialist author, campaigner, and prolific pamphleteer, whom Tom Mann, the first Secretary of the Labour Party, described as: 'a great character: he was terribly proud of being a Scotsman, and believed, or pretended to believe, that a very big share of all that was passable in the British Isles originated in Scotland.'[447]

As usual, barely able to control his gypsy impulses, in a book about Scotland, Graham whisks us off to the Argentinian *pampa*, where he relates an extraordinary encounter; two ships that pass in the daylight, so to speak, telling us all we need to know about the wandering Scot, and, incidentally, demonstrating a mastery of Scots dialect.

Age, nor class, nor ocean, are barriers to familiarity, and the unspoken bond between these strangers. Graham and his dishevelled compatriot share the sentiment expressed by Graham's friend and admirer Frederick Niven: 'We'll take Scotland with us, a kingdom of the mind,'[448] before we are removed to Graham's Arcadian, pre-Union, pre-Calvinist,[449] pre-industrialised Scotland, which he forlornly hopes might one day be reclaimed.

---

[443] Farm servants.
[444] Ireland, home of the mythical Gaelic Milesians who reputedly came from the Iberian peninsula.
[445] Joseph Conrad called Graham: "the Prince of Preface-writers."
[446] Davidson believed he had established that Graham, as a direct descendent of King Robert II, was *de jure* monarch of the United Kingdom. *The Edinburgh Evening News* (18 September 1895), p.3.
[447] Tom Mann, *Memoirs* (MacGibbon & Kee 1967), p.123.
[448] Frederick Niven, *The Flying Years* (Collins 1935), p.14.
[449] Despite his distaste for Calvinism, as a negative force in Scottish life and history, his wife's mystic Catholicism, his admiration for the old Jesuit missionaries in South America, and his own atheism, Graham had once declared himself 'a Protestant.' *The Coatbridge Express* (7 July 1886). Indeed, his father had donated the funds to build the first Free Church of Scotland (Wee Free) kirk in their home village of Gartmore.

**INTRODUCTION**: SCOTLAND FOR THE SCOTS: SCOTLAND REVISITED. (by Morrison Davidson), 1902.

Scottissimus Scotorum - Surely to no one more than to the author of "Scotland Revisited" does the above phrase apply. A Scot of Scots! although he apparently imagines that he has recently revisited Caledonia, I cannot think that he really left it for an hour.

Born in Buchan, perhaps to refute the saw,[450] "there's rowth o' a'thing in Buchan haud awa' freet"[451] - he carries Buchan with him everywhere he goes.

What is it that makes your true Scot, him I mean of the *perfervidum ingenium*,[452] so intensely national? It is, I think, because of those very qualities, the decay of which the Author bewails in his present book.

I remember once, in South America, having gone out to look for some strayed horses, and not having found them, that I ascended a little hill and sat me down to smoke. Below me rolled the Pampean ocean of brown grass: grass, grass, and still more

---

[450] A saying.
[451] Obscure. Perhaps: "There's an abundance of everything in Buchan, don't be concerned."
[452] Latin: '*Perfervidum ingenium Scotorum*': The intensely earnest character of the Scots.

grass: grass which the breeze from the south-west had set in motion in long waves: grass which, where rivers in the middle distance crossed it, was cut by strips of "Argentina," looking like silver bands: Grass in which deer and ostriches passed happy lives, so happy that the Gauchos knew the former as the "desert mirth": Brown waves of grass in which roamed cattle and sheep innumerable, and over which the Tero-Teros flew uttering their haunting cry.

And as I sat and smoked -

Upon a thin old chestnut horse, with a torn English saddle, over which a sheepskin had been laid, a man of about fifty years of age appeared. Dressed in a suit of Scottish homespun, - such as our farmers wore, but twenty years ago, before the looms of Bradford and of Leeds had clothed them all in shoddy, - with a grey flannel shirt without a collar, and the whole man surmounted by a battered, flat straw-hat, which might have made and indifferent strawberry pottle,[453] I at once descried a brother Scot. Dismounting and hobbling his horse, he drew a short clay pipe out of his pocket, capped with a tin cover that workmen in the North used to affect, in the pre-briar-root days, and greeting me in a strange Doric [454] Spanish, he sat down to smoke.

Some time he talked, till in compassion I said, "Friend, you appear to make but middling weather of it in the Spanish tongue." No sign he gave of the least astonishment, but between two draws, as he rammed the "dottle" [455] hard into his pipe, he said, "I see ye speak the English pretty well." I, though at the time, just at the age, when a man speaks, rides and shoots better than any other man in all the world, suppressed a smile, and said, "Yes; how do you like the view?"

"A bonny view, sir, aye, ou aye; I'd no say onything against the view: but man, maybe ye ken a hill - they ca' it the Dumyet [456] - just abune Brig o' Allan?" I did so, having climbed it as a boy, and watched the Forth wind out, a silver ribbon towards Aberfoyle.[457]

"Weel, weel, if ye ken it, ye'll ken there's a far brawer view frae the Dumyet than frae

---

[453] Scots: A conical punnet for fruit.
[454] A distinctive dialect spoken in the north east of Scotland.
[455] A plug of un-burnt tobacco.
[456] Dumyat ('Hillfort of the Maeatae tribe'). A hill to the north-east of Stirling, commanding the River Forth.
[457] A small town adjacent to Graham's old estate at Gartmore.

271

the wee boranty [458] that we're sittin' on the noo."

When he had got upon his horse and schauchled [459] down the hill, I fancied that I could smell the heather and sweet gale, hear the whawps [460] calling on the moor, and in the towns see drucken folk a-stotterin' [461] from the public house.

Something of this compound essence of the North our Author has. Something of the pre-bawbean [462] times, something of those old shirtless Scottish scholars who, in the Middle-Ages, over-ran Europe, "gaun aboot bodies"[463] with a tattered Homer in their hand, Andrew Ferrara [464] on their hip and with a plenteous lack of pelf in the lean deer-skin pouch they carried at their side. So, naturally enough, the Scotland of to-day seems to him wersh,[465] the national character becoming moulded after the Southern form; the whisky no sae nippy in the mooth, religion turned but a dreich [466] Erastian affair, and even hell-fire merely a wee bit spunky in the lum.[467]

But he has put his finger on the blot, and pointed out (his bagpipe certainly gives no uncertain sound) our national vice of snobbism. Pity to see a Scot "attempt the English" and essay in havering [468] tones to clip the Doric, and, worst of all, to see our country clean despoiled of brains, and all her sons run off to London, for the gatherin' o' the gear. The Highlands too delivered over to the Yank, and the whole land become a cross between a rich man's playground and a sweater's hell he marks with disapproval, and looks back to Fletcher, him of Saltoun,[469] who believed in the divine right of princes to be hanged.

He mourns our Scottish Parliament, that "lang auld sang" which Southern wiles and gold brought to an end, leaving the House disconsolate, and a mere stamping ground for Advocates, who, like the devil, walk to and fro seeking for those they may devour.[470]

---

458 Scots: A little mound or tumulus. The diminutive of 'burian.'
459 Scots: Shambled.
460 Scots: Curlews.
461 Scots: Staggering.
462 Pre-materialistic.
463 Scots: Wanderers, travellers.
464 More correctly: Andrea Ferrara, the generic name for the Scottish basket-hilted broadsword.
465 Scots: Flavourless.
466 Scots: Dismal.
467 Scots: A small spark in the chimney. Spunkie = Will o' the Wisp.
468 Scots: Babbling, talking nonsense.
469 Andrew Fletcher of Saltoun (1655-1716). Scottish writer, politician, and opponent of the 1707 Act of Union between Scotland and England.
470 1 Peter 5:8.

Therefore he advocates Home Rule.

Not a return to those blithe days when in Auld Reekie [471] folks cried "Gardey-Loo," [472] and on the causeway sword-and-buckler men fought for the "croon," whilst Highland chairmen carrying old gentlemen to routs, [473] paused not an instant though the bottom of the chair fell out, causing their fares desperately to run, and to exclaim on landing "that but for the honour o' the thing they had as lieve hae [474] walked."

But to return to a more national spirit and a revival of the ancient Scottish Type which ruled the roost before the Ten per Centlings [475] rose, making poor Scotland stink before the world with their base peddling ways.

~

Graham had expressed 'nationalist' sentiments from the very beginning of his Parliamentary career, including the following speech at Coatbridge immediately after his election to Parliament:

As Scotchmen, we should help the Irish with all their heart to gain Home Rule. (*Hear, hear.*) We must never forget that the idea of Home Rule originated with the Irish, and we should never lose sight of it till we see a Parliament legislating for purely Scottish matters in Edinburgh or Linlithgow. (*Loud cheers.*) Though the upper classes have become Anglified, yet I am glad to know that the working men have remained intensely Scottish, and I know that this name will be received with joy by you, and that you would not see the name of Scotland merged with England (*Cheers.*) But how should we act? It is all very well to say we should like a national Parliament. There were questions, as our worthy-chairman has said, that could be far better settled in Edinburgh than in London; but we have to bear in mind that we want no Englishman to represent Scottish seats. (*Cheers.*) We want none of their fine fellows coming down in the Pullman car from London (*Laughter and cheers.*) – giving a club address and talking in their fine English, and then, like swallows, flying away and leaving us and never coming near until the next

---

[471] Scots: Old smoky = Edinburgh.
[472] French/Scots: 'Beware of the water.' A common cry from an upper storey, before a chamber pot was emptied onto the street below.
[473] An evening assembly, sometimes 'a rabble.'
[474] Scots: Might as well have.
[475] Capitalists.

election. We want good hard-headed Scotchmen to represent us. (*Cheers.*) I will never believe for a moment that there was any necessity for Liberal Associations writing up to London and saying "Send us a candidate as per invoice." (*Laughter.*) Surely it is an insult to the Scottish people to have a candidate sent down bottled, preserved, and labeled in that way. (*Cheers, and a voice – "That's a good yin," and laughter.*) Scotchmen should never elect an Englishman, no matter of what party or how well qualified he was for an English seat. I think we should again take a lesson from the Irish, who would rather elect an Irish lamp-post than an English duke. (*Laughter.*)[476]

~

For many modern-day socialists, Graham's nationalism has been problematic – reactionary, seemingly at odds with his anti-racist, egalitarian, internationalist outlook, and as a consequence, he has been effectively written out of Labour Party history. But, reactionary is exactly what it was, a reaction against imperialism and its offspring – the untrammelled industrialisation that was obliterating distinctiveness, creating wage slaves, filling the slums and sweat-shops, dehumanising and alienating mankind, and it can only be fully understood in that context. Graham's brand of nationalism was neither narrow nor exclusive, it was a supposed antidote to imperial centralisation and to the standardisation that this so-called progress necessarily demanded. It was a desire to perfect the parts before a more rational, natural, holistic progression was ready to take place. For Graham it was a beginning, not an end.

In Graham's day, Home Rule for Scotland was seen by many as a cure for industrial exploitation; witnessed by the words of William Small, the Secretary of the Lanarkshire Miners Association, and a close associate of Keir Hardie:

> He assured them that dynamite was abroad, and that before many days, the Scottish miners would raise a revolution such as was never seen in Scotland. He only wished that the old mining laws of the country were being carried out. If they were, masters and landlords would be in prison charged with being thieves and robbers. They needed Home Rule in Scotland, and the sooner they had it, the better for all concerned.[477]

Home Rule had been an original guiding principle of the Labour Party, but as its share of the vote increased, and the realisation that Scotland was now one of its bastions,

---

[476] Transposed into the first person from *The Coatbridge Express* (28 July 1886), p.2.
[477] *The Airdrie Advertiser* (19 February 1887), p.5.

when it came to power in 1924, under Ramsay MacDonald's premiership,[478] the subject was off its agenda, and it formally renounced the policy in 1927. That vacuum would soon be filled and thus, ironically, the SNP would become the bastard child of the Labour Party, just as the Labour Party had been the bastard child of the Liberals, and the childless Graham was in attendance at the birth of both.

Graham was not a founder of the Scottish National Party as is often claimed, but, like the Labour Party, as a high-profile personality, he was certainly an inspiration and catalyst in its foundation. There had been a renewed resurgence of Scottish national feeling and culture after the First World War, particularly in the face of Scotland's catastrophic war losses, partly in the cause of freedom for small nations. In September 1927, following the rejection of yet another Scottish Home Rule Bill in Parliament, two young students, John MacCormick[479] and James Valentine, founded the Glasgow University Student Nationalist Association, and helped facilitate the creation of The National Party of Scotland in April 1928 (which subsumed the SHRA). Graham did not attend the inaugural meeting, but, such was his prestige, he was elected as its first President. Later that year saw a somewhat reluctant Graham stand as the 'nationalist' candidate for the rectorship of Glasgow University, against Prime Minster Stanley Baldwin,[480] and so successful was his campaign, supported by MacCormick, and Compton MacKenzie, that he came within 66 votes of winning,[481] gaining nationwide interest in the nationalist cause. As a direct consequence, two days later, an estimated 3,500 people attended a meeting of the National Party in The St Andrew's Halls, Glasgow, to hear him and others speak.

---

[478] MacDonald had at one time been Secretary of the London Branch of the Scottish Home Rule Association. The novelist Arnold Bennett records that Graham referred to MacDonald as a 'MacChadband' (Bleak House), because he preached so much, and as a "Judas." Arnold Bennett, *The Journals*, (Penguin Books 1954), p.480.

[479] MacCormick had been an active member of the Independent Labour Party between 1923 and 1927.

[480] Letter to R. E. Muirhead (22 July 1928): "I feel my chance for the university is not good for Baldwin is heavy metal." Muirhead (1868-1964) later became President of The Scottish National Party.

[481] "Glasgow University Rectorial Election took place yesterday and resulted in the return of Mr. Baldwin [. . .] The result was considered a triumph for Scottish Nationalists. The voting of the men students showed a clear majority for Mr. Cunninghame Graham, but the women's vote turned the scale in favour of the Premier." *The Observer* (28 October 1928), p.15.

Public meeting in The St Andrew's Halls, 29 October 1928, two days after the Glasgow University Rectorial Elections. Left to right: The Duke of Montrose, Compton MacKenzie, Cunninghame Graham, Hugh MacDiarmid, James Valentine, and John MacCormick.

## SCOTS NATION: THE NEW PARTY IN GLASGOW

*The Glasgow Herald*, 30th of October 1928.[482]

*A gathering of almost 3,000 Glasgow citizens attended a demonstration held last night in St Andrew's Hall by the National Party of Scotland. The Duke of Montrose[483] presided and delivered an address, and Mr. R. B. Cunninghame Graham was another of the speakers. The audience was very enthusiastic, and any pithy claim for Scottish self-government aroused great applause.*

It has been questioned whether there was any need for a National Scottish party. Are not the three existing parties sufficient to represent Scotsmen and Scotswomen? That these parties sufficed to represent Scotland in the way that the youth of Scotland wish it to be represented, I totally deny. (*Applause.*) There has been a tendency in Scotland for us to become pale copies of our Southern brethren. That is a tendency that I have always deplored. I have always hoped, always known, that Scotsmen and Scotland was a

---

[482] Transposed into the first person.
[483] James Graham, the 6th Duke of Montrose. The first Chairman of the centre-right Scottish Party, founded in 1932, and elected the first President of the SNP, when it merged with the National Party of Scotland in 1934. He had been a naval officer and engineer, and putatively, the designer of the world's first aircraft-carrier.

nation and nationality apart from any other nation or nationality in the world (*Applause.*)

The leaders of the three existing parties are all good men – and true, I dare say. (*Laughter.*) But they are not Scotsmen; their spiritual home is Westminster.

I have noticed that the Liberal leader [Lloyd George] has been pleased to complain the other day at Perth that we did not all of us wear kilts. That was Mr. Lloyd George's sole contribution, as he saw the matter, towards the immediate solution of our immediate Scottish problems. (*Laughter.*) The spiritual home of Scotland's Prime Minister should be Edinburgh. It is because I feel that that Scottish problems can be dealt with only in Edinburgh that I am here to advocate the aims of the Scottish National Party [sic] and the establishment of their own Parliament.

Why should unemployment in Scotland be larger far in ratio to population than it is in England; why should the housing in Scotland be a disgrace and scandal to the whole Empire; why should the mid-Scotland canal be hung up; lastly, why should 4,000,000 acres of our Highland territory be delivered over to American millionaires to exhibit their fat white knees and debauch the population with their dollars? (*Laughter and applause.*) I know that all these acres are not cultivatable, but most of them could carry sheep. Formerly they carried men – (applause) – men who carved their name with the claymore in the rock of fame. To-day these acres are deserted, the population negligible, the whole territory a stamping ground for rich men to take their pleasure in. A Scottish party alone can take these matters into consideration and solve them, if it is in the power of man to do so. (*Applause.*)

Any man can join the National Party without imperiling his convictions. In my own case I have not altered my convictions since the time when, with dear old Keir Hardie, I went through the mining districts.

Conservatives can join the party. Surely to a conservative the re-establishment of that old institution, the Scottish Parliament in Edinburgh, in which their fathers passed the simple Scottish statutes, amply sufficient for the needs of those days, should appeal. Liberals surely need not kick at this reform. Socialists can join – I am one myself; it would give them a better theatre in which to ventilate their grievances and with a better chance of being heard. Even Communists could join them; they send their men to Westminster, why not to a Parliament in Edinburgh?

Our rulers in Westminster have sent down to us the Secretary of State for Scotland[484] – a Scots himself, he thought – (*laughter.*) – who has become imbued so much with southern views, or perhaps those of Kelvinside,[485] that he has lost all touch with Scottish nationality. (*Applause.*) Take for instance the Bill which he is laying before us. Nothing more antagonistic to Scottish feelings could possibly have been devised. It was but another step more to stamp out local patriotism.[486]

We have become too tame in Scottish politics. When the whip cracks in London we are far too ready to come to heel. The Predominant Partner has always looked upon Scotland as a Cinderella not worthy of consideration. In appealing to Scots men and women to join the National Party, I can assure them that they will be joining no mean or inconsiderable cause; you have with you youth and the flowing tide. (*Applause.*)

~

Despite his optimism, his views, and those of the new party, were to face stiff opposition from the Unionist press, including, this piece in Dundee's *Courier & Advertiser*:

> Mr. Cunninghame Graham has a perfectly sound instinct when he turns to the use we make of the Highlands for his chief argument in favour of Scottish Home Rule. The Highlands ought to be a great source of wealth and strength to Scotland as the Alps are to Switzerland, and under the Imperial Parliament the subject is hardly ever even intelligently discussed. We are failing egregiously to turn to national account a great asset. But is there any ground for Mr. Cunninghame Graham's faith that a Scottish Home Rule Parliament would do better with it? If there is, we have never been able to find a hint of it in the kind of men who alone seem willing to give their time and brains to public representation. One of the most outstanding aspects of the times is the unwillingness of strong and capable Scotsmen to sacrifice their own business for work of this kind and the willingness to undertake it of hordes of individuals whose leading trait is their capacity for any business whatsoever and their eagerness to have a hand in the spending of other people's money. A Scottish Home Rule Parliament would be a howff [487] of cranks, visionaries, and second-raters

---

[484] Sir John Gilmour (1876-1940). He was appointed as Secretary for Scotland in 1924, and became the first Secretary of State for Scotland when the post was upgraded in 1926. He was a member of the Orange Order, but repudiated the Church of Scotland's 1923 report: '*The Menace of the Irish Race to our Scottish Nationality.*'
[485] Regarded then, as now, as the 'posh' part of Glasgow's West End.
[486] Gilmour proposed in his Reorganisation of Offices (Scotland) Bill, the centralising certain local government boards, under The Scottish Office in London, and the abolition of parish councils.
[487] Scots: A haunt.

elected for their gift of the gab, while the capable Scots would go on, as they are doing now, minding their personal affairs.

When Mr. Graham goes on to point the example of Europe and to lament that only Scotland and Wales lagged behind in the recrudescence of national sentiment which followed the Great War, he merely induces a shudder.

Of all the curses that afflict the Continent just now none is worse than the "recrudescence of national sentiment" which has Balkanised Europe. As an ideal, the Balkanising of Britain strikes us as worst of all.[488]

~

Graham remained a fervent and outspoken Scottish nationalist until the end of his life, but, like his involvement in the SPLP, he took no active role in party management, believing he could achieve more from outside: "the dunghill of active politics is a young man's game [. . .] It is a dunghill I know for I have been on (or in) the hill."[489] However, he was a popular figurehead, campaigner, and speaker, helping to attract large crowds to the new party's rallies, and, despite his advanced years, drew in many young, enthusiastic supporters.[490] When The National Party of Scotland merged with The Scottish Party in 1934 to form The Scottish National Party, Graham was elected Honorary President.

## SCOTLAND'S DAY: THE NEW COVENANT
*The Scots Independent* - June 1930.

A Demonstration of the National Party of Scotland at King's Park, Stirling, 21st of June, 1930.[491] (Editorial sub-headings are included)

Mr. Chairman, Ladies and Gentlemen,

*ASSERTION OF NATIONALITY*
We stand once more on this historic ground. The surroundings are unaltered. The eternal hills still form our background. Stirling Castle, a perennial monument to the power of Scotland when she shook the might of England to the core, makes our middle distance. Not far from where we are to unfold this banner is the historic Borestone whence the banner of the Bruce fluttered on the greatest occasion whereon victory has crowned the arms of Scotland. Three miles from here Wallace broke Cressingham[492] upon the long bridge over the Forth. Where'er I look, north, south, east or west, there is

---

[488] 'Scottish Home Rule,' *The Courier & Advertiser* (20 June, 1927), p6.
[489] Graham, Letter to R. E. Muirhead (27 July, 1928), Rauner Library, Dartmouth College, NH.
[490] 'Home Rule For Scotland,' *The Manchester Guardian, et al*, (24 November, 1932), p.5.
[491] Supplement to *The Scots Independent* (July 1930) pp.2-4.
[492] The commander of the English forces at the Battle of Stirling Bridge, 11 September 1297.

something that appeals to me as a Scotsman, there is something to stir one's heart, something to make one feel that we representatives of a distinct nationality – a nationality severed from all other nationalities and as different from our friends in England as we are from the Germans, the French, the Russians or any other nationality. The British Empire today has become a confederation of varying states. Australia, New Zealand, British Columbia, the Cape Colonies, and all the rest of the dependencies have got their parliaments and their separate legislatures. They are all practically self-governing States within their boundaries, and I ask you, is Scotland inferior to any one of these nationalities? Did we not send out the best and bravest of our sons to colonise Canada, New Zealand, Australia, and wherever the flag of the British Empire flies? I ask you as Scottish men and women whether it is not an injustice that cries to heaven and a sin against political science that the one nationality – the oldest of those that I have mentioned, and older perhaps than England itself, as a separate State – should be subservient to them, a mere appendage to the predominant partner, a mere county of England, such as Yorkshire, Lancashire, Nottingham or Middlesex. I, for one, cannot sit calmly under such a supposition. They tell us – triflers, pifflers and writers in the Press – that we rule the British Empire. That is untrue. What is true is that individual Scotsmen hold high posts in the British Empire. Why do they hold them? They hold them because of their abilities, not because of their nationality as Scotsmen.

*SHALL SCOTLAND LAG?*

If a man applies for any situation they do not ask him first, Are you a Catholic, a Protestant, a Presbyterian, a Czecho-Slovak, an American, an Englishman or a Scotsman, but they take the best man for their purpose, and that is why individual Scotsmen hold high positions in the Empire. To say that we rule the Empire is an untruth, and those who state it know it is an untruth. Let us assume for a moment that we did rule the Empire. What we do not rule is our own country, and I do not consider that even were the ruling of the Empire a fact instead of a myth, that it would in any wise repay us for the position of inferiority into which we have been relegated, perhaps not by the fault of Englishmen, but by our own apathy, and by our own dislike to go forward and face the petty martyrdom that we should have to endure. Nationality is the atmosphere of the world. Within the last ten years we have seen twenty nationalities come into being – Czecho-Slovakia, Yugo-Slavia, Poland, Lithuania, Esthonia, Ireland,

and perhaps there are others in the making even today. Shall Scotland lag behind all these nationalities? We talk about our prayer for a good conceit of ourselves. I used to think it was a prayer that was scarcely worth being put up by Scotsmen, but today it is a prayer that every Scottish man and woman should keep in mind and should perpetually put up until we have achieved that which we have in view, complete autonomy for our native land. When James the Sixth was a little boy they took him to the old Parliament House near Stirling, and looking up he saw there was a tile or two off the roof, and he said, "There is ane hole in this Parliament." The Parliament House still stands. As to the condition of its roof I know but little, but as for the condition of its interior I am well aware. No Scottish Parliament, no single representative of Scotland sits with plenary power to legislate for his own land, either in the old Parliament House of Stirling or in Edinburgh, and it is a disgrace to all Scotsmen that they do not sit there. I lay upon you as a sacred duty that you agitate until our old Parliament is restored to us, and once again Scotland takes her place as an independent nationality in the family of nations

*HOW WE ARE RULED.*

Let us for a moment survey what has been going on in the English Parliament. We have seen practically the bankruptcy of all political parties. Mr. Balfour and his happy family are struggling for leadership and for autonomy within their party. Mr. Lloyd George continues to twankle the Welsh harp and to deal out the dollars to those who have received his imprimatur. And the Labour Party is almost like a hornets' nest, each member of it, with true Christian unction, doing as much as possible to tread upon the hands of those who are slowly mounting the ladder. But let us be just, there is one thing the Labour Party have done for us. They have given us an increased income tax, and Mr. Lansbury has instituted mixed bathing in the Serpentine. That is about the achievement at present except the daily culture of the unemployed, who are growing like Jonah's gourd while they are sleeping. That is about the *summum bonum*[493] of the achievement of the Governmental party at present in power. In times gone by with old Keir Hardie and others, I was one of those who fought for the establishment of a Labour Party. I was young in those days and I had my illusions thick upon me. I hoped the coming of the Labour Party would be the coming of the millennium in England and Scotland. I was disappointed. They have simply become a party struggling for office and

---

[493] Latin: The highest good.

place like any of the other parties, and although every one of them are lavish of promises when they are out of office, I see no responsible statesman or highly placed member of one of the three parties who has devoted a speech or motion in the House of Commons, or introduced any legislation dealing exclusively with Scotland. Therefore I conclude that it is vain for Scotsmen to look for help in their struggle for autonomy to any of the existent parties.

## FALSIFIED HISTORY.

People have said that we shall lose by Scottish autonomy. They would have us imagine that we were mere barbarians before the Union. Some gentleman the other day painted an awful picture of Scotland before England took it by the hand. We believed in witchcraft, our feudal barons oppressed their people, the miners were practically serfs, and culture was unknown throughout the land. At that very time what was the state of England? Was England a paradise? Did the proletariat have any votes? Were not the feudal land-owners to the full as arrogant and as ignorant of the conditions of their fellow men as the feudal land-owners of Scotland? It is a pretence and a sham that Scotland owes its prosperity to the Union with England? Did England gain nothing by the Union? Were all the benefits upon one side? Was it no small benefit for any country to receive a population of hardy, industrious, grave and valiant men within their bounds, from which she could, and did, recruit her armies, putting the Scottish regiments always in the forefront of the battle? Had I lived in the time of the Union with England I would have resisted it to the best of my ability with Fletcher of Saltoun,[494] and had it gone to arms I would have been beside the Scottish patriots. The prosperity of Scotland was induced by the economic progress of the world. It was not in England's power even if she had wished to do so, to withhold the benefits that naturally accrued by the increasing wealth of Europe from Scotland. Scotland merely shared in the same development that touched France, Germany, Italy, Spain and the United States; and those who wish to take us back to these times, and paint a derogatory portrait are no true Scotsmen, and what is left for them is to bow before the golden calf of England, and to kiss the rod that chastises them.

There are many ways in which we can achieve self-government for Scotland. We are

---

[494] See passim.

not called upon to martyr ourselves and endure persecution, death or imprisonment, as were the Irish. It is a very simple process. We have merely to vote and to signify our wishes to the Parliament of Great Britain, and Scottish Home Rule would be as certain as that day follows night. I have been asked what should be the first movement of Scottish Nationalists were they returned to the British Parliament with a majority and a mandate, if the British House of Commons were against them. My answer has always been that they should withdraw to Edinburgh and start a Parliament which would be the beginning of our great and National Parliament. There is nothing very heroic in that.

*Idealism.*

There is no great self-sacrifice. In fact it is so easy and so manifest to the poorest intelligence that I need not elaborate the point. We want a renaissance, a re-birth of Scottish literature, art and sentiment. We can induce these things only by agitating for national self-government. Look at Southern Ireland. I do not hold it up as an example of all that mankind can achieve. I believe it is a very dull place since you do not hear the revolvers popping, but since she got self-government there has been a most marvelous renaissance of national sentiment and art, as displayed in drama, poetry and novel-writing. Irish painters and poets are deriving inspiration from the old legend[s] of their country, and from the actual conditions of their modern life. That is what I want to see in Scotland. I cannot bear to see Scottish writers take their inspiration from English themes. I cannot bear to see our painters paint entirely English subjects. Have they no themes in Scotland; are there no tragedies in the slums of Glasgow, in the mining districts of Lanarkshire, and in the Western Islands for men to write about; have our hills and straths lost their enchantment for painters? I say 'No'; but I do say that we want an increase of national sentiment in order to direct the attention of our artists and painters and poets more exclusively to the consideration of national subjects. No great movement has ever been carried to its end without idealism. A mere appeal to material improvement has never moved any mass of men; Scotsmen especially, under their somewhat hard exterior, are especially amenable to an appeal to sentiment.

*LIBERTY.*

When Bruce unfurled his banner did he harangue his soldiers upon yonder stricken field saying that they would make more money if they conquered England? Did he hold out to them increase of wealth or of position? No, if the Archdeacon of Aberdeen, Barbour,

283

is to be believed, he spoke to them of Liberty, an intangible thing, a mere idea. Did William Tell make his appeal to pure materialism? Let us come to the three great Mahatmas of modern life, Gandhi, Lenin and Mussolini. You may think, two of them may not appeal to sentiment, but Lenin and Mussolini were men imbued with sentiment, and Mussolini alone with his good and his bad qualities and rule in Italy has been able to do what he has done by the appeal to Italian national sentiment.[495] I hold no brief for Mussolini, but he found Italy, the Cinderella of Europe, almost in the dust, a prey to the worst kind of anarchy – an anarchy in which the anarchist has no ideal of freedom or liberty or any competent state. He held before them the emblem of the ancient Roman Empire, and by that he has appealed to them, by that he has elevated them, and has been able to make a united country, and to carry it to the position in which we see it today. Do you suppose the men he spoke to were urged by hope of individual gain? Do you think that Gandhi, when he started his salt making agitation imagined he was going to gain anything by it in a material sense? The salt the British Government made was no doubt one hundred times better than the salt that his Statagrayas[496] [sic] made upon the edge of the ocean. What he appealed to was the national sentiment of Indians, and by that he was enabled to inaugurate a movement that, good or bad, has shaken the British Empire to its very core.

*INDIVIDUAL RESPONSIBILITY.*

We must have Scottish sentiment, we must have that which elevates mankind, and makes mankind superior to the inferior animals, that which unites us intimately to every object that is loved and dear to us in our own country. We must have a sentiment that shows us that the slums of Glasgow are a slur not only upon the world, but upon each and every individual one of us, that shows us that the Highlands of Scotland are not only a crying scandal to Scotland and to the Empire, but that they call aloud to us as a scandal against humanity. Think of these regions once the abode of men, poor, violent, and perhaps uneducated, but still human beings, think of them today – mere playgrounds of rich men, with these mountains and straths debarred and cut off from

---

[495] Up until 1935, and the Second Italo-Ethiopian War, Benito Mussolini remained an heroic figure to many in Britain. On the 25th of March, 1926, Winston Churchill wrote to his wife Clementine: "My darling, I have two of yr dear letters. The description of Mussolini is vy vivid. No doubt he is one of the most wonderful men of our time. I am glad you have met him & been able to form a personal impression." And, three days later: "What a picture you draw of Mussolini! I feel sure you are right in regarding him as a prodigy."

[496] Followers of 'Satyagraha' - the concept of non-violent resistance developed by Mohandas Gandhi.

the use of the population of the country. Think of the roads closed, the cottages pulled down, and the desolate straths that once resounded with the laughter of children and the pibroch of the piper – silent but for the clacking of the grouse, the whirring of the black cock's wings and the grunting call of the deer. I say that it is wrong and must be altered, and it lies on us as Scottish men and women to alter it, and I call upon you all here under this flag which is to be unfurled, never to cease agitating until we get this autonomy for Scotland which alone can revive our ancient spirit, and make real Scotsmen of us.

~

## McSNEESHIN
*The Scots Independent,* January 1931.

From the beginning the McSneeshin clan have been the greatest enemy Scotland has known. The Spanish saying runs, "There is no worse thief than the thief in your own house" (*no hay peor ladron, que el de casa*). Scotland has suffered bitterly, if not from thieves, at least by traitors in her house. They, one and all, disguise it as they may, were but mere pensioners of England, taking her money quite contentedly, so that, as

Murray, Morton, and many other Scottish noblemen, they were allowed to browse upon the spoils of the monasteries, and to preserve their power and their position of pre-eminence inviolate. All were McSneeshins to a man, and anti-patriots, content to do the bidding of a foreign potentate, as long as a full mess of beef and beer supplied the absence of the soul that they had bartered for it.

## John Balliol McSneeshin

Balliol[497] was a good douce[498] noble. No doubt a gentleman, but not a "parfait knight." As a Norman noble, holding estates on both sides of the Tweed, and also in both Aquitaine and Normandy, he was more to be excused than were the above referred to English pensioners. Brought up in courts and probably speaking Norman French as his mother-tongue, no doubt he looked upon the Scots as mere barbarians. He saw that England was more advanced in arts and chivalry than Scotland. He probably admired sincerely the stern warrior Edward, perhaps the ablest king who ever sat on England's throne. He saw the English knights were sheltered in Milan steel and rode destriers[499] from Naples and from Spain, whilst those from Scotland had to be content with Galloways, or at the best with heavy flat-footed animals from Flanders. What he did not see was that the wildest Johnstone, Jardine or Turnbull, upon his little hackney, "that was never putte to hard meete," as Froissart[500] tells us, but who remained a Scot at heart, was, as far as Scotland was concerned, a prince compared to the McSneeshin chivalry.

Balliol bowed the knee, no doubt, in the first place for the crown, but perhaps as much because he saw something superior to the Scot in "Goddes owne Englishman." So he came beneath the spell, as so many of his spiritual descendants of today. Wealth, power, refinement, luxury, the gorgeous tournament, the cultured Court, the well armed knights, the ladies in bower, whose beauty was enhanced by all that wealth can bring (the Scottish lady had but her fresh complexion and her snood, except in rarest cases), all was designed to catch McSneeshin's eye.

He then, as now, had his excuse, that it was well to keep in with your neighbours, that we could use their wealth and better opportunities to our own ends. No doubt they

---

[497] John Balliol (1249–1314) King of Scots from 1292–1296. His father founded Balliol College, Oxford.
[498] Scots: Sober.
[499] A war-horse.
[500] Jean Froissart (c.1337- c.1405) A medieval author, and poet from Flanders.

286

said, just as they say today, a Scot, put him in far Cathay, remains a Scot at heart. No doubt the Scots of those days had their equivalent of "A Nicht wi' Burns," when round the festive bowl they trolled their ditties of some popular poet of the time. Without a shadow of a doubt they ate their haggis when it could be procured in exile, and over their French doublets or Italian silks they tied a tartan scarf. Just as they do to-day they thought that nationalism was a thing to put on once or twice a year. Meanwhile, the Saxon smiled beefily, and winked the other eye.

## The Modern McSneeshins

These were the members of the historic clan in former days. To-day their position, though in the main the same, that is spread-eagled (or perhaps better, frog-marched) to the south, they take a different attitude. We are the men, they tell us. We rule the British Empire. See how McWharble is Under-Secretary for Useless Affairs, McDoodle (of the Doodles of that ilk) the High Commissioner for Tristan d'Acunha [sic], and my Lord Moneypenny bears a pewter rod about the court! We are all proud of being Scots, they say, and prove it in the tongue of Grub Street, "up to the hilt," by wearing kilts at public banquets, and bellowing maudlin ditties about Alloway Kirk, and Bonnie Lassies O'. Thus having publicly professed their patriotism, and their descent from Wallace apostolically, they still continue to praise the Lord and cheat when the church bell chaps out, or competition renders it expedient.

## The McSneeshin Delusions

The pity of it is, the McSneeshin up-to-date is in the main an honest fellow, blinded by what he reads in newspapers, and never having peered beneath the surface of the society in which he moves. He takes for granted that such national prosperity as we enjoyed before the War, for he dimly perceives that all is not right in the state of Scotland to-day, came from the Union (bless the word!) with England. He thinks, apparently, that it has always been the keen desire of English legislators to forward Scotland's interests. Blinded to economic facts, he still believes that it is possible to build up once more our old prosperity on the old lines, not seeing that the whole conception of law, of order, commerce, and international relations has entirely changed, whilst he has been enjoying his after-dinner nap. Of course the typical McSneeshin of these days is a good Liberal, a member of that fast decaying race of pterodactyls that is being ground into extinction between the upper and the nether millstones of Toryism and Socialism.

Still, in the grinding he protests, just as the wheat emits a sound of gentle wailing during its attrition in an old-fashioned hand mill in Morocco or Spain. That kind of McSneeshin always wants to get back to Liberal principles, such as he remembered them in the halcyon days, when the pound sterling had hardly fallen to the level of the old Scots pound.

### The McSneeshin Consolations

What has been, clearly was ordained by Heaven, and one of Heaven's first laws was to hold fast to the union with the greater partner, brought about as we know by the venality of the Scottish aristocracy.

Our consolation is that somewhere in the selvage of the Union Jack a microscopic cross of St. Andrew still exists, but unobtrusively, "only a little," as the Frenchman said when asked if he was wed. Still it is there, and our good friend McSneeshin, when he sees it, rubs his belly like an old-time Gold Coast negro used to do before his fetish. Then looking upwards to his emasculated flag he thanks his Maker that his election is a dead sure thing, as after all he rules the British Empire, although the other fellow holds the whip.

### The Honest Scot

I have typified the honest, pig-headed Scot of these days under the name that I have chosen as a title to these lines. He is far from being a conscious traitor to his country, as were the anti-patriots of old. Our present representative of the type does not take bribes from English statesmen, nor would he take them, even if they came his way. His fault is lack of imagination, a fault that has made many more angels fall into the pit than did ambition.

Our fellow-countryman, who does not see that only he who wears the shoe can feel the pinch, is to be commiserated. Although he holds an antique creed, for him Triton will never wind his wreathed horn, or if he sounds it, it will fall upon deaf ears.

This little allegory, dip into history, or reflection on the present time, or what you will, I commend to all those Scotsmen who having eyes to see, see not, and having ears to hear, hear nothing.

### L'Envoi

Yes, fellow-Scots, the enemies of Scottish nationalism are not the English, for they were ever a great and generous folk, quick to respond when justice calls. Our real enemies are amongst us, born without imagination, bound in the fetters of their own conceit, impervious to progress, and who fail to see that what was right and just last year, to-day may have become through altering conditions, rank injustice.

~

Graham addressing the 'Scotland's Day' demonstration at King's Park, Stirling, in 1931. (Compton MacKenzie in kilt, seated left.)

## THE AWAKENING OF A NATION
*The Scots Independent*, October 1932.

Scotland has once again become race-conscious. Of course, our individual consciousness has never flagged. Nature has given us a good opinion of ourselves as individuals without the need of prayer.

Scotsmen have always felt that they were different, as individuals, from Englishmen. That consciousness has for a long time only manifested itself in "nichts wi' Burns", in sporadic jollifications upon St. Andrew's Day, in vague sentimentalities about the kilt, in glorification of the haggis, a dish we eat but rarely, and other matters of the like nature that have caused the Southron to wonder at us with a patronising air. I have no word to say against the haggis. It is a noble dish, a dish few southron stomachs can digest. As for the kilt, when kilted regiments pass down the street, with bagpipes singing i' the nose, I can no more restrain my admiration than I could when a boy at school. But all these things, as admirable in themselves as flies in amber, are a poor substitute, for me, at least, for race consciousness.

I know the papers are not likely to allow me to forget that several Prime Ministers have been born on this side of Tweed. I know that Scotland has furnished numerous ministers of state, governors of colonies, viceroys and dignitaries worthy of all respect. I am not ignorant that Scotsmen have risen high in the commercial world, in arts and sciences, and have shone brightly both as theologians and philosophers. But almost all of them have had to exercise their talents in English leading strings. Old David Hume, I think, was the one literary Scot of modern times imbued with the old Scottish feeling of the essential difference in point of view, in race and everything that goes to make a man, between a Scotsman and an Englishman.

Lord Byron, curiously enough, had a streak of the same feeling in him. Perhaps because in childhood he had roamed about Deeside, ascended Lochnagar,[501] and stood upon the fateful bridge that spans the Don. Burns, of course, had it also; but then both he and Byron felt it as poets and as men of genius, and genius has an intuition that forces those to whom it is vouchsafed not to take things for granted and to reject much that is taken and received as gospel by those less gifted than themselves.

Only in the last few years has there been a real national awakening. We have – at last – remembered that we gave kings to England, and at the Union perfect equality was understood, at least by Scotsmen. It was inevitable that the stronger party to that bargain would not look upon the partnership in the same light. Gradually she has assumed the airs of an elder brother, forgetting that the Union gave her the status of a twin.

Nothing more natural, for as the saying goes, "If the iron pot strikes the pot of clay it is bad for the clay pot, and if the clay pot strikes the iron, it is still bad for her."[502] This feeling of superiority that undoubtedly exists was natural in view of the difference

---

[501] George Gordon Byron (1788–1824). Poet. A scion, on his mother's side, of the Gordons of Gight in Aberdeenshire. Byron wrote the Scots song: 'Dark Lochnagar.' Like Graham, he attended Harrow School.
[502] A paraphrase of the Aesop fable: 'The Two Pots,' or La Fontaine's fable: 'Le Pot de Terre et le Pot de Fer.'

in wealth and size of the two countries. It was not reasoned out, but came about insensibly, as quietly and imperceptibly as the hands move upon a clock. Little by little Englishmen began to think that the two countries were really one, and not two ancient kingdoms that had entered into partnership. No doubt, had Scotland been the larger and wealthier of the two, she would have thought the same.

What is astonishing is that for so long most Scotsmen have taken the situation as quite natural. Even today there are not wanting members of the McSneeshin clan who think that Scotland's role is to play second fiddle in the orchestra that England rules over, wielding the baton as it pleases her. They all forget that the Union was brought about by bribery, chicane and wire-pulling, and that at least a half of Scotland was opposed to it.

They point out that since then, Scotland has made great strides towards prosperity and put it down to the advantages she has received from the Union with England. A hundred times at least I have insisted that the increase in Scotland's national wealth is due to the economic progress of the world. England was powerless either to help or hinder Scotland in her development. The self-same progress is to be observed in Holland, Belgium, Denmark, or Italy, and in all cases it came about from the same circumstances. England helped none of them, and she herself has shared just as did Scotland and the other countries in the same development.

At last our eyes have opened, and by degrees we are beginning to observe ourselves without the aid of English spectacles. What we observe does not give cause for self-congratulation. Our shipyards are paralysed. The Clyde, shipless and silent as a river in the moon, meanders noiselessly towards the sea. The Highlands, turned to a sporting desert, only receive a parliamentary grant (paid mainly out of Scottish money) to bolster up the sporting interest, for whose sole behoof it seems to have been created by an unwary providence. The unemployed are slowly eating up the nation's wealth in unproductiveness, and by degrees despair as to the future of the country has taken hold of everyone but Scottish Nationalists

We do not despair, for we remember Wallace, an outlaw, hiding in caves (one of them is on this property), Bruce's spider, Fletcher of Saltoun fighting a hopeless battle to the last, Sir Andrew Wood[503] aboard his "Yellow Frigate," when he engaged the English at such tremendous odds, and all our Scottish heroes of the past. Nor do we forget the heroic life of Muir.[504] We see him (or should see him) on his extraordinary "Trek" from Nootka Sound[505] to Mexico. Alone, footsore and weary, tortured by hunger and by thirst, steering by the stars, the heroic lawyer from Kirkintilloch eventually won through to liberty. What an example for all Scottish Nationalists!

What lies in front of Scottish Nationalism, compared to what those heroes of the past achieved? Nothing but the will to conquer. As it has been well said, "the world goes out to meet the conqueror; but he must conquer first."

All see the state of Scotland. No one can mark the unemployed in every street, our factories closed, our iron-works damped down, our industries all drifting southwards, banks, railways and commercial companies managed in London, without being, as Hamlet puts it, tempted "to fall a-cursing like a whore."[506]

We know that Scottish Nationalists cannot bring in the millennium, but as Conservatism, Socialism, and Liberalism all have failed, let us as Scotsmen try a national cure. Our platform is broad enough for all to join. Protestant, Catholic, Socialist, Conservative, Liberal, and Communist can find no fault that I can see in our idea. It gives them all a chance to push their schemes in a smaller theatre nearer home.

For us, all that we have to do is to unite and signify our will.

---

[503] Sir Andrew Wood of Largo, a Scottish sea captain who rose to become Lord High Admiral of Scotland following his exploits against the English Navy.
[504] Thomas Muir of Huntershill (1765-1799) A Glasgow lawyer and political martyr. Transported to Australia for his radical activities, he escaped to North America, travelling via Mexico and Cuba to Spain. En route he was badly injured in a sea-battle off Cadiz, and succumbed to his wounds as 'Citoyen Muir' in Paris, aged 33.
[505] Vancouver Island, British Columbia.
[506] Hamlet: Act II, Scene II.

# ☐☐☐☐☐
# POSTSCRIPT

It is a recurring but distracting theme in the many potted biographies of Graham that his life was extraordinarily diverse, preoccupied with his youthful adventures, his political activism, his travels, and his large literary output, and all too often he is cast as a romantic idealist or a fervent dilettante. It was certainly a singular life, but a closer examination reveals that his outlook was entirely pragmatic, and eventually, most of his aims and ambitions came to pass, although, that is beside the point. As Jocelyn Baines wrote: 'Cunninghame Graham championed causes because he was roused to do so, not because he expected them to triumph (if he had he probably would not have bothered).' [507] His philosophy, too, remained remarkably consistent, although his impulses and pronouncements tempered with age. Times changed, political friends and colleagues equivocated and compromised, but Graham remained resolute. This was not intransigence, nor lack of imagination – he was simply not a politician in the conventional sense, as he was only too happy to concede.[508] G. K. Chesterton wrote of him:

I felt much more kinship with the sort of Scot who, even when he was interested in politics, would never really be allowed in practical politics. A splendid example of this type of man was Cunninghame Graham. No Cabinet Minister would ever admire his Parliamentary style; though he had a much better style than any Cabinet Minister. Nothing could prevent Balfour being Prime Minister or MacDonald being Prime Minster; but Cunninghame Graham achieved the adventure of being Cunninghame Graham. As Bernard Shaw remarked, it is an achievement so fantastic that it would never be believed in a romance.[509]

Shaw might indeed have included Graham's name in the following passage:

The free-thinking English gentlemen-republicans of the last half of the nineteenth century [. . .] great globe-trotters, writers, *frondeurs*,[510] brilliant and accomplished cosmopolitans so far as their various abilities permitted, all more interested in the world than in themselves, and in themselves than in official decorations;[511] consequently unpurchasable, their price being too high for any modern commercial Government to pay.[512]

Graham's political ambitions were not based on dogma, party, or self-interest, but on an

---

[507] Jocelyn Baines, *Joseph Conrad: A Critical Biography* (Weidenfeld & Nicolson, 1960), p.198.
[508] "Mr Cunninghame Graham, strange as his statement may appear, at bottom is not a party politician." *The Airdrie Advertiser* (21 April 1888), p.5.
[509] G. K. Chesterton, *Autobiography* (Hutchinson & Co, 1936), p.269.
[510] Political rebels.
[511] Graham's name never appeared in 'Who's Who.'
[512] G. B. Shaw, *Pen Portraits and Reviews* (Constable, 1932), p.129.

unshakable sense of justice, and a deep compassion, but also on an ethical, broad-minded, all-encompassing practical morality, and if his political allegiances appear promiscuous to some, it was because he believed that the parties themselves had betrayed or compromised their founding principles, many of which he himself had set. Fundamentally, as Joseph Conrad pointed out, it was the human condition that Graham wished to see changed,[513] and, at a time of unprecedented and accelerating technological 'progress,' he remained a reactionary who deplored the inexorable disappearance of a more natural and diverse world, corrupted and laid waste by human greed.

In 1961, Moray McLaren recorded this memory of him in his declining years:
Cunninghame Graham came into the large and opulently furnished room. Immediately the life and the distinction seemed to drain out of everyone else. This old man of seventy-five made all the other notabilities at once appear not only undistinguished but unreal. It was an extraordinary thing to observe. It was as if a figure out of an old painting had stepped out of its frame and moved among the rest of us, to reduce us to dummies [. . .] the nearer he got to death the more vivid did he appear, and the more unreal did he render those around him.[514]

On a visit to Argentina, to attend the ceremonial naming of a town in his honour in Entre Ríos ('Don Roberto'), and to visit the birthplace of his old friend W. H. Hudson,[515] Graham, who had been suffering from periodic attacks of bronchitis, developed pneumonia, and died in the Plaza Hotel, Buenos Aires, on the 20th of March 1936. His body lay in state in the Casa de Teatro, where the President of The Argentine Republic paid his respects.[516] Large crowds lined the streets and followed the cortege that took his coffin to the pier-side, to be returned to Scotland on the ship he had intended to sail home on. He was buried in the chancel of the ruined Augustinian priory on the beautiful island of Inchmahome in the Lake of Menteith, next to his wife Gabrielle, whose grave he had dug thirty years earlier, attended by the great and good of Scottish life and letters.[517]

---

[513] "You are misguided by the desire of the impossible – and I envy you. Alas! What you want to reform are not institutions – it is human nature. Your faith will never move that mountain." Joseph Conrad, letter to Graham, dated "Sunday," February 1898. C. T. Watts, Ed., *Joseph Conrad's Letters to Cunninghame Graham* (Cambridge University Press,1969), p.68.

[514] Moray McLaren, *The Wisdom of the Scots* (Michael Joseph Ltd, 1961), pp.316-317.

[515] William Henry Hudson (1841-1922). Naturalist, ornithologist, and author of *Green Mansions* (1904). Hudson wrote to Graham in 1900: "You are rather like an Arthurian knight abroad in the great forest of the world in quest of adventure & ready at a moment's notice to lower your lance & and joust at any evil-minded person that may turn up."

[516] The Argentine Government apparently donated a large sum of money to have Graham's books translated into Spanish, and sent to schools throughout the country. *The Paris Daily Mail* (23 November 1936). p.25.

[517] The funeral procession was captured on film by The Scottish News Magazine, which is held by The National Library of Scotland. It can also be viewed online.

It would take another thirty years, and another World War, before the ideas gained momentum that 'progress' was not always beneficial, that some things were worth preserving, that small could be beautiful, that every person should have an equal opportunity, and, if the emotive word 'conservative' could morph into 'conservationist,' then, one day, 'reactionary' might transmute into 'prophet.'

In Graham's funeral oration, the author William Power bade farewell to:

The Scottish Arthur of our day. This was the noblest Scotsman of them all [. . .] As a literary artist, he was the peer of the greatest in any country [. . .] inasmuch as he had lived a whole Odyssey before he published a book. His love of Scotland expressed itself both in his writings and in his self-sacrificing efforts for Scottish causes. His "unutterable scorn" that Conrad perceived in him was the obverse of an infinite tenderness. He had the forthright simplicity together with the elusive subtlety of a great genius. His ultimate secret was an open one. He had a profound reverence for life.[518]

Death is a small thing: honour is all.
There is pardon for all sins except meanness and hypocrisy.
*The Saturday Review*, 26th of November, 1932, p.566.

---

[518] William Power, *In Memoriam: R. B. Cunninghame Graham* (Glasgow PEN Club, 1936).

Of course, the world could not go on if there were many like him,
but there is not the least danger of that.

*The Manchester Guardian*, 24th of November 1932, p.5.

Lachlan 'Lachie' Munro hails from Dennyloanhead in Stirlingshire, and is of Highland parentage. Most recently he has undertaken a PhD in History & Literature at the University of Glasgow, after previously studying History, and Political Philosophy at The University of Stirling, and London Metropolitan University, where he won the university history prize. In 2015, Lachlan was awarded the Tannahill Scholarship to carry out research in Dartmouth College, New Hampshire, and he is a visiting lecturer at The British Higher School of Art & Design in Moscow. He lives in North London with his wife Lesley, who works in the House of Lords.

## The Deveron Press

Originally founded in 1916 by James Leatham, printer and socialist pioneer, The Deveron Press was re-established at its centenary in 2016 to republish works formerly printed by James Leatham and to promote and showcase cultural and political writings from Scotland's past. The focus is on marginalised voices. It also promotes contemporary writing of the North East.

Our Catalogue Includes:
### The Centenary Collection

Volume 1: 'Sketches of Life Among My Ain Folk,' William Alexander (1875)
Volume 2: 'Daavit: The true story of a personage' James Leatham (1913)
Volume 3: 'James Leatham – profile of a Socialist Pioneer' Robert Duncan (2016)*
Volume 4: '60 Years of World-Mending' James Leatham (2016)**
Volume 5: 'Fisherfolk of the North East' James Leatham (1932)
Volume 6: 'Shows and Showfolk'  James Leatham (1934)
Volume 7: 'Socialism and Character'  James Leatham (1897)
Volume 8: 'William Morris and the early days of the Socialist movement' J.Bruce Glasier (1920)
Volume 9: William Morris: Master of Many Crafts: A Study' James Leatham (1897)
Volume 1 : 'Shakespeare Studies' James Leatham (2017)**

*    (New edition revised from 1978 edition)
**  (First paperback edition)

Also published by The Deveron Press in 2017:

'Sanners Gow's Tales and Folkore of the Buchan', Pat Hutchison
'Ploughing My Way', John Barron

The Deveron Press has also revived Leatham's *Gateway* Journal as a free online monthly magazine. Remaining true to the spirit of the original it offers in depth articles on culture and politics from Leatham and other writers past and present.

To buy books from our catalogue or find out more about James Leatham, The Deveron Press and The Gateway Journal, visit the website:

www.thedeveronpress.scot

Lightning Source UK Ltd.
Milton Keynes UK
UKOW01f2153210817
307610UK00002B/203/P

9 781910 601433